All material copyright Next Step Test Preparation LLC, 2( 
reproduced or distributed in any way or by any means el
or otherwise without the express written permission of N

LSAT is a registered Trademark of LSAC.

# TABLE OF CONTENTS

Introduction .................................................. 3
Introduction to Logical Reasoning .................................................. 4
Introduction to Reading Comprehension .................................................. 5
Introduction to Logic Games .................................................. 6

PrepTest 52
    PrepTest 52, Section 1 (LR) .................................................. 7
    PrepTest 52, Section 2 (Games) .................................................. 13
    PrepTest 52, Section 3 (LR) .................................................. 21
    PrepTest 52, Section 4 (RC) .................................................. 26

PrepTest 53
    PrepTest 53, Section 1 (LR) .................................................. 30
    PrepTest 53, Section 2 (Games) .................................................. 36
    PrepTest 53, Section 3 (LR) .................................................. 44
    PrepTest 53, Section 4 (RC) .................................................. 50

PrepTest 54
    PrepTest 54, Section 1 (RC) .................................................. 53
    PrepTest 54, Section 2 (LR) .................................................. 56
    PrepTest 54, Section 3 (Games) .................................................. 62
    PrepTest 54, Section 4 (LR) .................................................. 71

PrepTest 55
    PrepTest 55, Section 1 (LR) .................................................. 77
    PrepTest 55, Section 2 (RC) .................................................. 83
    PrepTest 55, Section 3 (LR) .................................................. 86
    PrepTest 55, Section 4 (Games) .................................................. 92

PrepTest 56
    PrepTest 56, Section 1 (Games) .................................................. 100
    PrepTest 56, Section 2 (LR) .................................................. 109
    PrepTest 56, Section 3 (LR) .................................................. 115
    PrepTest 56, Section 4 (RC) .................................................. 121

PrepTest 57
    PrepTest 57, Section 1 (Games) .................................................. 124
    PrepTest 57, Section 2 (LR) .................................................. 133
    PrepTest 57, Section 3 (LR) .................................................. 139
    PrepTest 57, Section 4 (RC) .................................................. 146

PrepTest 58
    PrepTest 58, Section 1 (LR) .................................................. 149
    PrepTest 58, Section 2 (RC) .................................................. 155
    PrepTest 58, Section 3 (Games) .................................................. 158
    PrepTest 58, Section 4 (LR) .................................................. 168

PrepTest 59
    PrepTest 59, Section 1 (Games) .................................................. 174
    PrepTest 59, Section 2 (LR) .................................................. 184
    PrepTest 59, Section 3 (LR) .................................................. 190
    PrepTest 59, Section 4 (RC) .................................................. 195

PrepTest 60
    PrepTest 60, Section 1 (LR) .................................................. 198
    PrepTest 60, Section 2 (Games) .................................................. 205
    PrepTest 60, Section 3 (LR) .................................................. 214
    PrepTest 60, Section 4 (RC) .................................................. 222

PrepTest 61
    PrepTest 61, Section 1 (RC) .................................................. 225
    PrepTest 61, Section 2 (LR) .................................................. 229
    PrepTest 61, Section 3 (Games) .................................................. 236
    PrepTest 61, Section 4 (LR) .................................................. 244

# Introduction

Thank you for choosing Next Step Test Preparation's Recent LSAT Explanations. We designed this document to fill a big hole in many students' LSAT prep. While students that take expensive prep courses (or our tutoring programs) get access to information like this, there wasn't a widely-available document that helped students think through problems on the most recent PrepTests. While LSAC's Super Prep does an admirable job of this task, its topic is several much older tests which don't include comparative reading, the more difficult reading comp passages, and modern logic games. And, while there are various explanations of single questions on some online forums, there was not one location where students could turn for a coherent document with authoritative explanations.

Our goal in this book is to give every student, no matter the starting level, insight into the logic underlying each question on the exam. You'll note that sometimes our explanations are brief – for example, a RC question that simply asks which answer choice is stated in the passage. Usually, however, we'll have an extensive explanation of the prompt and go in-depth on each answer choice.

## How to Use This Document

This document explains every question in the LSAC's "10 New Actual, Official LSAT Preptests." You will absolutely need to own that book as well; without it, this book will not be helpful. The worst way to use these books together would be to open the two books and just read through the answers and explanations. It's critical to your preparation that you try sections first, and only later look back at explanations.

We provide explanations of every problem, with extensive explanations of the hardest games and LR questions. While we hope you understand each question after reading the explanation, most students will still get some of the hardest questions wrong.

Particularly on logic games, you'll often have to read explanations a few times and compare back to the rules. This material is still complicated; the way you can use our explanations to improve is by taking the time to really understand how each question works – not just to see what the right answer is and move on. You should plan to spend several minutes reviewing each game, with our explanations.

## What This Book Can't Do

This book is not designed to be your primary prepbook for the LSAT. We don't go into the basic explanations and methodologies; this book assumes you've already learned basic concepts like understanding what a conclusion is, or finding the contrapositive. If you haven't learned these yet, we suggest ordering Next Step's Prepbook. Once you have a basic understanding of how to work through LSAT problems, these explanations should be quite useful.

www.nextsteptestprep.com/lsatbook or by phone at 888-530-NEXT

# Introduction to Logical Reasoning

Given that LR is half of your scored LSAT, understanding the logic that operates throughout each question is incredibly important. These explanations will be helpful by assisting you in learning that logic and the patterns of logic that recur frequently on the exam.

On most questions, we replicate the optimal process of answering a question by speaking a bit about the prompt itself before considering the answer choices. The best LSAT-takers predict answers in advance of even considering answer choices. That's why on many questions, the answer will be given in the discussion, then simply listed as "correct" within the answer choices along with explanations of the wrong answers.

We've listed the "question type" of each question in LR; the names may differ from specific prep books you may be using. Try not to focus on that; we see many students spending too much time memorizing categories when they should be learning about the logic that underpins each question on LR regardless of question type.

One specific point that may differ from other prep books or your own self-study deserves attention. On assumption questions, we always start by trying to make a prediction based on either an evident hole in the logic or a new "entity" in the conclusion that does not appear in the premises. When these strategies fail, the method that always works is what we call the "negation test." How does that work?

Remember that an assumption is an unstated premise in an argument which must be true for the argument to follow. That means that if we negate a necessary assumption, the argument would fail. The negation test does just this. If you are not sure whether an assumption is necessary, negate the assumption; does that hurt the argument? If so, you've found the assumption. If not, you've found the wrong answer.

Premise: Dan never does the dishes
Conclusion: Dan is a bad husband.

There's clearly an assumption here that not doing household chores makes one a bad husband. So, here's the negation test. What if we posited "chores has nothing to do with being a bad husband" – the negation of the assumption. Well, then the argument doesn't work at all because we've severed the link between doing the dishes and status as a husband.

While this is an elementary example, this logic can be used on every assumption question, and in fact is often the only way to solve more difficult assumption questions, often after eliminating a few clear wrong answer choices.

We'll make reference to the negation test on many assumption questions.

# Introduction to Reading Comprehension

Our explanations focus on the two things that should be valuable to students.

- A thorough write-up of the structure of the passage. We recommend that students make margin notes on each paragraph, underline key passages, and circle words that indicate a transition in the argument. Each explanation models this process for the passage.

- An explanation of each answer, focusing on questions where there is a wrong answer that is particularly tempting.

RC tends to be the section on which students can most easily review their own results and see what they did wrong. Students struggle much more with timing than with incredibly challenging questions (though there are still several questions that will be difficult even with unlimited time). In particular, students who have just started working with the most recent LSATS (since 2007) will notice that they are intentionally much more difficult than earlier practice exams.

For RC, we've focused more on correctly outlining and understanding the passage; we've also noted questions where the second-best choice is quite tempting. However, on many questions we have not listed out every answer choice so as to avoid 100 pages of "(D) Not mentioned in the passage" etc.

# Introduction to Logic Games

The logic games explanations deserve a little extra introduction since every student has likely learned different means of diagramming.

In our logic game explanations we've tried to do 3 things clearly: demonstrate the diagram, show the inferences to be made (if any), and show the logic of each question. We try to explain not only why the right answer is right, but what the process should be through the question.

**Diagramming Conventions**
Every prep company does logic games diagrams a bit differently, but the conventions are more similar than different. We'll go over ours here, but if you like another way better that will in no way affect the logic in each of the questions.

- A "~" sign will mean "not" in our diagrams
- In linear games, rules that must be consecutive and in a particular order will be listed in a square:
- Rules that must be consecutive but in any order will appear in a circle
- Sequenced rules will use the "<" sign. So, if F must go before G, we'll write "F < G". Here in particular, ad herents of a certain very large test prep company seem committed to using "F…G". That's just fine.
- Sequence rules that involve multiple variables will be stacked like so:

We list the contrapositive of every conditional statement immediately to that statement's right. You should do so as well. If you are not familiar with finding the contrapositive you should consult our prepbook separately.

When a particular variable isn't specifically constrained by a rule, we list it with a "*": "A*", for example. These "floaters" are important to identify. Knowing when you do (and don't) have a variable that can go anywhere often makes it much easier to fill in diagrams as you work through the questions.

When a variable can appear in one of two spaces only, we mark it with a /. For example,

$\frac{H/}{4}$   $\frac{H/}{5}$

In this diagram, H can go either 4 or 5 (but nowhere else).

The sign "=|=" means "not equal to."

We have denoted answer choice letters as "a)" to distinguish them from variable A. For your grammar buffs, this means we will start some sentences without a capital letter.

We made an effort to describe the process that you'll use while working these questions. We assume, for example, that you work through the questions in the best order – first the list question, then the "if" questions, then the rest. On some questions, we'll explain how you could eliminate particular answer choices by looking back at past diagrams. The goal is to help you understand how to navigate the process, not just get one particular question right.

In particular, we try to walk you through the inferences you'll make in an individual question. Very often, there will be one key inference which, if you found it, is essentially the answer. We hope this guide trains you to see those inferences, then quickly scan the answer choices for that inference as the correct answer.

In each game we have numbered the rules in the setup. This is done only for the purposes of easy discussion later; there's no need to number your rules during your practice. In addition, on many games there is a key rule which is written into the setup (rather than the indented list of rules). It's very helpful to actually write out these rules as well, so we've done so in the list of rules in brackets.

We write multiple variables, for example 2 instances of A, as A's. Yes, we know they are not possessive; we do this to distinguish multiple A's from As, which is "A" with subscript "s".

# PrepTest 52

## PrepTest 52, Section 1 (LR)

**1. Question type: Conclusion**
(A) and (B) both state facts that give background information in the stimulus.
(D) and (E) both state facts that suggest the practice is unfair, supporting the conclusion
**(C)** is the correct answer; it is the only statement in the stimulus that is opinionated, as shown by the word "unfair."

**2. Question type: Flaw in Reasoning**
(A) The stimulus never states this; it only says that students who take frequent naps are more likely to have insomnia.
(B) The stimulus is only comparing two groups: students who take frequent naps and sailors who take frequent naps. This is not enough to suggest that all insomnia has the same cause.
(C) No scientific definition of the word napping is necessary because the dictionary definition suffices.
**(D)** This is the right answer. The stimulus describes a correlation between two traits: those with insomnia tend to also take frequent naps. There is no reason to believe that a particular one of them causes the other, but the stimulus suggests that one does.
(E) The stimulus never suggests that fishermen have regular sleep schedules, only that most take naps frequently.

**3. Question type: Parallel Reasoning**
The stimulus can be diagrammed as:
vacuumed-->K&L-->fixed Then, the stimulus states that it was vacuumed, so he must have brought it in to be fixed.
**(A)** This is the correct answer. It can be diagrammed as:
wet-->morning water-->medication       Then, the glass is wet, so she must have taken her medication.
(B) S or B,      B,       therefore S. This reasoning is not similar to that in the stimulus.
(C) John bill-->kitchen table,       ~~kitchen table,~~      therefore ~~John bill~~. This reasoning is not similar to that in the stimulus.
(D) grumpy-->no coffee-->runs out,       therefore, grumpy-->runs out. This reasoning is not similar to that in the stimulus.
(E) G or C,       allergic to G,       therefore C       This reasoning is not similar to that in the stimulus.

**4. Question type: Strengthen**
(A), (B), (D), and (E) do not strengthen the argument; we need to know how the key interests of the shareholders relate to the corporation's profits.
(A) refers to satisfaction, which is unrelated.
(B) mentions the board of directors, which is unrelated.
(D) suggests that shareholders are interested in more than just profits, which would actually weaken the argument.
(E) suggests the president has other things to worry about, which does not suggest a strong relationship between the key interests and profits.
**(C)** This is the correct answer. It tells us there is a positive relationship between key interests and profits, making the "therefore" statement of the stimulus stronger.

**5. Question type: Must be true**
(A) There is nothing in the stimulus that determines how many children under six there are in the neighborhood.
**(B)** This is the correct answer. The stimulus says everyone in the neighborhood is allowed to go to the pool at some point. The child under six cannot go from noon to 5 or from 5 to closing. Therefore, there must be a time before noon when the child under six can go.
(C) There is no information about how many adults and how many kids over the age of 6 use the pool. There could be more adults swimming after 5, making the pool more crowded.

# PrepTest 52, Section 1 (LR) Continued...

(D) Just because people are able to visit the pool at some point during the day does not mean someone will visit the pool.
(E) A child over the age of six is allowed to swim between noon and 5, so they would not be breaking the rules.

### 6. Question type: Flaw in Reasoning
(A) The stimulus suggests that consistent numbers prove accuracy, not that consistent numbers are more important.
(B) Other tasks are irrelevant to the argument in the stimulus.
(C) Beck assumes that consistency means accuracy, so he could not believe that the numbers would be consistent even if the data was not accurate.
(D) The stimulus is about the accuracy of the program; there is no reason to judge it on anything else.
**(E)** This is the correct answer. Beck assumes that consistency means accuracy, which is a flaw in his reasoning.

### 7. Question type: Support
**(A)** Correct. The last sentence indicates that inductance is like the flow of water pipes; since we're talking about the rate of water flow, the analogy suggests that inductance strongly influences the rate of electric "flow" as well.
(B) The stimulus suggests that electrical flow is related to inductance in the same way that water flow is related to inertia. There is no suggested relationship between electricity and inertia.
(C) The stimulus suggests that inertia occurs in every pipe with water flowing, not just those with electric pumps. Therefore, the inertia could not be caused by the electric pump.
(D) The stimulus says nothing about electrical engineers, so there is no support for this statement.
(E) This is a trick. Inertia will keep the water flowing temporarily, but that does not mean the pump is still pumping.

### 8. Question type: Justify
(A) The reasoning is related to economic status, not health or illness.
(B) The journalist thinks that having a nationwide price is unjustified because some people in poor countries have more money than some people in richer countries. He doesn't mention a requirement to help those in need.
**(C)** This is the correct answer. Being from a poor country does not mean you must be poor, and being from a rich country does not mean you must be rich. The journalist thinks that prices should reflect the ability of each individual to pay, not the average individual's ability to pay.
(D) The problem is not a disparity of access between countries but between people within the same country.
(E) The fairness of these two things does not have an effect on the argument.

### 9. Question type: Strengthen
(A) This would not help Robert's case; it supports Samantha's idea that no extra time would be added.
(B) This does not help either side of the argument, as the argument centers on whether there will be extra time added to the school year.
(C) This is a trick. The point at issue is whether the plan will add extra time, not whether adding time will be beneficial.
**(D)** This is the correct answer. It suggests that the same number of school days, when spread out over the whole year with no three-month break, can be used to teach more. It supports Robert's idea that eliminating the summer break will allow teachers to teach more material.
(E) Students' preferences have nothing to do with the argument.

### 10. Question type: Assumption
**(A)** This is the correct answer. The conclusion is that when the plan is implemented, it will not be effectively enforced for some time. However, this depends on when the plan is implemented. If the plan is not implemented until the new system is in place, then there will be no problem with enforcing the plan when it is begun.
(B) The stimulus does not mention anything about the city's budget, just that it wants to raise revenue.
(C) This is not an assumption but rather a conclusion that could be drawn.
(D) An assumption is an unstated premise that would allow the conclusion to be properly drawn. Knowing

# PrepTest 52, Section 1 (LR) Continued...

that either raising revenue or alleviating congestion is desired over the other has no effect on the argument, as both are only affected when the plan is implemented and enforced effectively.

(E) Assuming this is true, the conclusion still cannot be properly drawn. Under this assumption, the plan could still be implemented only once the system is in place, making the conclusion false.

### 11. Question type: Resolve the paradox

(A) Having better nutrition could help people recover from illnesses, which would explain the difference. This is not the right answer.

(B) Having a higher level of stress could hurt people's recoveries from illnesses, which would explain the difference. This is not the right answer.

**(C)** This does not explain the difference. If there is no correlation between prestige of school and patient recovery rate, then more doctors from prestigious schools at large hospitals does not explain a lower recovery rate at larger hospitals. This is the correct answer.

(D) Being in the hospital for observation for a shorter length of time could make it less likely that a patient will recover, which would explain the difference. This is not the right answer.

(E) Doctors having less time to help treat patients could hurt people's recoveries from illnesses, which would explain the difference. This is not the right answer.

### 12. Question type: Weaken

(A) Perry has not made an argument for lending to businesses with the most extensive divisions of labor, so this does not weaken his argument.

(B) and (C) Because Perry has argued that worker-owned businesses are riskier, these both support his argument.

(D) Perry has argued that investors want to stay away from worker-owned businesses, which would be supported by this.

**(E)** Perry has argued that worker-owned businesses involve inefficiencies that lead to low profitability. This answer suggests a way that these inefficiencies are compensated for, weakening his argument.

### 13. Question type: Complete the argument

(A) is too extreme. Having one counterexample to a piece of evidence does not mean that evidence is false.

(B) is also too extreme. We could find other pieces of evidence that would tell us about this phenomenon.

(C) is too extreme as well. One example of nests being used in a particular way is not enough to decide how all nests are used.

(D) does not fit with the rest of the stimulus.

**(E)** is the correct answer. Because of the counterexample, paleontologists will have to look to other evidence to determine the truth. Therefore, the evidence they are using is not very strong.

### 14. Question type: Resolve the Paradox

(A) would not allow the conclusion to be drawn, as it would still mean that many students who studied less got higher grades.

(B) would not help either; all students' grades would go down, so there would be no overall effect.

**(C)** is the right answer; students who studied more in a harder course could get lower grades than those who studied less in an easier course. Comparing the grades only within individual courses takes this possibility out of the picture.

(D) would not help. Because the study only looked at study time, the amount of participation in extracurricular activities would not have an effect on the results.

(E) would explain the conclusion but not the data. Therefore, it does not resolve the paradox.

### 15. Question type: Most supported

(A) does not capture all of the implications because group C had negative psychological effects.

**(B)** is correct because the intensity of the pulses had a correlation with the changes in mood professional cyclists experienced.

(C) is incorrect because there is no data in between 60 and 70; 65% might improve mood just as much as 60.

(D) There is no reason to believe that the two are equal in affecting depression

(E) is incorrect because we don't know how moderate cycling affects them physically, only emotionally.

# PrepTest 52, Section 1 (LR) Continued...

**16. Question type: Parallel reasoning (flaw)**
believe in ET -->believe in UFOs,
UFOs refuted
therefore no extraterrestrials exist
The stimulus assumes wrongly that the relationship between believing in two things is the same as the relationship between the actual existence of those two things.

(A)     believe in unicorns-->believe in centaurs,
        centaurs refuted,
        therefore no unicorns
Correct. It uses the same logic that the stimulus does, confusing a relationship between beliefs as identical to the relationship between the actual existence of uniforms.

(B)     believe in unicorns-->believe in centaurs
        you don't believe in centaurs
        therefore you don't believe in unicorns
This is incorrect because it is logically sound, which the stimulus was not. Note that it deals only with beliefs, not making the incorrect transition to an argument about the actual existence of uniforms.

(C)     believe in unicorns-->believe in centaurs
        you don't believe in unicorns
        therefore you don't believe in centaurs
This is incorrect because it makes a different mistake in reasoning; it assumes that since the necsary (if) clause is false, the sufficient (then) clause will also be false. This is a very frequent fallacy on the LSAT.

(D)     believe in unicorns-->believe in centaurs
        no reason to believe in centaurs
        therefore no good reason to believe in unicorns
This is similar to the logic of the stimulus, but slightly different. In this case, it assumes that the relationship between believing in two things is the same as the relationship between how reasonable it is to believe in those things.

(E)     believe in unicorns-->believe in centaurs
        unicorns refuted
        therefore no centaurs
Note that in the stimulus, it's the necessary (then) clause that's refuted. Here it's the sufficient (if) clause.

**17. Question type: Assumption**
(A), (B), and (D) are incorrect because they do not cause the conclusion to be properly drawn; the problem with the conclusion is that the arguer jumped from premises about what can cause resentment to a conclusion about something being prudent or not. The assumption will have to relate prudence and resentment to each other somehow.
(C) is incorrect because it would suggest that one would be resented no matter what s/he did (appearing prudent would cause resentment due to the second premise, while appearing imprudent would cause resentment due to (C)). This does not allow the conclusion to be properly drawn.
(E) Correct. It defines a relationship between what is prudent and how much one is resented that allows the conclusion to be properly drawn.

**18. Question type: Cannot be true**
(A) could be true because all we know is that a regular smoker who smoked a cigarette has better short-term memory than a non-smoker who did and didn't smoke a cigarette. We do not know how one group of non-smokers did compared to the other.
(B) Correct. The stimulus states that a regular smoker who has smoked a cigarette has better short term memory than a non-smoker who has smoked a cigarette, so (B) is false.
(C) is possible, as we don't know anything about nonsmokers compared to smokers who have not smoked cigarettes.
(D) is possible, as we don't know anything about the effect of a heavy smoking session; it could heighten a smoker's short-term memory skills.
(E) is possible, as the data suggests that many regular smokers maintain better short-term memories for eight hours following smoking.

# PrepTest 52, Section 1 (LR) Continued...

**19. Question type: Principle/justify**
(A) is incorrect because the argument does not suggest one's vote would ever be more influential than an other's; rather, the argument suggests that one's vote is more influential if used in one way than in another way.
(B) is incorrect because it side-steps the issue and does not help the argument.
(C) is incorrect because it supports the argument but not for the reasons given in the argument.
(D) is incorrect because it runs counter to the argument.
**(E) Correct.** The educator suggests that voting should be done in a particular way because that way would increase the influence of each vote. (E) supports this reasoning.

**20. Question type: Assumption**
The conclusion suggests that there is "influence" between the two parts of the brain, which is not mentioned in any of the premises; up to this point we have only been discussing signals. Therefore, the missing assumption must relate signals to influence.
(A) does not allow the conclusion to be properly drawn; knowing that one depends on the other does not suggest that one is greater than the other.
(B) is incorrect; suggesting A exerts more influence on C than other things does not mean that A exerts more on C than C does on A.
(C) is incorrect; it involves similar reasoning to that used in (B) and is incorrect for the same reason.
(D) is incorrect; it fails to establish a connection between influence and brain connections that implies the conclusion.
**(E) Correct.** This is a clear link between signals and influence.

**21. Question type: Weaken**
(A) has no effect on the argument; if those poems attributed to Homer are in question, then having other poems attributed to him does not help or harm the argument.
(B) does not weaken the argument; minor copying errors may or may not contribute to differences between the two stories.
**(C) Correct.** It severely weakens the argument by denying the evidence's relevance.
(D) does not weaken the argument because it was never claimed that the two works were internally consistent.
(E) This strengthens the argument.

**22. Question type: Principle**
(A) is incorrect because according to the principle, something must be true for a statement to be wholly truthful. While he did not lie, his statement was not wholly truthful.
(B) is incorrect because his statement was a lie; it was intended to deceive.
(C) is tricky, but it is incorrect. Siobhan's statement was not wholly truthful, so either it was not true or it was intended to deceive. But we know that the statement was true, so it must have been intended to deceive. But if it was intended to deceive, then it was a lie. The statements taken together cannot all be true while using the principle in the stimulus.
**(D) is correct;** because Walter intended to deceive the interviewer, his statement was a lie according to the principle.
(E) is incorrect because a statement is a lie if it is intended to deceive, even if one would clarify a misinterpretation.

**23. Question type: Principle**
The principle can be diagrammed as:
intellectual development healthy --> does not detract social dev.
(A) is incorrect because the principle is not a claim based on experience but an idea of what would be good.
(B) is incorrect; in applying the principle, this was not done. It is possible that the principle neglects this idea, but this is not a problem with applying the principle. Rather, it is a problem with the principle itself.
(C) is incorrect because the application never claimed something was unhealthy; rather, it claimed that something was not healthy (it could be neutral).
**(D) is the correct answer;** in applying the principle, it was assumed that spending less time with other kids detracted from social development, making the activity not healthy.

# PrepTest 52, Section 1 (LR) Continued...

(E) is incorrect because the argument's application correctly used the sufficient->necessary relationship.

### 24. Question type: Support
(A) is incorrect because the stimulus contains no information about other companies' citrus juices.
(B) is incorrect because there are bacterial infections in the apple juice but not the citrus juices.
(C) is incorrect because only intense pasteurization is known to destroy original taste.
(D) is incorrect because the method is not MOST likely to destroy flavor but simply likely to do so.
**(E)** Correct. Intensely pasteurizing apple juice kills bacteria more effectively than any other method, and there are bacteria in McElligott's unpasteurized apple juice.

### 25. Question type: Assumption
The conclusion is the second sentence. There's a disconnect between "looking after their own welfare" and the sort of behavior that doesn't hurt others.
(A) is incorrect because the argument specifies what legislators who value democracy should do, so it does not assume that all legislators value democracy.
(B) is incorrect because it simply restates the last sentence in different words.
(C) and (D) are incorrect because assuming either one will not help prove the conclusion. They are both mere statements of fact that do not affect what legislators who value democracy should do.
**(E)** Correct. If (E) is assumed, it follows that the legislation in question would be injurious to democracy, so those valuing democracy should not support that legislation.

# PrepTest 52, Section 2, Game 1

This is a basic linear game as each valve is opened once, and only one at a time.

GHIKLNOP = 8

___  ___  ___  ___  ___  ___  ___  ___
 1    2    3    4    5    6    7    8

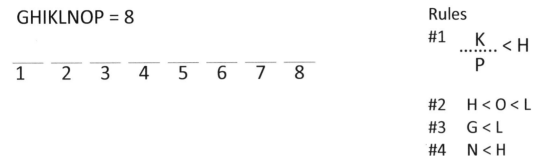

Rules
#1  ...K... < H
       P
#2  H < O < L
#3  G < L
#4  N < H
#5  K < I

Discussion: In all sequencing rules, it's imperative to combine rules as thoroughly as possible.

Use exclusion rules to get some key inferences. Always start with first and last spaces. Only I or L can go last, a key time-saver. Only K, P, G, or N could go first.

|    |    |    |    |    |    |    | I/L |
|----|----|----|----|----|----|----|-----|
| 1  | 2  | 3  | 4  | 5  | 6  | 7  | 8   |
| ~I | ~H | ~O | ~L |    | ~K | ~K | ~K  |
| ~H | ~O | ~L |    |    | ~P | ~P | ~P  |
| ~O | ~L |    |    |    |    | ~H | ~N  |
| ~L |    |    |    |    |    |    | ~H  |
|    |    |    |    |    |    |    | ~O  |
|    |    |    |    |    |    |    | ~G  |

1. List question; go rule-by-rule eliminating answer choices as you go.
a) Violates 5th rule
b) Violates second rule
c) Violates 4th rule
d) Violates third rule
e) **Correct**

2. Use prior diagrams for process of elimination
   a) Works, example: K P G N H O L I
   b) Works, example: K P G N I H O L
   c) **Correct**, K cannot be 5th; I, H, O, and L all have to go after it. (This is an inference we could have made in our initial diagram, but most students will miss it and it's not critical. Add it now.)
   d) Works, example: K P G I N H O L
   e) Works, example: K P G N H O L I

3. If I is second, K must be first.
   a) G can be third after K and I
   b) **Correct**; H must have N, K, and P before it. Since K and I must go first, there is not room for both P and N to also go before H if it is fourth.
   c) Works, example: K I N G P H O L
   d) Works, example: K I P N H O G L
   e) Works, example: K I P N I H G L

4. If L is seventh, think about what could go after it. I is the only variable that could go last.
   a) Works: K G P N H O L I
   b) **Correct**; I cannot go second because it must be last
   c) Works: G K N P H O L I
   d) Works: K N P G H O L F
   e) Works: N P K G H O L I

5. Use past diagrams to eliminate when possible.
   a) There's no reason P couldn't be first
   b) G could be first
   c) We know that L MUST go after O, but I and G could both also go after L
   d) 4 valves could be after H including O, I, L, and G
   e) **Correct**. N is before the sequence of H < O < L, so K, P, I, and G could go before N but no other variable could

6. K is usually an early variable, so we should think about the implications if K goes later. If K goes 4th, what has to go after it? I, H, O, and L, so P, N, and G go before K (in no particular order).
   a) We know I must go after K, 5th or later
   b) **Correct**. We know N goes before K, and there are not restrictions on the order of P, N, and G other than that they go before K in 4th
   c) G must go before K in 4th
   d) O must go after K and also after H, so the earliest it could go is 6th
   e) P must go before K here

7. If G is 1st and I is 3rd you can solve most of the game. L is the only other variable that could go last; if I isn't last, L will be last. Then, we can fill in O in 7 and H in 6. K has to go before I, so it must go in 2. Everything is filled in except for P and N, which could go in either 4 or 5.

   G K I _ _ H O L

   a) Must be true.
   b) **Correct**. N could be in 4 or in 5
   c) Must be true.
   d) Must be true.
   e) Must be true.

# PrepTest 52, Section 2, Game 2

This is a simple grouping game. There are 6 spots for 6 children.

J K L S T V = 6 children
MOP = 3 adults

M ___ ___
O ___ ___
P ___ ___ T

**Rules**

#1    Jm → Lp

#2    ~Km → Vo

#3    [JK] (crossed out)

#4    [LS] (crossed out)

#5    [TV] (crossed out)

**Contrapositives**

~Lp → ~Jm

~Vo → Km

Discussion: There aren't critical inferences to be made here. While you could work out the options given by the conditional rules, they don't lead to any significant insights. Better to just move on to the questions.

---

8. List question.
   a) Violates first rule
   b) **Correct**
   c) Violates second rule
   d) Violates fourth rule (L cannot be with S)
   e) Violates third rule

9. If L and T are with M, we know that the second rule is triggered and V must be with O. (That is, K cannot go with M because M is full with L and T). Then consider your exclusion rules. J and K need to be split up, though we aren't sure where exactly they go. That leaves S as the final variable which must go with P, as all other spaces are full.

M  L   T
O  V   J/K
P  J/K  S

   a) Could be false
   b) Could be false
   c) Could be false
   d) Could be false
   e) **Correct**: must be true.

10. Since P is full, we can deduce that M and O will each have one of L/S, and each have one of T/K since neither of those variables can be together by rule. That gives us:

$$
\begin{array}{ccc}
M & \underline{L/S} & \underline{T/K} \\
O & \underline{L/S} & \underline{T/K} \\
P & \underline{J} & \underline{V}
\end{array}
$$

We can then easily eliminate answer choices B and C. Then we start working through.

a) **Correct**.
b) K and T must be split.
c) L and S must be split
d) Violates the second rule. K is not with M, in which case V would have to be with O, but that's not possible
e) Similar to D, violates the second rule

11. What are the 2 things we know about T? He must go with M or O, and he cannot be paired with V. A quick scan reveals the answer:
a) Works
b) Can be eliminated by looking at #9's diagram
c) Can be eliminated by looking at #9's diagram
d) **Correct**. T can never be accompanied by P.
e) Works


12. This is simple process of elimination. **c) is the correct answer** since K and T cannot go with O. If K and T are with O, the second rule is in play: If K is not accompanied by M, V must be accompanied by O. Since O is full, it doesn't work. A, B, D, and E all work in this configuration.

# PrepTest 52, Section 2, Game 3

This is a hybrid game. At first, it looks like simple grouping since you need to fit 6 seminars into the 3 days of the conference. However, you also need to order within groups and across days linearly; it matters in which order the seminars go on a particular day. Your diagram should reflect this.

Short = G O P
Long = H* N T

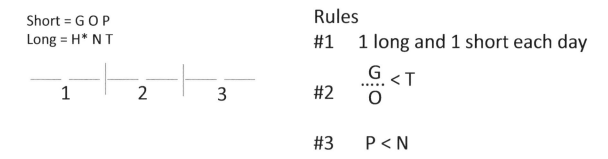

**Rules**

#1   1 long and 1 short each day

#2   G / O < T

#3   P < N

Discussion: Think about how the sequencing rules here interact with the need for 1 long and 1 short each day. While there aren't any big breakthroughs, you know, for example, that the earliest T can go is 4th because it must go after G and O, and if either G or O is in day 1 it must be accompanied by a long seminar. That means that G, O, and either N or H must go before T.

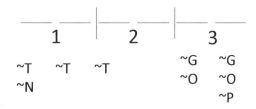

---

13. List question – use rule-by-rule process of elimination
    a) Violates second rule
    b) **Correct**
    c) Violates third rule
    d) Violates first rule – G and O are both short
    e) Violates second rule

14. Redraw your diagram and fill in G. We don't yet know if G goes first or second on Day 1.
    a) Since P goes before N, this won't work
    b) We can't have 2 shorts on any day
    c) We can't have 2 shorts on any day
    d) If H is on day 2, we need to place the other 2 long seminars. However, both T and N are highly restricted; neither of them can go in Day 1 under this arrangement, and they can't both go in day 3
    e) **Correct.** G H O T P N

15. It's very helpful to combine this new rule (N < O) with your other sequencing rules to get P < N < O < T, with G coming before T and H still floating.
    a) Could be true – G can go anywhere before T, and could go before or after N
    b) Could be true
    c) **Correct**. Our new rules clearly demonstrate this.
    d) Could be true
    e) Could be true

16. We can do a lot of eliminating here. H can always go anywhere. We can also look at our diagram for #15, where we see a lot of options for going fourth (second on the second day).
    a) Eliminated
    b) **Correct**. You run into problems with the short lectures. If P is the second day's short lecture, that would mean that either G or O would go 1ˢᵗ and 3ʳᵈ. However, we also know that N is the long lecture on Day 3 because it has to follow P. Then we have a problem with T; it has to go after O and G, but day 3 is full
    c) Could be true
    d) Could be true
    e) Could be true

17. If H is the long lecture the second day, immediately consider where our other long lectures go. We know from our inferences that T can't go on the first day, so it must go on the third day; therefore, N would be on the first day. We also know P has to go before N, so we get:

    P   N   H/   H/

Now we have to place our G O T sequence. T will have to be last, behind the short lecture on day 3. We don't have any direction on the order in which G/O go, so we get:

    P   N   H/G/O   G/O   T

    a) Can't be true
    b) Can't be true
    c) Can't be true
    d) **Correct**
    e) Can't be true

# PrepTest 52, Section 2, Game 4

This is another basic linear game, though it includes a conditional rule with a sequence, which has become popular on recent LSATs.

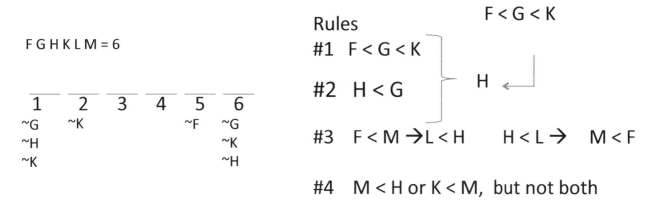

F G H K L M = 6

```
  1    2    3    4    5    6
 ~G   ~K              ~F   ~G
 ~H                        ~K
 ~K                        ~H
```

Rules
#1  F < G < K
#2  H < G
#3  F < M → L < H     H < L → M < F
#4  M < H or K < M, but not both

Combined
F < G < K
        ↑
        H

Discussion: Give some thought to what actually happens given the two options in Rule 4. Keep in mind that since only one of the options can be true (M < H or K < M), the *other* option must be false. So if M < H, we can infer M < K as well; if K < M, we can infer H < M.

**If M < H (implies M < K):**

M < H < G < K
        ↑
        F

Note: We moved H up into the main sequence here so we could add M and have a somewhat neater diagram. The relationship between F and other variables has not changed.

OR

**If K < M (implies H < K):**

F < G < K < M
        ↑
        H

This also triggers the conditional rule, Rule 3; since F < M is true, we know L < H as well:

F < G < K < M
        ↑
        L < H

---

18. List question – use rule-by-rule process of elimination
    a) Violates third rule
    b) Violates 4th rule (neither M<H or K<M)
    c) **Correct**
    d) Violates first rule
    e) Violates second rule

19. If F is 4th, G and K will be 5th and 6th respectively. Does an answer choice hinge on that insight? Yes.
    a) **Correct** – we see instantly that this is the inference we just found

We don't need to evaluate B-E here, each of which could be true.

20. There is a ton of variability here. You still have to place F, H, G, and K. We know the conditional rule is not triggered, and we don't get help from Rule 4 (M<H is true implying M<K, but that's obvious). However, when we examine the relationships of F, H, G, and K what do we see? Either H or F could start the sequence. What has to go last? Only K can go last!
a) Could be false
b) Could be false
c) Could be false
d) False; this configuration can't be true.
e) **Correct**.

21. This must be true question revolves around your understanding of the sequencing rules as given. Scan through and see if the right answer pops out.
a) Could be true
b) Could be true
c) **Correct**. This is definitely true because H < G and G < K
d) Could be true
e) Could be true

22. Make sure to write out your new rule K<L and combine it with what you already have. Only M is not represented, but we can learn more about it. Does this trigger any rules? Right – the contrapositive to Rule 3. If H < L → M < F.

## M< F < G < K < L

H

a) If F < M then we know that L < H from Rule 3. However, our diagram says that H goes before L, so this doesn't work
b) The same logic as in A works here
c) **Correct**. We could have M F H G K L
d) Only L can go last here since M has to go before F (because of Rule 3)
e) This one is more complicated. Remember that of the two options in Rule 4, if one is right the other's opposite is also right. We know from the discussion above that M will go before F, so we also know M < K. Since K < M is FALSE, M < H must be true as the other option. M therefore can't be second because it has to go first

23. Use past diagrams to eliminate, then move to process of elimination.
a) Could be true
b) Could be true
c) Could be true
d) Could be true
e) **Correct**. If M is 4th, we an deduce that H will have to go before M since at least G and K must still go after H and M. According to the 4th rule, either M < H or K <M. We know H < M, so we deduce K < M. But that doesn't work at all!

# PrepTest 52, Section 3 (LR)

## 1. Question type: Principle
The correct choice in this type of question will give a general principle that is applied by the argument in the prompt. To find the principle, state the argument more abstractly and generally, which will help predict the answer. Here, the argument is that a particular stamp's red ink would be damaged if the stamp is put on display, so to preserve the stamp, it should not be displayed. This general argument is given by choice **(D)**, which is therefore the correct answer.

The prompt never mentions public perception, so (A) is wrong.

(B) is perhaps appealing, but the author of the prompt appears to assume that museum cases, of any kind, would allow ultraviolet light to damage artifacts—roughly the opposite of (B).

(C) focuses on the red ink—the specifics of the situation, not the general principle involved. (It also gets the argument backwards.)

(E) states a principle that is at odds with the author's argument: the author seems to assume that educating the public is secondary to the museum's role as an archive.

## 2. Question type: Main Point
The main point should already be stated in the passage, so your mission is simply to choose the answer that restates the conclusion that the argument reaches. Restated simply, the passage argues that food with "fake fat" is unlikely to help with weight loss, because consumers compensate by replacing the calories in other ways. This conclusion is stated even more succinctly by choice **(D)**, the correct answer.

(A) gives merely a premise on which the conclusion rests.

(B) is initially appealing, but the passage focuses on weight loss, not nutrition. These are not the same thing, so (B) is incorrect.

(C) overstates the author's case. The author argues that "fake fat" foods are neither more likely nor less likely to lead to obesity, but the passage never states that the "fake fat" foods are actually worse.

(E) gives a statement made in the prompt, but does not focus on the prompt's main idea.

## 3. Question type: Strengthen
The best choice will often support an unstated assumption made by the argument. The argument here is that it is a poor business decision for banks not to offer special deals to long-term customers rather than new customers.

(A) states that most banks have similar charges, which is irrelevant to the argument.

**(B)** is correct: it states that banks that give deals to long-term customers fare better, providing evidence that doing so is good for business.

(C) actually weakens the given argument.

(D) too, would actually weaken the argument.

(E) states that offering incentives to new customers can be successful, which is approximately the opposite of the prompt's argument.

## 4. Question type: Find the flaw
The difficulty with this argument is that it assumes that correlation implies causation. The author reasons that because articles that are cited in the popular press are also cited more frequently by subsequent researchers, that the subsequent researches were influenced by the popular press. But it could be that both the appearance in the press and the subsequent citations are both caused by the original articles' excellence.

(A) is incorrect. The prompt gives nothing that seems to be a counterargument.

**(B)** is correct: it identifies that the press and subsequent researchers may be influenced by a third cause (like excellence).

(C) is incorrect: the assumption it gives is not one the prompt seems to make.

(D) is true, but does not identify a flaw in the argument, so is not correct.

(E) states that the author is guilty of circular reasoning; that isn't the problem here.

## 5. Question type: Method of argument
The question asks you to analyze the structure of the argument. In this case, the author lists three options for deciding a meeting agenda. He rejects two of the three for various reasons, and settles on the third option. The correct choice describes that structure.

(A) is incorrect, because constitutional grounds are never mentioned.

## PrepTest 52, Section 3 (LR) Continued...

(B) is incorrect, because the author never says that one procedure will always be appropriate.
(C) is incorrect, because constitutional changes are never suggested.
**(D)** is correct. The argument is by elimination of alternatives.
(E) is incorrect. The argument never references other persons who have advocated alternatives.

### 6. Question type: Weaken
One way of weakening a conclusion is to find a consideration that was overlooked by the author of the argument. Here, the argument is that a municipal tax on cigarettes would cause sales of cigarettes in the city to drop, and would thus reduce smoking. We wish to weaken this argument.
(A) if true, would strengthen this argument.
(B) may seem attractive, but it discusses consumer behavior under one price increase relative to another; here, we do not have two types of price increases to compare.
**(C)** is correct. One consideration that was overlooked by the argument is the fact that even if cigarette sales in the city go down, consumers simply may buy their tobacco elsewhere, thus resulting in no actual reduction in smoking.
(D) is irrelevant to the argument at hand, since it addresses education programs.
(E) likewise, deals with the education program rather than the tax, and is incorrect.

### 7. Question type: Assumption
The correct assumption will bolster a weak argument. In this case, the argument is that because children are several years old before they can voluntarily produce vowels and consonants, that speech acquisition is a motor control process. The missing link in this argument is the one between producing vowels and consonants and speech acquisition.
**(A)** correctly states this missing assumption.
(B), (C), (D), and (E) give details about the development of motor control; none of them are relevant to the link between producing sounds and speech acquisition.

### 8. Question type: Find the flaw
In this case, the biggest flaw is that the argument overstates its conclusion. The author makes a fair (but not rock-solid) case that knocking down the base may have been inefficient. But there is no premise that would support a leap to the further conclusion that the government's action is also immoral.
**(A)** is correct. It states the chief problem with the argument: an action may be moral even if it is inefficient.
(B) is incorrect. The author in fact assumes the opposite: that consequences are relevant to an action's morality.
(C) is incorrect: no such assumption is made.
(D) is incorrect: while the author seems to assume that an inefficient action is immoral, the author does not also assume the inverse of that statement.
(E) is incorrect: no false dichotomy is presented here.

### 9. Question type: Assumption
The correct assumption will give an unstated premise on which the conclusion depends. Here, the author considers a study showing that patients who hear music require less anesthesia than those who hear conversation; he reaches the conclusion that reducing stress lowers sensitivity to pain. The missing element is the link between music or conversation and stress level. This is given in **(C)**, the correct choice.
(A) is incorrect, since the reasoning of the argument does not depend on this assumption.
(B) makes a statement that is irrelevant to the argument.
(D) is incorrect—the variable in the study is music vs. conversation, not whether either is changed by painkillers.
(E) likewise, misunderstands the point of the study: analyzing music vs. conversation, rather than anesthesia vs. painkillers.

### 10. Question type: Point at issue
One easy technique, in deciding where the two speakers disagree, is to eliminate the answer choices that mention something only one speaker (or neither speaker) discussed.
(A) A trend towards dissolution of social bonds is discussed only by the first speaker.
(B) The idea that purely private behavior dissolves social bonds is mentioned by only the first speaker—and

## PrepTest 52, Section 3 (LR) Continued...

even he did not go so far as to say that all such behavior does so.
(C) is not a point which either speaker directly addressed.
(D), likewise, is a point addressed by neither speaker.
(E) is correct. The speakers differ on what people would be doing if they weren't using their computers.

### 11. Question type: Principle

The correct choice will give a general principle that is applied by the argument in the prompt. One easy technique is to restate the argument in more general terms, which will help predict the answer. According to the author, seeding the oceans with iron has side effects that are not understood; until these side effects are known, the oceans are too valuable to experiment with.
(A) states the inverse of that argument, and is therefore incorrect.
(B) is correct: it states the above argument in more general terms.
(C) is incorrect: the argument does not weigh the relative consequences of the solution and the problem.
(D) is incorrect: it misses that we don't understand the consequences of a given action, which was important in the argument.
(E) is incorrect: it, too, overstates the argument.

### 12. Question type: Find the flaw

Here, the conclusion drawn is simply unsupported by the premise. If historians are necessarily affected by their biases, would that problem really be solved by interpreting contemporary reactions rather than the events themselves?
(A) While the fact that historians with different biases tend to agree might actually weaken this author's argument, this isn't a strengthen-weaken question. This fact isn't a flaw in the author's argument.
(B) Scholars in other disciplines simply aren't relevant to the argument.
(C) The fact that the biases have been identified is in fact a restatement of the author's premise.
(D), if true, would actually support the argument.
(E) is correct. It accurately identifies the problem.

### 13. Question type: Assumption

The assumption is an unstated premise on which the conclusion depends. Here, the author reasons that because trauma centers can save lives, those persons' earnings would improve Country X's GDP. The missing link is that between saved lives and earnings. That link is provided by answer (D).
(A) compares country X and country Y, but the argument has nothing to do with the two countries' relative per-capita income.
(B) is not relevant to the argument.
(C) is appealing, since it gives an apparent "hole" in the argument, but it is not the best choice since the argument does not actually depend on this assumption.
(D) is the correct choice.
(E) is irrelevant to the question of transportation to trauma centers.

### 14. Question type: Inference

You are asked to draw the conclusion that is supported by the given premises. Here, we know that urban societies require farming, that farming requires irrigation, and that irrigation required rivers or lakes until recently. Therefore, urban societies required rivers or lakes until recently. That's what (C) says.
(A) is incorrect, since it requires a statement that most people lived in urban societies; we don't have that premise.
(B) references societies, not urban societies, so cannot be correct.
(C) is the correct inference.
(D) makes a statement that is not supported by the given premises.
(E) draws a conclusion about rural societies; we don't have information about those.

### 15. Question type: Assumption

Despite the unusual wording of the prompt, you are asked to identify an unstated premise on which the conclusion depends. The author reasons that rapid recovery requires investment, and that investment requires public confidence. He then concludes that countries that put collective goals before individual goals do not re-

# PrepTest 52, Section 3 (LR) Continued...

cover rapidly. The missing link is that between public confidence and valuing collective goals over individual.
(A) incorrectly states the inverse of one of the premises.
(B) makes a statement that is irrelevant to the argument.
(C) is supported by the economist's argument, but isn't a conclusion on which the argument depends.
**(D)** is the correct answer: it provides the missing link between public confidence and the relative value of the collective and the individual.
(E) is irrelevant; it deals with experiencing a recession rather than emerging from one.

### 16. Question type: Find the flaw
One common flaw with LSAT arguments is incorrectly drawing inferences from averages, especially when juxtaposed with absolute numbers. Here, we learn that the average hospital stay at University Hospital is longer than at Edgewater, yet recovery rates are similar at the two hospitals for patients with similar illnesses. The author draws the conclusion that patients stay at University longer than they need to. This conclusion arises from incorrectly understanding what the average hospital stay implies. It could just as easily be that University treats a greater proportion of patients with serious illnesses. This problem is given by choice **(C)**.
Both (A) and (B) raise points that are not even addressed in the argument.
(D) is incorrect: the article makes no such sweeping assumption.
(E) is irrelevant: the preferences of the patients are not germane to the argument.

### 17. Question type: Method of argument
The question asks you to analyze the structure of the philosopher's argument. He is clearly presenting a counterargument to Graham. But how is he attacking Graham's argument? Graham stated, as his premise, that a person is only happy when he is doing something; the philosopher points out that happiness is possible even during sleep. This statement is aimed at Graham's premise.
(A) is untrue: the statement is a premise of the philosopher's argument, not Graham's.
**(B)** is correct: the statement attacks Graham's premise.
(C) is inaccurate, since there is no analogy presented here.
(D) is not the best answer: the philosopher is not (directly) attacking Graham's conclusion that the best life is an active life. Instead, he is attacking the premise that we are only happy when active.
(E) is false. The main conclusion of the philosopher's argument is simply that Graham should not be believed.

### 18. Question type: Inference.
Each of the historian's statements is designed to show that West influenced Stuart. The fact that Stuart used West's terminology and that Stuart often met with West support that inference. Thus, the correct answer is choice **(D)**. The other answers all list inferences that cannot be drawn from this evidence.

### 19. Question type: Weaken
The argument is that dinosaurs died from angiosperm poisoning. Mammals were immune to this poison, so survived. The author suggests that strong evidence for this is derived from the contorted positions of dinosaur skeletons that have been found (suggesting that the dinosaurs had been poisoned). If that strong evidence were weakened, the theory would also be weakened. That's given by choice (A): if mammal fossils were also contorted, it would suggest either that they were not immune to the poison, or that the contorting was for some other reason than the poison. Choices (B) through (E) are irrelevant to the argument.

### 20. Question type: Strengthen (strengthen one portion of the argument)
The argument is that continuous maintenance is cheaper over the long term than radical reconstruction. Yet continuous maintenance almost never happens. You are looking for evidence that would explain why this is so.
(A) is incorrect, because if true, it would make radical reconstruction less common than continual maintenance.
(B) is irrelevant to the difference between continuous maintenance and radical reconstruction. Choice (C) is possibly true, but does not explain the discrepancy.
(D) like choice (A), would make radical reconstruction more difficult, not less.
**(E)** Correct. The lack of urgency explains why the continuous method is not adopted despite the fact that it saves in the long-run.

## PrepTest 52, Section 3 (LR) Continued...

**21. Question type: Find the flaw**
The argument is that because one-time parachuters report being frightened, while repeat parachuters do not, that repeatedly engaging in an activity can help one overcome fear. Essentially, this is sample bias: people who find parachuting frightening are unlikely to repeat the experience. So naturally, the sample of repeat parachuters is likely to contain far more of those who did not initially find it frightening.
This is reflected in answer choice (**E**).

**22. Question type: Discrepency/paradox**
You are asked to reconcile two apparently contradictory statements. Here, we have the general economic statement that reducing a product's price can increase demand for the product, and the statement that reducing the price of domestic wine can increase demand for imported wine. The two statements are not inconsistent—we hear nothing about whether demand for the domestic wine went up or down. So what we are looking for is some way in which the price of domestic wine and demand for imported wine can be economically linked. That is given in choice (**E**).

**23. Question type: Inference**
The passage suggests that the H2S waste product helps the bacteria by both eliminating O2 and by killing off competitors. Dense colonies can do this indefinitely. Choice (**A**) states this inference conservatively. Choices (D) and (E) word this same inference too strongly, and are therefore incorrect. Choices (B) and (C) make statements not supported by the passage.

**24. Question type: Parallel reasoning**
The passage states that because utopian books are popular, dystopian books must be unpopular. The flaw with this reasoning is assuming that the inverse of a true statement is also true. (That is, taking A->B and reasoning that Not A -> Not B. This is a fallacy.) This reasoning is replicated by choice (**C**), which starts with the statement that action movies are expensive, and reasons that non-action movies must be inexpensive.

**25. Question type: Principle.**
The argument states that study of the present can provide clues to the distant past; however, the more distant the past in question, the less helpful that study will be. This is paralleled in choice (**A**). Choice (C) seems appealing, but refers to distance between one's world view and that of the author; such distance is not necessarily distance in time. The other choices are not close to being parallel.

# PrepTest 52, Section 4 (RC)

**Passage 1.** The beginning, "Many critics..." should alert you to the fact that the author may disagree. "But his originality as a filmmaker lies most strikingly in having successfully adapted film...to the needs, pace, and structure of West African culture" states the passage's main idea, and should be underlined. The first sentences of the remaining paragraphs indicate that they introduce specific examples of this idea.

1. Main idea. The passage is about this filmmaker's use of West African storytelling techniques and motifs within the context of contemporary film. Having predicted that answer, look for the choice that most clearly expresses that. Here, it's **(E)**.

(A) is appealing, but is not stated as generally as the author does.
(B) focuses on only one of the specific examples the author gives.
(C) takes an idea suggested by the passage and overstates it.
(D) states an idea not contained in the passage at all.

2. Information explicitly stated. Read each answer choice. **(E)** states an idea that is explicitly mentioned in the passage (lines 35-38). The other four answers do not.

3. Strengthen. Reread the sentence pointed to in the prompt; it makes the claim that binary oppositions in Sembene's films derive from West African tradition, not from Marxist thought. This argument would be strengthened by other evidence that West African tradition can be a source of such binaries, independently of Marxism.

**(A)** is correct: it suggests that other West Africans use this technique, including those who have not been exposed to Marx.
(B) would weaken the argument: it suggests that binary juxtaposition is an element of all storytelling, not just West African tradition.
(C) would weaken the argument by suggesting that Sembene's technique was explicitly Marxist.
(D) is appealing, but incorrect because it demonstrates only that the binaries are neither European nor North American; it does not demonstrate that they are West African.
(E), likewise, suffers from the problem that it fails to tie binaries to West Africa.

4. Inference. The question asks you to identify the choice that is supported by evidence within the passage.
(A) No reference is made in the passage to Sembene's popularity.
(B) and (E) The government reaction to the films is not given any consideration.
(C) While it is true that the passage gives a different interpretation of his films than is advanced by "many critics," there is no indication that Senegalese critics misunderstand the films.
**(D)** is correct. See lines 20-24.
(E) Censorship is not mentioned.

5. Word meaning. Refer to the sentence indicated. From context, "initiatory" is used to describe a journey that brings about a change in a character's worldview. This is expressed by choice **(C)**. (A) and (E) are appealing, but lack that "initiation" sense that is intended. (B) and (D) miss the mark entirely.

6. Inference not supported. You are asked to identify an inference not supported by the passage. While the passage makes it clear that Sembene is interested in social commentary, it does not state his actual opinions of the Senegalese government, or attempts at reform. **(A)** thus overstates the author's position, and is correct (because the passage does not support this choice). (B) through (E) all make statements that are supported by the passage.

**Passage 2, Comparative reading**
Passage A argues that history professors assign dry reading to their students. However, in response to this, some historians have begun to incorporate stories into their writing, which has become a trend.

Passage B begins similarly by noting that legal writing follows strict rules. The author argues that lawyers write

## PrepTest 52, Section 4 (RC) Continued...

badly, with one solution being narrative. The author is concerned that narrative could be incorporated into curricula without actually changing matters but believes it should be done anyway.

Consider where the passages overlap. Both are arguing that narrative should play a bigger role in their respective fields.

7. Common theme. Based on the above analysis, **(D)** is the correct choice.
(A) is an idea developed only in Passage B.
(B) is an idea suggested only by Passage A.
(C) states an idea that neither author agrees with.
(D) is correct.
(E) states an idea not relevant to either passage.

8. Inferences. Both authors seem to speak from within their professions—knowledgeable about how they operate, yet critical of that operation. Choice **(B)** is therefore correct.

9. Common theme. The two passages are alike in that they suggest that both professions focus too little on storytelling, and too much on ideas. See lines 9-14, 48-51. Choice **(A)** expresses this, and is correct.

(B) Hyperbole—exaggeration—is not mentioned.
(C) Subversion—undercutting commonly held ideas—is mentioned in Passage B only.
(D) Narrative is mentioned in both passages as desirable, but not typical.
(E) Imagination, likewise, is suggested as being atypical of the professions' writing.

10. We know these passages are more alike than different. Only choice **(C)** accurately describes a difference between the passages; Passage A in the first paragraph offers examples of the sort of dry historical writing it critiques, while Passage B lacks example.

11. The sentence referred to in the prompt essentially states that the problem with historiography is the lack of appeal to emotions. The correct answer will give a phrase from passage B that highlights a similar problem with legal writing. That response is choice **(B)**.

12. The author of Passage B states that most legal writing is devoid of emotions. You can infer from that that he would expect a lawyer's summary of a case to be equally dry. That is reflected in choice **(D)**.

**Passage 3**
1st paragraph describes the "traditional" theory. This should alert you that the author's point of view may contrast. Second paragraph: population of the spider, "however," exhibits different behavior. Reichert argues that this behavior is explained by evolutionary game theory. Similarities and differences between evolutionary and traditional game theory are discussed. Third paragraph: if game theory is correct, a prediction is made.

The main of the passage is the relative success of evolutionary game theory (rather than the traditional method) to predict spider behavior.

13. Main idea. As noted, the passage focuses on the use of game theory to explain spider behavior. This is given in choice **(C)**. The other choices give ideas contained in the passage, but they are not the main idea.

14. As noted, the first paragraph describes the traditional theory that the author wishes to contrast with game theory. The tortoises are given as an example of that traditional theory. **(E)** is correct.

15. (Not scored)

16. This focuses on the third paragraph: the point of game theory is that the more desirable the habitat, and the scarcer it is, the more likely the spiders are to fight over it. You're looking for evidence that would refute that. (The passage states that desirable riparian habitat is less scarce than desirable grassland habitat.)

# PrepTest 52, Section 4 (RC) Continued...

Each of the answer choices is consistent with this point of view except (D), the correct answer.

17. As noted, the third paragraph is a prediction. Having marked that, you can scan the answers quickly to arrive at **(E)**.

18, The passage mentions at least two main reasons why the spiders will vary their approach to fighting: value of disputed resource, and likelihood of injury (lines 31-34). Choice **(B)** is correct because it states both facts. Choice (A) is appealing, but it states that the differences are "primarily" because of the differing levels of competition—the passage never directly states the relative importance of this factor versus likelihood of injury. The other choices are unsupported by the passage.

19. The main idea, again, is that game theory, rather than traditional theories, predicts spider behavior. This is an alternative theory, so choice **(A)** is correct.

**Passage 4**
The first paragraph contains several reversals—read carefully to reach the main idea. "Most people" acknowledge that governments sometimes prescribe immoral conduct. But it is "commonly" supposed that that is an exception, and that law carries moral weight. The passage then describes philosophical anarchism, which holds that law never carries moral weight. "Some commentators" have rejected this view for two stated reasons. "In fact, however," those two reasons are ill-founded.

Add it all up, and you can see that the author is defending philosophical anarchism against one particular line of attack—the two points argued "some commentators." The paragraph beginning with "First" refutes the first of those points (that governments are all equally legitimate); the paragraph beginning with "Second" refutes the second (that people will not follow laws absent a moral obligation). Mark your passage accordingly.

20. Main point: As noted, the passage defends philosophical anarchism against two specific charges (helpfully marked as (1) and (2) in the passage). This is given in answer choice **(C)**.

21. The "commonly held" beliefs listed in the passage are in the first paragraph—these are the points of view that are contrasted with philosophical anarchism. Choice **(A)** gives one of those points of view.

22. The author is defending philosophical anarchism, so his point of view towards that philosophy is unlikely to be negative. Thus, eliminate (C), (D), and (E). The difference between choice (A) (ardent approval) and choice (B) (apparent acceptance) is one of tone. The author is not vociferously arguing that anarchism is correct; he's merely refuting one line of attack against it. **(B)** is therefore more accurate.

23. The question essentially asks you to define "counterintuitive" in context. The best definition is given by choice **(A)**. Counterintuitive means "contrary to intuition"; intuition is a combination of basic assumptions and common sense. Choices (B) (contrary to evidence), (D) (contrary to each other), and (E) (contrary to logic) misstate the meaning of the word. Choice (C) is backwards—the commentators believe that anarchism defies common sense, not that it follows it.

24. Refer to the section of the passage indicated. You should have noted the topic of that paragraph is anarchism's belief that individuals have moral duties to each other, even outside of governmental context. Choice **(B)** is the only example of someone behaving morally despite lack of formal governmental punishments for not doing so.

(C), (D), and (E) are examples of someone behaving immorally. (A) is an example of someone acting morally but only in order to avoid government punishment.

25. You are looking for a point of view that can reasonably be inferred from the passage. The only choice supported by the passage is **(C)**; according to the author individuals will support good initiatives even without moral force of law. (A) is incorrect—the author seems to believe that there are fewer moral obligations than normally supposed. Choices (B), (D), and (E) all link morality with government, the opposite of the passage's

*PrepTest 52, Section 4 (RC) Continued...*

point of view.

26. The discussion of individuals' moral duty to care for one another appears in the third paragraph; it's part of the author's refutation of point (2). The opposite of point (2) is that philosophical anarchism recognizes that people may not do as they please, and do have moral obligations. Thus, choice **(D)** is correct.

27. As noted, the structure of the passage is a refutation of an argument against philosophical anarchism. This is given by choice **(D)**.

# PrepTest 53

## PrepTest 53, Section 1 (LR)

**1. Question Type: Strengthen EXCEPT**
The conclusion here is that consumers should be skeptical of claims made in advertisements. Four of the answers should help this claim, while the correct answer should not.
(A) This supports the conclusion by suggesting many claims will be inaccurate.
(B) This supports the conclusion by showing that claims have been inaccurate in the past.
**(C)** Correct. This does not support the claim, as it does not suggest that consumers should be skeptical; it only states that many consumers are.
(D) This supports the conclusion by suggesting that ad creators are okay with inaccuracies.
(E) This supports the conclusion because this would make it easy to get away with inaccurate claims in advertising.

**2. Question Type: Point at Issue**
Elaine is concerned with acquiring pieces of art from every genre, while Frederick is concerned with preserving the greatest pieces of art, regardless of genre.
(A) Elaine suggests this is possible, and Frederick does not say it is impossible, so they do not disagree on this issue.
**(B)** Correct. Elaine thinks that museums should try to get the best artwork from every genre, while Frederick thinks they should just try to get pieces from recognized masters, regardless of which genres are represented. Thus, the two disagree about this statement.
(C) Elaine and Frederick both mention that this is one of the purposes of a museum.
(D) Neither has suggested this should be done or not done, so it is not the issue they disagree about.
(E) Neither has suggested this should be done or not done, so it is not the issue they disagree about.

**3. Question Type: Weaken**
A flaw in the argument is that no premise has stated that diseases shared between humans and cats are genetically based; this is simply assumed. The weakness will likely expose this flaw.
(A) This does not affect the argument; resistance to a disease is unrelated to having it in common with another species.
**(B)** Correct. This answer correctly exposes the assumption made and shows the author was incorrect to assume it. Therefore, the statement weakens the argument.
(C) This does not affect the argument as we do not know how genetically related the non-human primates are to cats, only that non-human primates are more closely related to humans than cats are.
(D) This does not affect the argument as how mild a disease is does not alter the number of diseases shared between species.
(E) This was stated as a premise, so it cannot weaken the argument.

**4. Question Type: Conclusion/Main Point**
The conclusion of this argument is the first sentence, so we should look for an answer that paraphrases the first sentence.
**(A)** Correct. This is a paraphrase of the first sentence, so it expresses the conclusion accurately.
(B), (C), (D) and (E) do not paraphrase the first sentence, so they do not express the conclusion.

**5. Question Type: Principle**
(A) This answer is too extreme. It is possible that a technical or scientific solution could fix the problem described.
(B) No prescription for the problem is given, so this does not fit the situation.
(C) This answer is too extreme. We don't know about EVERY enhancement, just one.
(D) No institution is preoccupied with prolonging life, so this cannot be the answer.
**(E)** Correct. One set of problems (early death) has been solved, but created a different set of problems (underfunded welfare programs).

## PrepTest 53, Section 1 (LR) Continued...

**6. Question Type: Strengthen**

The main point of the argument is that Jackie will probably like the new album. So the answer will probably support this idea.

(A) Correct. This supports the idea that Jackie will like the new album, so it strengthens the argument.
(B) There is no reason to believe that Jackie will be impressed by the new producer.
(C) There is no reason to believe that where the band plays will affect Jackie's disposition.
(D) This does not affect whether she will like the new album or not.
(E) This does not affect what Jackie will think about the new album by a different band.

**7. Question Type: Must Be True**

The statement can be diagrammed as follows:
If SC economically feasible -> a substance conducts above -148
Conducts above -148 -> it is an alloy of N and G
There is no alloy of N and G that conducts above -160

Following the logic, since anything conducting above -148 must be an alloy of N and G, and there is no alloy of N and G, we conclude that superconducting will not become feasible. (To see why this is so, write out the contrapositives as well.

(A) Correct. This correctly states what we inferred above from the statement.
(B) This would contradict the second statement in the diagram above, so it is not supported by the stimulus.
(C) This would contradict the first statement in the diagram above, so it is not supported by the stimulus.
(D) We know only that such an alloy conducts at temperatures no higher than -160; we know nothing about when it does not super-conduct.
(E) This is not supported by the stimulus, which only makes a statement about the economic feasibility of superconductors, not N and G.

**8. Question Type: Weaken**

Because this stimulus includes statistical data, any answer that attacks the use of this data to imply the conclusion would weaken it. (This is a common pattern on the LSAT).

(A) This does not weaken the argument because it does not give the age of the children in the study. They could be old enough to fit with the conclusion given.
(B) This does not weaken the argument, which states that near-sightedness caused by night lights disappears with age. The argument does not suggest or assume that having a night light makes someone more or less likely to be near sighted.
(C) This could be seen as strengthening the argument; at best it is neutral.
(D) Correct. This answer suggests that the data cannot be used because the sample is too small, which would weaken the argument.
(E) This could be seen as strengthening the argument; at best it is neutral.

**9. Question Type: Assumption**

If you read closely, you should have noticed that the stimulus states that the population of nesting females has fallen by two thirds. This is different from the entire population of the species, which may or may not have fallen by two thirds. The correct answer should make a link between the female population and the population as a whole.

(A) Correct. This creates the link we were looking for with our predicted answer. If we negate this statement, it makes the conclusion incorrect, therefore passing the negation test.
(B) This does not have an effect on the argument, which says that leatherback turtles are in danger of extinction due to a specific criterion.
(C) This sounds like it could be the link we are looking for. However, because the argument refers to proportions, the answer should also be in proportions.
(D) This could strengthen the argument, but it is not an assumption of the argument. Whether or not they exist in captivity has no bearing on whether or not the conclusion is sound.
(E) The argument does not suggest anything be done about the situation, merely that leatherback turtles should be given a new label.

# PrepTest 53, Section 1 (LR) Continued...

**10. Question Type: Strengthen**
The flaw in reasoning here is an assumption; it is assumed that teaching people how to make vegetables more appetizing will get them to eat more vegetables. The answer will likely support this assumption.
(A) This does not strengthen the argument, as making vegetables more appetizing would not have any effect on those who already love vegetables.
(B) This would actually weaken the argument, as it would suggest that we don't want people to make their vegetables more appetizing.
(C) This would also weaken the argument, as it would suggest that knowing vegetables can be made more appetizing would not help people eat more vegetables.
(D) Correct. This answer supports the assumption we identified, therefore strengthening the argument.
(E) This answer is too extreme, and it does not get rid of the flaw in reasoning.

**11. Question Type: Method of Reasoning**
The claim is that they will not pay for pure science, which suggests the conclusion that public funds should be used to fund pure science. As such, the claim is a premise that rules out an alternative and supports the conclusion.
(A) It is a premise, not the conclusion.
(B) Pure research is described in the first sentence, not the sentence regarding private companies.
(C) It is not used to distract from anything but rather to support the conclusion.
(D) Correct. This answer correctly describes our predicted answer.
(E) The argument does not mention anything about consequences, so this cannot be what the claim about private companies was about.

**12. Question Type: Flaw**
Jack seems to misunderstand Melinda's use of the word risk. He thinks she means that buying insurance will reduce the risk of his home catching on fire. She is merely talking about the money someone would have to pay for repairs.
(A) and (B) Jack does not mention either of these terms, and neither seems to have an effect on his answer to Melinda.
(C) Correct. This correctly identifies risk as the term that caused the misunderstanding.
(D) They both use the term decrease to mean lessen, despite the different contexts.
(E) He clearly knows what insurance is and believes it is the same thing Melinda does.

**13. Question Type: Assumption**
The argument assumes that if the effect of the drug did not go away after not having the drug for three months, then it must not have been an effect of the drug. The correct answer will paraphrase this.
(A) Correct. This correctly paraphrases the predicted answer. If we negate this statement, it makes the conclusion incorrect, therefore passing the negation test.
(B) If this is assumed, then the conclusion would be incorrect. Therefore, this cannot be the assumption.
(C), (D), and (E) all strengthen the argument by adding facts that suggest the conclusion. However, none of them identifies the assumption that makes the conclusion sound.

**14. Question Type: Method of Reasoning**
This statement is a sub-conclusion, supported by the sentences that follow, and it supports the main conclusion that some government control is needed.
(A) The statement is given as evidence for the conclusion, so it cannot be a view it is attempting to discredit.
(B) and (C) The argument disagrees with the idea that a TV should only be subject to market forces, so these cannot be the correct answer.
(D) Correct. This answer paraphrases our predicted answer. It describes the role played by the statement in the argument.
(E) This reverses the role of the statement and one of the premises.

**15. Question Type: Assumption**
The conclusion is that if we spread limestone, the soil will be more attractive to worms by balancing the acid. There's an assumption in here that if we spread alkaline on top of acid, the two will counter-balance.

(A) The argument makes no claim about the function of earthworms; it simply states one way that soil could be made more attractive to earthworms.
(B) Correct. Since the limestone has to interact with the layer underneath, if it got washed away too quickly the conclusion wouldn't follow.
(C) The argument does not suggest that the limestone is there to make the soil healthier, so this is not assumed by the argument.
(D) The argument does not attempt to explain what makes dead plants decompose, so this is not the correct answer.
(E) The argument suggests the soil should be neutralized, not made alkaline. Therefore, this is not an assumption of the argument.

### 16. Question Type: Most Supported
(A) The argument does not mention those who write statutes, so this is not supported.
(B) The argument suggests that a moral code is the only way to choose between sets of laws, so this is not supported.
(C) This answer choice might seem attractive, but it actually goes against what was stated in the passage. The argument suggests that moral behavior and compliance with laws can be distinguished, and it also suggests that it is not legally forbidden to violate some moral rules. Therefore, it directly contradicts this answer.
(D) This answer is too extreme; the argument suggests that there should be exceptions to equating a moral code with law, not that it should never be done.
(E) Correct. Given that a nation's laws are an expression of a moral code and that some laws can be violated without violating that moral code, there must be some laws that do not fit with the moral code. This line of reasoning supports this answer.

### 17. Question Type: Principle
The principle can be summarized as: correlation does not imply causation, and the correlation is often the result of a third factor causing both.
(A) The argument here is that while some say one thing caused another, they are really the same thing. This is not the same as two events being caused by the same phenomenon, so it does not illustrate the principle.
(B) Correct. This correctly illustrates the principle. Two correlated phenomena, high blood pressure and being overweight, are suggested not to be causally linked, and it is suggested that a third factor, an unhealthy lifestyle, causes both.
(C) This correctly illustrates the first part of the principle but not the second part.
(D) This fails to correctly illustrate the second part of the principle by suggesting one does in fact cause the other, though we don't know which one.
(E) This fails to illustrate the second part of the principle and is only slightly related to the first part of the principle.

### 18. Question Type: Flaw
The flaw here is a mistaken reversal. The statements can be diagrammed as follows:
        conclusion:     successful salesman → 3 years
        premise: successful salesman → client base
        premise: 3 years → client base
The conclusion only follows if the second premise (last sentence) is reversed. Therefore, the argument fails to consider that people could take less than three years to develop a client base.
(A) The argument does consider this possibility and rules it out.
(B) Correct. This correctly paraphrases our predicted answer.
(C) The argument does consider this and in fact suggests that it is true.
(D) The argument does consider this and suggests that it takes at least three years to develop a strong client base.
(E) While the argument does not consider whether or not salespeople are able to do this, its failure to do so does not weaken the argument.

# PrepTest 53, Section 1 (LR) Continued...

### 19. Question Type: Parallel Reasoning
The reasoning can be described as follows:
> A subset of the group of people who sleep less than six hours a night was found to become less anxious when they began sleeping 8 or more hours a night. This is used as evidence that most of those who sleep less than six hours a night will become less anxious if they do the same.

(A) Correct. This answer follows the same pattern of reasoning, generalizing results from a subset of a population to the larger population.
(B) The subset of the population is too limited in this answer. Certain small businesses suggest that it could be talking about a select few. The prompt says that people who switch their sleeping schedule "typically," fell less anxious, meaning it is typical of any group.
(C) This answer is too extreme; the prompt only says "most," while this answer says "any."
(D) The "only if" makes the reasoning different from that in the prompt.
(E) This answer takes the reasoning too far; the people became less anxious, not anxiety free. As such, small businesses should become stronger, not necessarily strong.

### 20. Question Type: Assumption
The argument assumes that if skeletal anatomy cannot be used in one case, it cannot be used in any case.
(A) Whether their skeletons are similar or different to other skeletons has no bearing on whether skeletal anatomy can be used to determine hunting behavior.
(B) This has no bearing on the argument as well; the point was that lions and tigers are indistinguishable in skeletal anatomy but have different hunting behaviors.
(C) Correct. This paraphrases our predicted answer and would make the conclusion sound. If we negated this statement, it would make the conclusion incorrect, therefore passing the negation test.
(D) This statement reverses the inferences made in the prompt and thus is incorrect.
(E) This statement fails to pass the negation test, as negating the statement still allows the conclusion to be true.

### 21. Question Type: Parallel Flaw
The argument can be diagrammed as follows:

| | |
|---|---|
| rainfall exceeds 5 cm → trees blossom in May | ~trees blossom → ~exceed 5cm |
| rainfall exceeds 5 cm → reservoir full May 1 | ~reservoir full → ~exceed 5cm |
| ~(reservoir full) | |
| therefore, trees will not blossom | |

The flaw in reasoning is a mistaken reversal. While the contrapositive of the second statement suggests that rainfall failed to exceed 5 cm this April, that does not imply that trees will not blossom. (Note that there's actually no logic that would lead us to that conclusion here since ~(trees blossom) is nowhere a necessary condition).
(A) Correct. This argument has the same structure, with a correct contrapositive but a mistaken reversal.
(B) and (C) have no flaw in reasoning, so neither can be the right answer.
(D) This argument involves a mistaken negation in addition to a mistaken reversal.
(E) This argument has no flaw in reasoning, so it cannot be the right answer.

### 22. Question Type: Flaw
The flaw in this argument seems to be the use of "healthier". Just because those who are slightly overweight are healthier than those considerably underweight does not mean that slightly overweight people are healthy.
(A) The argument mentions the medical opinion against the conclusion but suggests it is wrong because of a piece of evidence.
(B) This is close, but the problem isn't the definition of healthy. Rather, it is the doctor's assumption that being healthier than someone else makes you healthy.
(C) Whether someone is overweight or underweight takes their appropriate weight into account, so this is not a flaw.
(D) The argument does not suggest this, so it is not a flaw of the argument.
(E) Correct. The argument mistakes being healthier, a relative property, for being healthy, an absolute property.

*PrepTest 53, Section 1 (LR) Continued...*

**23. Question Type: Assumption**
The argument suggests that robust crops are better at dealing with insect damage and that killing insects is not enough. The conclusion is that we should give plants better soil. There is a missing link between robust crops and better soil, which the correct answer will show.
(A) This statement does not affect the argument because the argument does not suggest anything about how to achieve better soil, only that it should be achieved.
(B) The argument suggests that there is no way to keep insects from attacking plants, which goes against this statement.
(C) The argument never says that pesticides will not reduce the extent of damage but rather says that the un derlying problem of weakness to insect attack should be solved, which pesticides does not.
**(D)** Correct. It correctly supplies a link between robust crops and good soil. Additionally, if we negate this statement, it makes the conclusion incorrect, therefore passing the negation test.
(E) The argument does not suggest that pesticides affect how robust crops are, nor does it require that they do so. Negating this statement does not make the conclusion false, so it is not the right answer.

**24. Question Type: Resolve Paradox EXCEPT**
The paradox is that some people who can tell the difference between red and green are unable to tell the difference between shades of red. Four answers will explain this, while one will not.
(A) This explains why people would be able to tell red apart from green but not apart from other shades of red, so it is not the correct answer.
(B) This would explain why many people failed to distinguish between shades of red while they were able to distinguish red from green, so it is not the correct answer.
(C) This would explain seeing the difference between red and green but not different shades of red, so it is not the correct answer.
**(D)** Correct. This only explains why people cannot distinguish red from green; it does not address the issue that many failed to distinguish shades of red. Therefore, it fails to resolve the paradox and is the correct answer.
(E) This would explain the failure to distinguish between shades of red, so it is not the correct answer.

**25. Question Type: Flaw**
The flaw here is that the argument suggests that using math and astronomy makes something science, while it is possible that one can use those to do non-scientific things.
(A) This reverses what the argument presumes, which is that complicated math suggests something is science. Therefore, it is incorrect.
**(B)** Correct. This is a paraphrase of our predicted answer.
(C) The argument does not deny this but ignores it.
(D) The argument does not infer this; it infers that astrology is scientific because it uses astronomical knowledge, which it presumes is scientific.
(E) This reverses what the argument presumes, which is that the use of symbols suggests something is art.

# PrepTest 53, Section 2, Game 1

This is a relatively simple matching game. When creating a diagram for matching games, it's best to pick as a base the variable set that doesn't get repeated. In this game, the performers are a good base because they will each be assigned exactly one agency, whereas some of the agencies will get multiple performers.

F P S = 3

$$\frac{\phantom{T}\;\;\phantom{W}\;\;F\;\;\phantom{Y}\;\;\phantom{Z}}{T\;\;\;W\;\;\;X\;\;\;Y\;\;\;Z}$$

**Rules**
(Each agency has at least one performer)
#1  X signs with F (insert into your diagram)
#2  X =|= Y
#3  Z = Y
#4  T star → W star     ~W star → ~T star

Inferences: X is involved in 2 rules, so it makes sense to examine them together. We know that X signs with F, so Y must not sign with F. There are only 2 other options (P or S) so play it out as a limited option split. We also know that Y and Z are together so that will help us fill out our limited options.

Option 1  $\dfrac{\phantom{T}\;\;\phantom{W}\;\;F\;\;P\;\;P}{T\;\;\;W\;\;\;X\;\;\;Y\;\;\;Z}$      Option 2  $\dfrac{\phantom{T}\;\;\phantom{W}\;\;F\;\;S\;\;S}{T\;\;\;W\;\;\;X\;\;\;Y\;\;\;Z}$

We can go even further with the last rule. On the left side, we still need someone to sign with Star. If T does, W does as well and we are all set. However, consider the contrapositive. If W doesn't sign with Star, T doesn't either, and we have no one to sign with Star. Therefore, W must sign with Star. Note that this DOES NOT imply that T must sign with Star.

Option 1  $\dfrac{\phantom{T}\;\;S\;\;F\;\;P\;\;P}{T\;\;\;W\;\;\;X\;\;\;Y\;\;\;Z}$

In our second option (on the right above), we already have 2 Stars. If T signs with Star, that means W would as well, and no one would sign with Premium. Therefore, T cannot sign with Star.

Option 2  $\dfrac{F/P\;\;\phantom{W}\;\;F\;\;S\;\;S}{T\;\;\;\;\;W\;\;\;X\;\;\;Y\;\;\;Z}$

These 2 options will simplify this game enormously.

1. List question. Use rule-by-rule elimination.
   a) Violates 4th rule
   b) **Correct**
   c) Violates 3rd rule
   d) Violates 1st rule
   e) Violates 2nd rule

2. Our options will be very helpful here.
a) **Correct,** see Option 1.
b) Doesn't fit either option. If Y and Z sign with P, W must sign with S.
c) This can't be true by rule since Z = Y and Y=|= Z
d) Again doesn't fit our options
e) Option 1 is out. It's worth checking in Option 2. If T signs with Fame, then W would have to sign with Star (so someone signs with Star)

3. Here again, examine the 2 split options.
a) We see from our options that they could in Option 2
b) **Correct**. In Option 2, either T or W must sign with Star, so there cannot be 3 that sign with Fame
c) Could be true, but many options where it is not
d) Could be true
e) West could sign with Fame in Option 2

4. You're looking for the answer choice that not only helps you decide between the two split options, but also resolves the uncertainty.
a) T could sign with Fame in either option
b) **Correct;** we know we're dealing with Option 1 because T can't sign with Star in Option 2. If T signs with Star, Option 1 is complete
c) Limits to Option 2, but we don't know for sure where F signs
d) This is true in every configuration – it doesn't help at all
e) We know it's Option 1, but T is still undetermined

5. If Z signs with Star, we know we're on Option 2.
a) Both T and W could sign with premier
b) W, Y, and Z could all sign with Star
c) **Correct.** We know for sure that in Option 2, T must sign with either Fame or Premier
d) W isn't limited in option 2
e) T, W, or both could also sign with Fame

# PrepTest 53, Section 2, Game 2

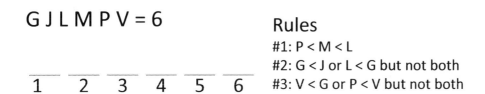

**Rules**
#1: P < M < L
#2: G < J or L < G but not both
#3: V < G or P < V but not both

Discussion: Note that with rules 2 and 3, if one option is true, the other option is false. Taking that logic one step further, if one option is true, the *opposite* of the other option *must also be true.* I.e. if G < J, we know "L < G" must be false, and we can deduce G < L. On the other hand, if L < G then J < G. So there are really 2 options for each of those rules:

These don't lead to any huge deductions, but will be invaluable as you move through the game. It's also a lot more efficient to put them in this visual format as choices.

---

6. List question. Use rule-by-rule elimination.
a) Violates 2nd rule
b) Violates 1st rule
c) **Correct**
d) Violates 3rd rule
e) Violates 1st rule

7. This question is very straightforward if you've written out rule 1.
a) **Correct**. Since L must follow M, M cannot be last

8. If L is last, what can we deduce? Think about the other rules that involve L. Look at the options for Rule 2. If L goes last, the second option is active: G< J and L. Is that deduction represented in the answer choices? Yes!
a) **Correct**. We deduced that the second option of Rule 2 is active, so G must be before J.
B through E could be true or false.

9. Make sure you've re-written your combined rule with the new local rule:

   P < M < L

   J ⤶

Since the question is looking for "could be true EXCEPT," you are looking for the option that must be false. When you scan the choices does one stand out as violating the combined rule?
a)  Could be true, e.g. P J M L G V. The easiest way to proceed quickly is to put J in 2nd, then rapidly fill in the rest of your local rule. IT's also easiest to put G and V last so you don't have to spend as much time thinking over those rules.
b)  Could be true.
c)  Could be true.
d)  **Correct** (must be false). J must have both M and L behind it, so it cannot go 5th.
e)  Could be true.

10. An easy one! You only have one definitive sequencing rule, so see if you can use that to find the answer quickly.
**C) Correct!** We know that L must come after both P and M so it clearly cannot go first.

11. It will be much quicker to re-draw the diagram and insert each option rather than trying to visualize.
a)  M can never go first because P must go before it.
b)  **Correct**. Since we know where P goes and there are only 2 spaces after, M must be 5th and L must be 6th. That leaves V first for V G P J M L, which is valid.
c)  Violates Rule 2; if G is before J, as it is here, then L must also be after G, which isn't possible.
d)  There is no room for M after P.
e)  Violates Rule 2; G is after V, but P would have to be before it.

# PrepTest 53, Section 2, Game 3

S T V W X Y Z

Confessed? (C or ~C)

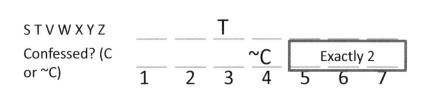

## Rules
#1: (add to diagram)
#2: (add to diagram)
#3: W < S
#4:

$$Z < \genfrac{}{}{0pt}{}{V}{X}$$

#5: no confessions after W questioned
#6: (add to diagram)

Discussion: W is in two rules, so let's give it a look. We know that S goes after W and also that anyone after W does not confess, therefore S does not confess:

```
S
X
```

No one can confess after W, but we also know that 2 suspects after T must confess. Where can W go then? It can't go 4th or 5th because that wouldn't leave us two spots for confession. It can't go 7th because S must go after W. Therefore we find a major deduction: *W can only go 6th*, and, therefore, S must go 7th and must not confess. That also helps us identify the only two slots left to confess after T: 5 and 6.

```
              T           W   S
                  ~C  C    C  ~C
         1    2   3   4    5   6   7
```

---

12. This is straightforward if you found the inferences.
    a) X can never go first as it must go after Z.
    b) **Correct**. This means Z would go first and X/Y could go 4th/5th.
    c) Z in 4 doesn't leave space for both X and V after.
    d) We know W is on day 6.
    e) S must go on day 7.

13. The new local information helps us fill our suspects. We know X and V must follow Z, and there are only two spaces. That leaves Y for first.

| Y | Z | T | X/V | X/V | W | S |
|---|---|---|---|---|---|---|
|   |   |   | ~C | C | C | ~C |
| 1 | 2 | 3 | 4 | 5 | 6 | 7 |

Be careful here; the question says that Z is the second suspect to *confess* (not just to be questioned). Since Z must go second, Y must also confess.

a) through d) are all possibilities given this configuration.

**e) Correct.** Y must confess.

14. This gives us the sequencing rules V < Y < X. You should automatically combine that with other sequencing rules. We know that Z must go before V and X, so we end up with Z < V < Y < X. This completes our order:

| Z | V | T | Y | X | W | S |
|---|---|---|---|---|---|---|
|   |   |   | ~C | C | C | ~C |
| 1 | 2 | 3 | 4 | 5 | 6 | 7 |

a) **Correct.** We do not know whether or not V confessed.
b) through e) are ruled out by the diagram.

15. Think about the spacing here. There are 2 spots before T and 2 empty spaces after (not counting W and S). Our sequencing rule tells us that Z must come before X and V, so Z is a logical place to start when we consider what must come before T. Test the opposite proposition: could Z go in 4$^{th}$? No, because there would not then be room for both X and V. It certainly can't go 5$^{th}$ for the same reason.
**e) Correct**

16. Make sure you are drawing lots of diagrams – this one is very challenging to work mentally as there are several options. You will likely need to try each diagram quickly.

**a) Correct.** If V confessed, it couldn't go 4$^{th}$. It also can't go 1$^{st}$ because it must go after V. If V went second, it doesn't work because one of X or Y would have to go 4 or 5; that can't happen because they must both confess. Can V go 5$^{th}$? No; again, that would mean that X and Y would have to go 2/4, and one of them would not confess.

b) through e) all could be true in this configuration.

17. If neither X nor V confess, they must go in 2 and 4. (They can't go first because they must go after Z, and they can't go 5$^{th}$ because we are saying they do not confess. That gives us Z first and Y 5$^{th}$.

| Z | V/X | T | V/X | Y | W | S |
|---|---|---|---|---|---|---|
| ~C | ~C |   | ~C | C | C | ~C |
| 1 | 2 | 3 | 4 | 5 | 6 | 7 |

**d) Correct.** Y must confess.

All other answers could be true but do not have to be true.

# PrepTest 53, Section 2, Game 4

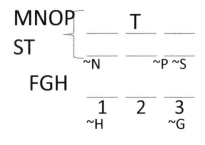

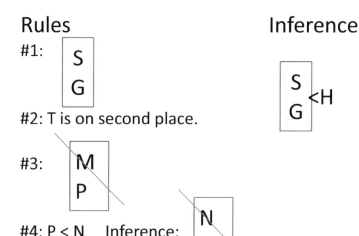

#2: T is on second place.

#4: P < N     Inference:

#5: G < H

Discussion: It's useful to fill in the negative rules from rules 4 and 5 here, but there aren't breakthrough inferences. We can combine rule 1 and rule 5 to learn that S cannot be last.

---

18. List question.
    a) Rule 2 eliminates
    b) Rule 3 eliminates
    c) Rule 4 eliminates
    d) This is harder. When you run our of elimination options, put the options into the diagram. When you do so on D, you quickly realize that S cannot go last because it has to go with school G, which must go before school H.
    e) **Correct**.

19. Write out your new rule, then combine it with other rules that use the same variables.

    | P |   then combine:           | P |
    | H |                    G < | H | < N

    As you can see, we now have all 3 days represented and we can fill in:

        T                                  M/O  T  M/O
        P   N      Then fill in the easy    S   P   N
                   inferences, leaving M/O
        G   H      as uncertainties:        G   H   F
        1   2   3                           1   2   3

    a) **Correct.** O (or M) could each be on the first place team.

20. If O goes second with T, second place is full. That means we'll have to put P in first and N third based on Rule 4. S will have to go first with G, since it can't go second, and G can never go last. M will have to go third. Everything is solved except for the schools; H and F could go second or third.

```
P   T   M
S   O   N

G  H/F H/F
1   2   3
```

a) Can't be true.
b) **Correct.** N could be on the team from either H or F.
c) Can't be true.
d) Can't be true.
e) Can't be true.


21. If P and T are teammates in second place, N must go last because it must go after P. S must go first because it has to go with G, which can never go last. M and O are still uncertain. **C is correct** – we know P, T, S, and N but not M or O.


22. If M is higher than H, M must go first or second. We'll have to do some elimination as there is not a major inference. You will go much faster if you put each of these quickly into a diagram to eliminate.
a) If F goes first, G must go second and H last. S would have to go with T in second place. Then we'll have to split up P and N, so P will go first. That's a problem – we now have M and P together. Doesn't work.
b) This is exactly the same scenario as A above, and it still does not work.
c) If N is second, P must be first. Since M must place higher than Hilltop, M must be first (second is full with N and T). This forces M and P together, which doesn't work.
d) If O is first there are a few options but try them – nothing works. If S goes first and M goes second, P and N would have to be together. If P goes first, M would go second (because it must be higher than H), putting S last which doesn't work. (S can't be last because it must go with G, which can't be last.
e) **Correct**, could be true. If P is first with S, M second with T, then O and N can be third.


22. You can save a ton of time here by eliminating from past diagrams where we've seen S teamed up with various others successfully. We've seen S be teammates with P (#18) and with M and O (#19), so we are left with B and E.

**b) Correct**. If S and N were to be together, the can't go first because P < N, and they can't go last because S < H. They also can't go second because T must go in second place.

# PrepTest 53, Section 3 (LR)

**1. Question Type: Strengthen**
The flaw in the argument is that some problems will occur after the manufacturer's warranty, and there is no reason to believe that they will cost less to repair than the extended warranty. The answer that strengthens the argument will get rid of this flaw.
- **(A)** Correct. This fixes the flaw by removing the possibility of costly repairs needed after the manufacturer's warranty.
- (B) This answer fails to describe the relative cost of the repairs and the warranty, so it does not fix the problem that repairs could cost more, making the warranty a good idea.
- (C) This has no bearing on the argument, as only the cost of the warranty and repairs matters.
- (D) This would weaken the argument, or at best remain neutral.
- (E) Why extended warranties are offered has no bearing on whether they end up costing more than the repairs they would cover.

**2. Question Type: Flaw**
The argument assumes that the regulations have not slowed the worsening of the environment, so the correct answer will probably point this out.
- (A) The argument says nothing about the environmentalists, so this is not the right answer.
- (B) The argument only suggests that regulation is not the solution to a problem, not that its absence is the solution to that problem.
- **(C)** Correct. This answer correctly points out that the environment could have been worse if there had been no regulation, a possibility the prompt did not consider.
- (D) The argument never suggests this. Rather, it suggests that because regulation hasn't prevented the worsening of the environment, more regulation will not do so either.
- (E) While the argument does not consider the argument of opponents, it does not simply argue for the environmentalists. Therefore, opposing arguments are not necessary.

**3. Question Type: Conclusion**
The main conclusion is that musical knowledge does in some sense grow over time. Each of the following statements supports this statement, and this statement is not used to support any other statement.
- (A) This is not the conclusion but a premise supporting the conclusion.
- (B) The argument does not suggest that dissonant sounds are now pleasing but rather that they have been made consonant.
- (C) This view is given as one the conclusion contradicts.
- (D) While this is suggested by the passage, it is not the conclusion. No premises support it, so it cannot be the conclusion.
- **(E)** Correct. This is the predicted answer.

**4. Question Type: Weaken**
The argument assumes that twelve mosquitoes is a very small number because it is much smaller than the total number of insects killed. However, what really matters to the conclusion is how large twelve is compared to the total number of mosquitoes. The correct answer will likely point this out and say the assumption is incorrect.
- **(A)** Correct. If there were no mosquitoes near the device, then it must have killed all of them, meaning it is actually pretty good at killing mosquitoes. This weakens the argument, making it the correct answer.
- (B) This is simply stated in the argument, so it cannot weaken the argument.
- (C) This would strengthen the argument.
- (D) This would strengthen the argument.
- (E) This does not weaken the argument, as the argument's point was that it was not good at killing mosquitoes.

**5. Question Type: Conclusion**
The main conclusion is that researchers need accurate verbal reports to understand how the brain enables us to think. It is supported by the premise in the next sentence and does not support any other sentence.
- (A) This is never suggested in the argument, so it cannot be the conclusion.
- (B) This is a premise supporting the conclusion.
- (C) This is never suggested in the argument, so it cannot be the conclusion.
- (D) This is never stated in the argument, so it cannot be the conclusion.

## PrepTest 53, Section 3 (LR) Continued...

(E) Correct. This is a paraphrase of our predicted answer.

### 6. Question Type: Flaw
The argument assumes that the data collected from the same spot at the same time every day will be representative of the birds' behavior in different locations and at different times. The correct answer will likely point out this assumption and suggest it is incorrect.
(A) This was not assumed without justification, as a camouflaged blind was used.
(B) What type of animal food sources does not make a difference, as any animal food source is not vegetation.
(C) The argument does the opposite of this; it takes a well-established viewpoint and collects evidence before suggesting that it should be overturned.
(D) Correct. This reveals one of the assumptions mentioned in the predicted answer, so it reveals the flaw in reasoning.
(E) Whether or not the diet used to be mostly vegetation, if it does not consist of mostly vegetation now, a belief that it does is erroneous. Therefore, this is not a flaw in reasoning.

### 7. Question Type: Complete the Argument
Assuming the teacher's job is to get students to learn as much as possible, a predicted answer must include something about instilling curiosity in students and satisfying that curiosity.
(A) Correct. This answer includes both aspects of our predicted answer.
(B) This does not follow from the prior sentences. The first sentence makes clear that such devices would not cause students to learn.
(C) This would not make sense, as these topics would be learned least successfully by the students.
(D) Whether students take responsibility or not, they will only learn if they are genuinely curious, as stated in the first sentence. Therefore, this does not complete the argument.
(E) Even if a student understands some learning is not enjoyable, s/he will not learn unless s/he has curiosity and that curiosity is satisfied. Therefore, this does not complete the argument.

### 8. Question Type: Assumption
There is a missing link between landfills and the bacteria that break down cleaning products. Therefore, the answer should provide that link.
(A) Correct. This establishes a link between bacteria and landfills. If this statement is negated, the conclusion is incorrect, so it passes the negation test.
(B) This would not help the argument, as it does not establish that the bacteria the produce harmful vapors will be in the landfill.
(C) The vapors themselves do not cause problems, it is the vapors from bacteria that break down cleaning products. Meanwhile, this does not suggest that there will be harmful vapors in parks converted from landfills.
(D) Even if this is assumed, it does not allow the conclusion to be drawn. The argument only references toxic vapors from bacteria, which this answer does not address.
(E) We are concerned with the public health, which is supposed to deteriorate if landfills are converted to parks. Even if some people are harmed by vapors from a landfill, this does not address the situation in the prompt.

### 9. Question Type: Weaken
The argument assumes that the correlation between those who drink camellia tea and kidney damage implies causation between the two. There is no reason to believe this. The correct answer will suggest that this assumption is incorrect.
(A) and (B) do not affect whether camellia tea causes kidney damage or not, so they are not the right answer.
(C) While this does express something positive about camellia tea, it does not rebut the claim that camellia tea helps cause kidney damage.
(D) This does not affect the argument, as it would still be the case that a higher proportion of camellia drinkers developed kidney damage than those who do not drink it. Therefore, it does not suggest that the conclusion is incorrect.
(E) Correct. This answer suggests that the assumption in the predicted answer is incorrect. It suggests that a different factor could cause kidney damage, and that its correlation with camellia tea is accidental.

# PrepTest 53, Section 3 (LR) Continued...

### 10. Question Type: Method of Reasoning
The artists claim that avant-garde artwork that becomes popular is successful. The main conclusion of the argument is that this is incorrect. The correct answer should mention that it is a claim that the argument ultimately decides against.
(A) The claim is at odds with the conclusion, so it cannot be used to bolster it.
**(B)** Correct. This paraphrases our predicted answer.
(C) The claim is not supported by the initial premise, so this is not the right answer.
(D) The claim does not support the initial premise, so this is not the right answer.
(E) The argument does not suggest that the initial premise is incorrect, so there was no counterargument against it. Therefore, this is not the correct answer.

### 11. Question Type: Strengthen
The flaw in the argument is that it assumes one of two correlated phenomena causes the other (in this case, that international travel causes insomnia). The answer will most likely be a statement that supports this causal relationship.
(A) This either weakens the argument or is neutral to it. It could be suggested that having contiguous border makes it less likely that there will be a dramatic climate or cultural change. Thus, this would suggest the travel did not cause insomnia, weakening the argument. Otherwise, it is neutral.
(B) This would weaken the argument, as it would suggest the stress it not that great. This would make it less likely to cause insomnia.
**(C)** Correct. This supports the idea that international travel causes insomnia by showing that insomnia is not the cause of participating in international business travel. This rules out the possibility that the researchers had the causal link reversed.
(D) This does not affect the argument, which suggests that insomnia is caused by international travel. Whether those with insomnia benefit from international travel does not affect this idea.
(E) Sleep-related ailments are too general to relate to this argument. Even if it had said insomnia, the statement would only have a bearing on the argument if the people did not have insomnia before traveling internationally.

### 12. Question Type: Principle
It is suggested that people should not attempt to achieve the ultimate achievement if it has a high risk of death and injury, especially since it will not bring spiritual discovery.
(A) The prompt only writes about those projects for which spiritual discovery is not likely, so this principle does not justify the prompt.
**(B)** Correct. This correctly paraphrases the predicted answer. It mentions both the risk of death and the lack of spiritual discovery.
(C) The prompt has nothing to do with legal prohibitions, so this is not the answer.
(D) This does not justify the argument that people should not climb Mount Everest; it merely suggests that those seeking spiritual discovery could do something different.
(E) Mountain climbers could easily examine the underlying reasons and decide they still wanted to climb Mount Everest; therefore, this principle would not justify the reasoning in the prompt.

### 13. Question Type: Parallel Reasoning EXCEPT
The reasoning used is generalizing from aspects of pieces of a whole to the whole itself. In this case, it is assumed that because the parts are simple, the whole will be simple, which does not follow. Four answers will use similar reasoning, and the correct answer will not.
(A) This answer generalizes from the parts of a car to the whole car, so it does have similar reasoning. The flaw is similar in that having perfect parts does not require a perfect whole.
**(B)** Correct. While this answer does generalize from part to whole, the generalization is correct. If every part is made of metal, then the whole must be made of metal.
(C) This answer generalizes from part to whole. Just because the part has one shape does not mean the whole will also have that shape. It has a similar generalization and flaw, so it is incorrect.
(D) This answer generalizes from part to whole. Just because the parts are sturdy does not mean the whole is sturdy. It has a similar generalization and flaw, so it is incorrect.
(E) This answer generalizes from part to whole. Just because the parts are well-constructed does not mean the

## PrepTest 53, Section 3 (LR) Continued...

whole is. It has a similar generalization and flaw, so it is incorrect.

### 14. Question Type: Weaken
The flaw in reasoning is that it is assumed hesitation will lower the rate of violent crime. The correct answer will likely expose this assumption and suggest it is incorrect.
- **(A)** Correct. If violent crime is not premeditated, then it is a crime committed in the moment. This means criminals will not have time to think things out and hesitate.
- (B) While it would be unfortunate for innocents to go to jail, this does not weaken the argument. It is still possible that criminals will be deterred from violent crime if innocents are jailed for violent crimes.
- (C) This does not weaken the argument, as whether it is a first or third time committing a crime does not alter the crime rate.
- (D) The argument does not suggest there will be no trials, just that tricky maneuvers will be removed to speed the process up.
- (E) This would strengthen the argument.

### 15. Question Type: Assumption
The argument assumes that some people will decide to continue working past 65 if mandatory retirement is cut.
- (A) This is suggested by the argument, but it is not necessary for the conclusion to be true. Some people who have worked 40 years could be under 65, and this would not suggest the conclusion is incorrect. It therefore fails the negation test.
- (B) The argument only claims that youth are trained, not that they are highly trained professionals. This would make no difference to the argument, though.
- (C) The argument doesn't need to say this is unfair because it has already stated that the issue is widespread dissatisfaction among the young.
- (D) This would actually go against the conclusion, so it is not an assumption of the argument.
- **(E)** Correct. This correctly paraphrases our predicted answer. It also passes the negation test.

### 16. Question Type: Weaken
The conclusion of the argument is that teaching preschoolers is not especially difficult. The correct answer will likely suggest this is not the case.
- (A) This strengthens the argument.
- **(B)** Correct. This suggests it would be difficult to work with preschoolers, weakening the argument.
- (C) and (D) have no bearing on how difficult it is to teach preschoolers.
- (E) This strengthens the argument.

### 17. Question Type: Flaw
The main assumption here is that each piece of evidence has the same amount of influence on the strength of the case. The correct answer will likely point out this assumption.
- **(A)** Correct. This paraphrases the predicted answer.
- (B) This is not assumed, as the body is supposed to remain strong despite losing a few parts.
- (C) While this is not specifically mentioned, it is not necessary to make the argument. Even if this possibility were true, it would go against the argument. The argument only made a claim about a few pieces of evidence being discredited, not many.
- (D) This is incorrect because the lawyer does suggest that the two share similarities.
- (E) This is not done in the argument, so it is not the correct answer.

### 18. Question Type: Principle
The answer must fit every piece of the given details.
- (A) This is not correct because the argument suggests beauty makes the natural environment worth preserving.
- (B) This is not correct because it adds an extra argument and leaves out another. The prompt never suggested that moral value is not a good enough reason, just that it is not as strong as beauty because it is open to logical objections.
- (C) This does not fit any of the prompt, which never said we should remove anything from the environment.

## PrepTest 53, Section 3 (LR) Continued...

(D) This fails to consider the second half of the prompt, which suggests that arguing beauty will be less vulnerable than arguing moral.

(E) Correct. The argument regarding the beauty of nature is "less open to logical objections" because that beauty belongs indisputably to nature.

### 19. Question Type: Most Supported/Must be True

At most two of the authors can be included, and if K is included, J is.

(A) Correct. If L is included, K cannot be included because it would force J to be included as well, and only up to two can be included. Therefore, this statement must be true.

(B) It could include one by K and one by J.

(C) It could include one by K and one by J.

(D) It could include just an essay by L.

(E) It could include one by K and one by J.

### 20. Question Type: Assumption

The assumption here is that the temperature dependence of chemical reactions will affect the development of the brain and intelligence. While it is clear that animals that regulate temperature stabilize the temperature chemical reactions occur at in the brain, it is not clear that this would affect their brain/intelligence. The correct answer will likely point this out.

(A) This does not affect the missing link. If we negated it, the conclusion could still be true.

(B) This is not necessary; the argument is only about mammals. Even if some non-mammals could regulate their temperature, it would have no bearing on the argument.

(C) This answer is too extreme. Even if the brain could support intelligence with uncontrolled temperatures, the conclusion could still be true, so it fails the negation test.

(D) Correct. This correctly identifies the link needed. If the development of intelligence was independent of the chemical reactions, then the conclusion could not be true. It therefore passes the negation test.

(E) This answer does not affect the argument. What happens to organisms incapable of controlling temperatures does not have any bearing on what happens to those capable of controlling temperature.

### 21. Question Type: Most Supported

(A) This is not supported by the argument; it could be that the location it is in was the safest when the waste was put there, but there is now a safer place for it.

(B) This is denied by the argument, which states that it simply needs to be moved to a safer place without trying to find the safest possible place.

(C) Correct. This is supported. The author believes moving the waste to the new site will reduce risk because the new site is safer. Therefore, he must believe that moving the waste would reduce the threat.

(D) This is not necessarily true. The argument only talks about one case, which is when there is a safer place and the current place poses a risk.

(E) This is not necessarily true. The argument only talks about one proposed site being a better place for the waste. It is possible that other sites are less safe than the current location.

### 22. Question Type: Resolve the Paradox EXCEPT

The paradox is that people are reading fewer books, but bookstores are making more money. Four of the answers will explain how this is possible, while the correct answer will fail to do so.

(A) If this were the case, more books would be bought, while readership would decline. Therefore, this explains the difference.

(B) Correct. This fails to explain the drop in readership, and it fails to explain the increase in profits. Because it does not explain the difference, this is the answer.

(C) The coffee shops would bring more money to the bookstores while allowing people to read less. Therefore, this explains the difference.

(D) If people bought fewer books but more expensive books, bookstores would make more money while people would read fewer books. Therefore, this explains the difference.

(E) The increased purchase of magazines at bookstores would increase profits, while having little time would suggest less reading. Therefore, this explains the difference.

## PrepTest 53, Section 3 (LR) Continued...

**23. Question Type: Parallel Reasoning**
~(change too rapid) → species can survive
Therefore, threats to woodlands species are caused by rate of destruction, not destruction itself.
(A) There is no conditional in this statement, so it cannot be the right answer.
(B) The conditional is not a premise but a conclusion in this answer, so it is incorrect.
(C) There is no conditional in this statement, so it cannot be the right answer.
**(D)** Correct. A conditional is used as a premise to support a non-conditional conclusion.
(E) Despite the conditional, the reasoning is flawed. The conditional does not logically imply that there is not good soil now.

**24. Question Type: Method of Reasoning**
The conclusion is that meaningful freedom is comprised of both number of choices and differences between alternatives. The first sentence is an example used to prove this statement.
**(A)** Correct. The general principle about meaningful freedom is supported by the example of soda choices.
(B) This answer reverses the premise and conclusion.
(C) There is no analogy, so this is not the right answer.
(D) This method of argumentation was not used.
(E) Only one general principle is established, so this is not the right answer.

**25. Question Type: Principle**
(A) and (B) Presenting at the meeting is not discussed in the principle, so these are not the right answer.
**(C)** Correct. If no issue is relevant to a majority, it should not be discussed, and if no issue is relevant to Terry, he should not be required to go. Thus if no issue relevant to Terry is relevant to a majority, he should not have to go.
(D) This would not suggest that Terry did not need to go.
(E) Even if there was one issue that was relevant to Terry, he would still have to go.

# PrepTest 53, Section 4 (RC)

**Passage 1**

Mark the passage. The first sentence includes the word "generally," which should be a clue that the author is either going to give a specific example or else an exception to the "general" rule. So read what comes next carefully. "In this light, the recent work of Wing Tek Lum...is striking for its demand to be understood on its own terms." In other words, Lum's work is an exception to the general rule—that Asian-Hawaiian writers focus on either multiculturalism or Asian-American themes. This is likely to be part of the main idea.

The rest of the first paragraph (lines 9-20) give details of Lum's approach. Paragraph 2 (lines 21-40) describe specifics of two poems. This is an example of a paragraph that contains more than one idea; you might want to mark the place where the author switches subjects (the sentence starting at line 34).

The final paragraph describes another poem that exemplifies Lum's approach to Asian culture in a Hawaiian context.

1. Predict the main idea of the passage. As noted above, the point is that Lum is an exception to the run-of-the-mill Asian-Hawaiian poet. That idea is expressed most closely in **(A)**. Note that (B) and (D) both describe aspects of Lum's poetry that are addressed in the passage, but they miss that main idea—that Lum differs from other poets of his background.

2. The main feature of Lum's poetry that is identified by the passage is his attempt to harmonize his Asian background with American values and Hawaiian context. Only **(C)** expresses a point of view that is in accordance with this.

3. You're asked to say what a phrase means in context, so read the context. Jump a sentence or two back from where the prompt points you to. "Flux" means change; in context, we're talking about immigrants, so the change in question is the continual inflow of new cultures from east and west. That's expressed in **(D)**, the correct choice. (C) is wrong because the change is happening to Hawaii, not the immigrants themselves.

4. The Asian-Hawaiian literature to which Lum's work is contrasted is described in the first paragraph (you know this from having marked the passage). Read the first sentence—the two concerns identified are multiculturalism and generational conflict. **(C)** is one of these (generational conflicts).

5. As noted above, the word "striking" is used to show that Lum's work is different from that of other Asian-Hawaiian poets. That's choice **(D)**.

6. When you're asked to find something that the author would agree with, you're looking for a statement that's supported by evidence in the passage. **(D)** conveys that balance between heritage and context (lines 25 through 30, though also a general theme of the passage).

**Passage 2**

Each of the three paragraphs here moves in a different direction. Paragraph 1 (lines 1-15) describes the common law as being "derived largely from English judicial custom and precedent," and states that it "cannot properly be understood without taking a long historical view."

Paragraph 2—beginning with "Yet," alerting you to a change of viewpoint, states that common law has seldom been seen this way. Note the word "consistently" (line 24): modern jurisprudence "consistently" treats common law as a unified system of rules that can be treated as a logical whole.

Paragraph 3—introduces Goodrich for the first time, and tells you that "however," he treats common law as an evolving tradition rather than a set of rules. Emphasis is placed on his study of law as if it were literature.

So what's the main idea here? We have a paragraph describing a development-based view of English common law, a paragraph stating that the conventional viewpoint among legal experts is different, and a paragraph

## PrepTest 53, Section 4 (RC) Continued...

outlining the work of one scholar that has departed from that conventional viewpoint. If the author has a position, it's probably that reflected in the first and third paragraphs rather than the second. So he believes that the conventional view—in which the study of the development of law is de-emphasized in favor of studying it as a coherent, logical whole—is misplaced, as Goodrich suggests. Look for something like that.

7. The main idea that we just identified (above) is stated in **(D)**.

8. When asked for something the author believes, you're looking for a statement that is supported by evidence in the passage. **(A)** is correct (lines 20-30); there are apparently many ways in which modern jurisprudence misinterprets legal tradition. Choices (B), (C), (D), and (E) directly contradict the passage in one way or another.

9. Read the sentence suggested by the prompt: the "interpretive theory" mentioned (lines 18-20) is one in which although the historical roots of law are analyzed, their contemporary significance is ignored. That's **(C)**.

10. Remember, you're asked for an inference. So the answer might not be found in the passage itself, but must be consistent with its reasoning. The point the author is making is that the development of law over time is important. This is because the law changes over time. Thus, he would most likely agree with **(E)**.

11. "Political" in this context refers to the political system abstractly; the other, less high-minded definitions of "political" (choices A and B) aren't referred to. So that means you're looking at **(D)**.

12. The passage mentions choice **(B)**. (See line 5 ("medieval cases").)

13. What's the author's point of view towards modern jurisprudence? That it basically fails to take into account the importance of the historical development of the law. In other words, **(B)** fits the bill. (D) may be attractive, but the author specifically mentions that students are required to study old law.

14. As noted, we've got an author disagreeing with the traditional approach to jurisprudence, and discussing a theorist whom he feels resolves the problem. Both of those aspects of the passage have to be reflected in your choice. The right answer is **(A)**. (Where's the paradox? It lies in the disconnect between the importance of historical development of the common law and the fact that traditional theorists ignore that development.) (D) and (E) are incorrect because the author is not advocating a return to an earlier theory: apparently, legal experts never took adequate account of legal development.

**Passage 3, Comparative reading**

Look at the main idea of each passage separately. Passage A states the point of view that treating research as a commodity has harmful effects, largely because it gets in the way of free exchange of ideas, and creates perverse incentives against exploring all ideas—especially non-profitable ones. Passage B points out that since science is such a critical part of the "information economy," the line between discovery (to be shared) and invention (to be patented) has been blurred.

Before moving on to the questions, take a moment to think about what the two passages have in common: both are talking about how business interests have transformed scientific research. Passage A is bemoaning the loss of pure science; Passage B simply points out that patent law has been affected

15. As noted, **(A)** is something that is brought up in Passage B but not Passage A.

16. Both passages talk about the effect of market economy on scientific research. The correct choice is **(C)**: the dichotomy is between research as a public good and research as a commodity. (A) may be attractive, but there really isn't much here about "commercially unsuccessful research." Note that (D) is incorrect because it mentions something that's only contained in Passage B.

17. Biotechnology is used as a prime example in both Passage A (line 22) and Passage B (line 44). That's **(D)**.

The other choices are only mentioned in one (or neither) of the passages.

18. As noted, both passages talk about the effect of the market economy on scientific research. So both authors believe that commercialization of science has led to change in scientific culture. The only choice that reflects that is **(C)**.

19. Read the choices. The only one that is consistent with both passages' point of view is **(D)**. Both authors believe that commercialization has restricted common access to scientific research. That means that both authors believe that access used to be easier.

**Passage 4**

We've got two flavors of mites. The cyclamen mites (CM) eat strawberry plants, and the Typhlodromus mites (TM) eat CM. These mites are used as an example of how the best way to control an agricultural pest is sometimes to simply let the pest's predators run free. That's the point of the first paragraph (and the point of the whole essay).

The second paragraph describes TM, and how they live on CM. The third paragraph describes an experiment in which it was demonstrated that the insecticide parathion (which kills TM) causes CM to run rampant. The final paragraph states that this is a clear case where using insecticide can actually make things worse.

20. The main point is given by **(C)**: the TM/CM case is an example of how natural predation can be more effective than insecticide. (A) is attractive, but the main problem with it is that it's phrased categorically. Control of pests isn't always better using natural predation—the first word of the passage is "sometimes," after all.

21. This is a difficult question. The author mentions several aspects of the relationship between TM and CM, some of which are echoed in the choices. Your task, really, is to pick out which one of those principles is fundamental. Well, the key thing about predators is that they eat their prey, right? So focus on the choice that talks about eating—that's **(D)**. Choice (A), which focuses instead on reproduction of the predators being in sync with the prey, isn't quite right. You can imagine a situation in which predators and prey are born at different rates—so long as the predators are eating enough, it'll work. The other three choices miss the mark still further.

22. **(E)** is correct. It's the only one that states something actually mentioned in the article. (See lines 27-32.)

23. Pesticide X lowers the reproductive rate of CM (meaning there will be fewer of them). TM eat CM (meaning there will be fewer CM). So, whether a field is treated with pesticide X or not, there will be fewer CM. That's **(A)**.

24. The author's point of view towards using predation rather than pesticides seems to be positive. So you can eliminate (B) and (D). There's no support in the article for (E). As for choice (A), parathion actually fails to kill CM. Choice (A) suggests that parathion be used for that purpose, so it can't be right. That leaves **(C)**, which is correct.

25. To analyze why the article mentions something, take a look (in context) at the place where it's mentioned. In this case, that's lines 18-23. To get the context, look a couple lines up from that, and you see the following sentence: "Its population can increase as rapidly as that of its prey." And that's answer **(D)**.

26. Which one of the choices is good news if you want to use TM to keep your strawberries free of pests? **(E)** is: a strawberry's winter isn't fierce enough to kill off TM. Note that choice (C) is similar, but it's wrong: it tells us that the plants endure mild winters, but it doesn't tell us that even mild winters won't kill TM.

27. The answer is **(A)**: if a strawberry field has both TM and CM, the TM will keep the CM in control, thereby limiting damage to the crop. Other choices are not supported in the passage.

# PrepTest 54
## PrepTest 54, Section 1 (RC)

**Passage 1**

Paragraph 1 states that the Internet poses problems when it comes to legislation and law enforcement, since it represents information freely crossing borders. Traditional approaches to legislation are based on borders, which is the source of the problem. This paragraph appears to give the main point.

Paragraph 2 states that part of the problem is a lack of ability to control the information that crosses borders (see lines 13-16). The rest of the paragraph expands on this enforcement problem.

Paragraph 3 talks about the particular problems the internet raises for trademark law. Paragraph 4 talks about jurisdictional issues with the internet that have gone completely unaddressed under the current system.

1. Predict the main point before you answer: it appears to be about the fact that internet information flow has led to problems with law and law enforcement, since information so easily crosses political boundaries. That's choice (**A**).

2. Why did the passage mention France? Well, a good strategy is to start reading a sentence or two earlier. You'll read there (lines 53-57) what turns out to be choice (**C**).

3. The main issue here is being able to quickly find the part of the passage they're referring to. The traditional approach, and the problems it creates, are mentioned in paragraph 1, but fleshed out in paragraph 2. Take a look at the beginning of paragraph 2 (lines 10-11), and you'll see (**D**) pretty much spelled out right there.

4. You're told to look at paragraph 2. Scanning quickly, you find the sentence there, "Such a draconian measure would almost certainly be extremely unpopular..." Clearly, the author describes the measure as draconian, but merely predicts that it'll be unpopular. So (**D**) is better than (C).

5. You're asked what the purpose of the fourth paragraph is. You know (from your notes, see above) that it isn't calling anything into question, and it's not a summary. So you're left with choices (D) and (E). Does it continue the argument in the third paragraph, or supply an additional argument in support of the first paragraph? Well, your notes reflect that paragraphs 3 and 4 aren't related. So you're looking at (**E**).

**Passage 2, Comparative reading**

Passage A deals with drilling mud; it describes the function of this substance, describes what it usually contains, and mentions that because there are myriad possible ingredients (many of them secret), evaluating the mud's toxicity can be daunting.

Passage B is also about drilling mud. It describes the distinction between water-based and oil-based mud. The latter is used for deeper wells than the former. It is also more toxic, and so its release by offshore drillers is more heavily regulated.

6. The only thing the two passages have in common, really, is that they're about drilling mud. So that leaves us with choice (**B**). Note that (C) is too broad: while both passages do mention environmental impacts, they only allude to impacts of the mud itself, not environmental impacts associated with oil drilling in general.

7. Both passages mention that barite is a heavy mineral (line 15; line 50-51). That's choice (**E**), which is correct. The other items are mentioned either in only one of the passages (A, D) or not at all (B, C).

8. The best strategy is to read the choices, and mark the ones that you don't recall having been mentioned in the passage. Choice (**E**) is correct: it directly contradicts statements made in Passage B, whereas Passage A does not mention offshore drilling at all.

## PrepTest 54, Section 1 (RC) Continued...

9. You're asked to make an inference from both passages which cannot be drawn from just one. So you need a choice that synthesizes some information from Passage A and some info from Passage B. That's choice **(B)**. Note that the first passage mentions the "barium meals" used before x-rays, while only the second passage mentions that barite can kill sea creatures. Choice (A) is nearly correct: the problem is that while the second passage does mention that barite is environmentally damaging, it falls far short of saying that it's the most damaging thing in drilling mud.

10. The first passage made a great deal out of the fact that drillers keep their recipes for drilling mud secret. The second paragraph, which describes the regulation of drilling mud, doesn't mention anything about disclosing the ingredients. So that means **(B)** is correct.

11. The second paragraph tells us that OBMs are used in deeper wells. So OBMs will be used more if deeper wells are used more. So the correct answer will be something indicating that there will be more deep-drilled wells in the future. That's **(C)**.

12. Choice **(A)** is stated directly in the passage (lines 53-54).

**Passage 3**
Break it down by paragraphs. Paragraph 1 mentions Walker as having popularized the cakewalk; the dance's origin in West African sources is mentioned. Paragraph 2 describes the fact that European dance influences were added; part of this was a parody of white slave owners. The cakewalk itself was then parodied by whites. Paragraph 3 notes that this "mimetic vertigo" added to the dance's cross-racial appeal. Paragraph 4 returns us to Walker, who used these aspects of the dance to popularize it.

What's the point? Well, largely the essay describes the development of the cakewalk, in such a way that makes it clear why it became popular across racial divides; Walker took advantage of that to bring "authentic" cakewalk to black and white audiences. Let's predict an answer something like that, before moving on to...

13. Answer choice **(C)** matches the prediction we just made.

14. In our markup, we noted that paragraph 3 was about explaining why the cakewalk appealed to a wide range of people. That's reflected in answer **(D)**.

15. The cakewalk became popular among white people because it parodied elements that were themselves parodies of white dance. So we're looking for a response that includes that same sort of feedback loop. That looks like choice **(C)**.

16. Read the choices. **(E)** is the only one supported in the passage. See lines 22-24.

17. You're looking for a statement with some support in the passage. That's **(E)**; take a look at the last sentence of the passage. The other choices mention other art forms, other dances, etc.; the passage contains no evidence to support claims about them.

18. Walker's role, according to the passage, was to popularize the cakewalk. A good definition of "popularize" is "to broaden the appeal of." So **(A)** is probably right. Choice (B) isn't correct, since if anything, it sounds like Walker made the dance less satirical (she claimed to do an "authentic" cakewalk).

19. Basically, you're asked whether the passage contains information on a particular subject. Choice **(A)** is correct; look at lines 10-14.

**Passage 4**

This one takes a long time to get to the point. Read carefully.

Paragraph 1 describes how cohesiveness—agreement and support among group members—is generally a

## PrepTest 54, Section 1 (RC) Continued...

good thing, because it allows group members to express candid opinions without fear of reprisal.

Paragraph 2, which begins with the transition word "but," describes how cohesiveness can also lead to "groupthink," in which members of a group agree with the consensus because of group pressures or habit rather than because of actual substantive analysis.

Paragraph 3 discusses analysis of diplomatic fiascos, in which the characteristics of "groupthink" are identified. It states that it's important to work towards identifying the factors that allow the good things about cohesiveness to decay into groupthink.

We have good things and bad things about cohesiveness identified here; that's really the point. It's good, but it can lead to groupthink.

20. The main point is **(A)**, as predicted above.

21. Groupthink is where excessive agreement leads to problems. The scenario in the prompt is where excessive disagreement led to the problem. We don't know what to call that, but it certainly isn't groupthink. So zero in on choice **(C)**.

22. The author posits that groupthink results from cohesiveness. Thus, it would be unlikely to result when a group is not cohesive. That means that choice **(C)** is correct.

23. Only **(B)** gives an element of groupthink; the other choices list aspects of either individual thinking or outright disagreement.

24. The author clearly believes that groupthink is bad; the researchers who found groupthink at work in diplomatic fiascos clearly thought so, too. So that's choice (E). Choice (D) might be inferred from the author's point of view, but not from the description of the researchers' work. The other choices seem to contradict the passage.

25. **(E)** is correct. Cohesive groups allow disagreement to be expressed; in non-cohesive groups, there is pressure to conform. That's what paragraph 1 says.

26. The prompt points to paragraph 1. From your notes, you know that that paragraph is about how cohesiveness is a good thing. The description of low cohesiveness is designed to bolster that argument. That's reflected in choice **(A)**.

27. By now you know that cohesiveness is good, groupthink is bad, and cohesiveness can sometimes lead to groupthink. The only one of the choices that's consistent with this point of view is **(B)**.

# PrepTest 54, Section 2 (LR)

**1. Question Type: Flaw**
The argument cites statistical data (95%), so we should see if this data is flawed in anyway. The survey was only of retirees, so it is most likely a biased sample and not representative. The correct answer will most likely point this out.
(A) There is more than one premise, so this cannot be the answer.
(B) The evidence can be verified, it just doesn't necessarily suggest what the company says it does.
(C) To equivocate means to use a term ambiguously with the intent to deceive. Fairly is not used ambiguously, so this is not the correct answer.
**(D)** Correct. This correctly paraphrases our predicted answer and calls the generalization from the survey into question.
(E) The company does not say anything about how its treatment of employees has changed or not changed over the years.

**2. Question Type: Assumption**
There is a missing link between feeding pets meat and contributing to cruelty to animals. The correct answer will likely create this link so that the conclusion can be properly drawn.
(A) The argument has not suggested that contributing to animal cruelty affects whether one can love a pet, so this is not the answer. If it is negated and added as a premise, the conclusion can still be true, so it fails the negation test.
(B) Even if it is not the case that those opposed to keep dogs and cats are opposed to cruelty to animals, the conclusion can still be true, so this answer fails the negation test.
(C) The argument did not mention anything about laboratories, so there is no reason to believe that it has assumed anything about what people who work in laboratories think.
(D) This answer could actually weaken the conclusion, meaning it cannot be the assumption that would make the argument sound.
**(E)** Correct. If feeding meat to pets did not contribute to cruelty to animals, then the conclusion would not follow. This answer passes the negation test, so it is assumed by the argument.

**3. Question Type: Weaken**
On both strengthen and weaken questions, there's often an assumption made by the argument which can be strengthened (affirmed) or weakened (denied). The argument assumes that because fiction revenues have declined at bookstores, readership of fiction has declined. The correct answer will likely point out this assumption and suggest it is incorrect.
**(A)** Correct. This answers gives a situation that suggests the assumption identified in the predicted answer is incorrect, so it weakens the argument.
(B) This is either neutral or strengthens the argument.
(C) Markdowns in biographies does not affect revenues from fiction, so this is not the right answer.
(D) This would not affect fiction revenues or readership, so it does not affect the argument.
(E) It is unlikely that they were trying to get people overseas to read more fiction, as this is the National Book Association, so this does not affect the argument.

**4. Question Type: Resolve the Paradox**
The correct answer must explain how those who consume honey avoid cavities.
(A) This does not explain why they would not get cavities from the honey itself.
(B) Since the sugar would still pass through the mouth, this does not explain the absence of cavities.
(C) This does not explain why most honey eaters have fewer cavities.
(D) Health problems is too broad a term, and the argument has not mentioned anything about refined and unrefined sugars.
**(E)** Correct. Eating honey reduces tooth decay, suggesting that those who eat honey should have fewer cavities.

**5. Question Type: Flaw**
The argument says that being late to a board meeting or missing two general meeting results in suspension. However, this does not mean that there is no other way to get suspended. The flaw in reasoning is that a sufficient cause is taken to be necessary.

*PrepTest 54, Section 2 (LR) Continued...*

(A) It would not matter if he was late to a general meeting, only missing two results in suspension.
(B) Correct. This correctly states the flaw we predicted. There could be another event sufficient to cause suspension.
(C) This would be taking the necessary as sufficient, which is the reverse of the mistake in the argument.
(D) This does not matter; whatever the definition, if they're late, they're suspended.
(E) The length of time he has been an officer has no bearing on the argument.

**6. Question Type: Assumption**
The conclusion here is a little complicated, but the argument is essentially that if recycled paper becomes the norm, paper manufacturers will have to use more filler. This is because recycled paper requires more filler to look white. This reveals the assumption that paper needs to be white.
(A) The argument is only about writing paper, so this does not affect the argument.
(B) The argument does not mention anything about the environment, so this is not the answer.
(C) Correct. If grayish paper became an acceptable alternative, then the conclusion would not be correct.
(D) Even if there was no limit, the conclusion could still be correct. This answer therefore fails the negation test and is incorrect.
(E) Even if the amount of writing paper did not increase significantly, it could still be the case that manufacturers use more filler, so this fails the negation test.

**7. Question Type: Complete the Argument**
The argument suggests that emissions can only be curbed by regulation and that no nation will single-handedly impose regulation. So, if emissions are to be stopped, nations must impose regulation together. The answer is likely to paraphrase this statement.
(A) This would not fit into the sentence at all.
(B) The argument suggests that regulation is necessary, so this does not seem like something it would agree with.
(C) Correct. This paraphrases the predicted answer.
(D) The level of distrust has no bearing on whether or not emissions are reduced.
(E) This does not seem to be what the argument is driving toward. The argument states that one nation will not do it alone, which suggests that it is going to speak about more nations doing it together.

**8. Question Type: Principle**
The prompt mentions a specific character of digital technology that is an advantage in one sense (less waste), but a disadvantage in another sense (easier to destroy). The generalization must mention both of these.
(A) Correct. This correctly mentions both the advantage and disadvantage.
(B) There is no reason to believe that there are more problems, so this is incorrect.
(C) Accessibility is not mentioned in the argument, and the argument does not suggest anything is more important than anything else.
(D) This completely leaves out the reduction of waste and goes against the increased risk.
(E) This fails to mention the added risk of destruction.

**9. Question Type: Assumption**
The assumption here is pretty well hidden. The argument is that raising minimum wage will cause the museum's expenses to go up. To deal with this, the museum will either have to raise revenue by increasing ticket prices or decreases expenses by cutting services. The missing link is between raising minimum wage and the museum's expenses going up; this link only exists if raising minimum wage will cause employees to be paid more. Therefore, it is assumed that some employees are paid below the proposed minimum wage value.
(A) Correct. This correctly paraphrases our predicted answer. If all employees were already paid significantly more than minimum wage, the conclusion would not follow, so this answer passes the negation test.
(B) It does not matter what has happened over the past five years. Even if the revenue has gone up or down, the conclusion can still be true. This answer fails the negation test.
(C) This would actually hurt the conclusion, so it is not an assumption.
(D) Even if the number of visitors has not increased, the conclusion can still be true. This answer therefore fails the negation test.
(E) Even if all visitors are required to pay an admission fee, the conclusion can still be true. This answer fails

*PrepTest 54, Section 2 (LR) Continued...*

the negation test.

**10. Question Type: Method of Reasoning**
Helen makes a claim about reading any book, and Randi suggests that some books do not fit this claim. The correct answer will likely mention this.
(A) He does not question her evidence, so this is incorrect.
**(B)** Correct. This paraphrases the predicted answer, by suggesting that Helen's scope was all books where it should just have been certain books.
(C) There is no absurd conclusion, so this is not correct.
(D) While Randi does draw an analogy, Helen did not have an example, so it was not an analogy to her example.
(E) Helen did not give any examples, so this is not correct.

**11. Question Type: Conclusion**
The conclusion is that no hardware store will be opening in the shopping plaza. It is supported by the following two sentences, and it does not support any other statement.
(A) This is not the conclusion but something implied by the first half of the first sentence.
**(B)** Correct. This is a paraphrase of our predicted answer.
(C) This is one of the premises supporting the conclusion.
(D) The prompt never mentioned that anything would be unwise, so this is not the conclusion.
(E) This is one of the premises supporting the conclusion.

**12. Question Type: Most supported/Must be true**
The conclusion of the argument is that science has its own value system.
(A) This claim is not supported by ordinary morality, which says a person is morally responsible if they could foresee the consequences.
(B) This is not necessarily true, as something could have consequences the scientist could not foresee.
(C) The argument says that science is not morally neutral, so this is incorrect.
**(D)** Correct. This is possible. If a scientist does research that has foreseeable and terrible consequences, s/he has not broken science's value system but has broken ordinary morality.
(E) The argument suggests that uses and effects of science can be foreseen sometimes, so this is not correct.

**13. Question Type: Assumption**
The argument must be assuming that consumers are only attracted to the highest quality and the lowest price in their purchases, rather than some middle ground of quality and price.
(A) If a company did have both, the conclusion could still be correct. This fails the negation test.
**(B)** Correct. This correctly paraphrases the predicted answer. If this did attract customers, the conclusion would be incorrect, so this passes the negation test.
(C) Even if a company that had one of these went bankrupt, the conclusion could still be true, so this fails the negation test.
(D) Even if all consumers did continue through brand loyalty, the conclusion could still be true, so this fails the negation test.
(E) Even if a company was driven from the market for this reason, the conclusion could still be true, so this fails the negation test.

**14. Question Type: Weaken**
The argument uses statistics to support its conclusion. However, just because the two are correlated does not mean that one caused the other. The correct answer will likely suggest that the causation attributed to the data is not the correct explanation.
(A) This does not weaken the argument, as speeding is relative to the speed limit. It could be that speeding after the limit is lowered is still slower than the old limit.
(B) This would not affect the argument, so it is not the correct answer.
**(C)** Correct. This answer suggests the causation is not the correct explanation, therefore weakening the argument.
(D) This would not affect the argument, which only pertains to serious accidents.

(E) This suggests that more accidents were called serious after 1986, which would not explain the drop, therefore failing to weaken the argument.

### 15. Question Type: Flaw
The argument has made a leap from one instance in which people do not act rationally to the generalization that people are not rational. The correct answer will likely point this out.
(A) There is no problem with the definition of rational, which he states is well-considered thinking and behavior. It is not well-considered behavior to pollute and deplete the soil we eat from. There is no internal contradiction.
(B) He never suggests that humans are aware, nor is this needed to prove his argument.
(C) He doesn't need to suggest this, as he is only arguing that humans are not rational.
(D) He only states that humans are no better, and he uses evidence to attempt to prove this claim.
**(E)** Correct. This answer points out the jump from one example to a generalization that we predicted.

### 16. Question Type: Must be True
(A) This does not have to be true. The only statement made about the ratio is that all good hunters have a high ratio. This does not suggest that some with high ratio are not good hunters.
(B) We only know that most wild and some domestic are good hunters and thus have high ratios. We do not know anything about concrete numbers; some domestic could be a higher number than most wild.
(C) All good have high ratio does not mean that all bad have low ration; this is a mistaken negation.
**(D)** Correct. If some domestic cats are good hunters and all good hunters have high ratios, then some domestic cats have high ratios.
(E) This is a mistaken reversal of the statement that all good hunters have high ratios.

### 17. Question Type: Method of Reasoning
The conclusion is that moral responsibility differs from legal responsibility. The statement mentioned in the question is a premise used to prove a sub-conclusion, which is used to prove the conclusion.
(A) This claim is not made, so it cannot be supporting that claim.
(B) The argument does not suggest that legal responsibility includes moral responsibility, so this is not correct.
(C) This is not correct; the argument shows that people are sometimes responsible for something legally but not morally.
**(D)** Correct. This is the sub-conclusion used to prove the conclusion, so this is the correct answer.
(E) This premise does not support that claim, so this is not the correct answer.

### 18. Question Type: Principle
Each principle should be tested to see if it matches each aspect of the prompt.
(A) The prompt did not say when it was reasonable to take a strong position, so this does not fit the prompt.
(B) This fails to mention the piece of the prompt regarding understanding an issue fully.
**(C)** Correct. This answer essentially just paraphrases the prompt.
(D) This fails to conform to the reasoning in the prompt by applying connections between topics incorrectly and failing to mention the main point.
(E) The prompt does not suggest when it is reasonable to take a strong position, so this does not fit the prompt.

### 19. Question Type: Flaw
The argument assumes that two phenomena that have been correlated in the past will continue to occur together in the future.
(A) The argument does not make this mistake, as it correctly uses the contrapositive.
(B) The argument says that no computer was necessary, suggesting that the computer was reliable enough since it was double-checked by hand.
(C) There is no conclusion about the use of computers in sports.
**(D)** Correct. This paraphrases the predicted answer. Just because the team has only lost without Jennifer in the past does not mean this will continue to be the case in the future.
(E) There is no conclusion about the value of computer analyses.

## PrepTest 54, Section 2 (LR) Continued...

### 20. Question Type: Most Supported/Must be True
(A) This is not implied by the argument. Eggs are only among the easiest, which suggests there are others that are similarly easy, which could also require less cleaning.
(B) The argument does not suggest that anything could not be packaged in Styrofoam, just that certain things require more cleaning and are more difficult to package.
(C) The argument days nothing about what is on the old Styrofoam being recycled.
(D) This is not necessarily true; it could still be easier or cheaper to use non-recycled containers.
(E) Correct. This is suggested by the argument. If it is easier to recycle containers for eggs because the container doesn't touch the actual food, then it follows that the more difficult items do touch the containers.

### 21. Question Type: Parallel Reasoning
The argument suggests that a correlation implies causation. The correlation is between something earlier in time and something later in time. It is assumed that if the earlier thing is true, the later thing is likely to be true.
(A) Correct. This infers causation from correlation and does so with a similar time relationship, so it is the answer.
(B) This does not infer causation from correlation, so it is incorrect.
(C) This does infer causation, but it also mistakenly negates the result, making it an incorrect answer.
(D) This does not have the time relationship used in the argument, so it is incorrect.
(E) This does not infer causation from correlation, so it is incorrect.

### 22. Question Type: Flaw
Just because there is not enough evidence to prove something is true does not mean that it is false. The student makes this mistake, so the correct answer will likely point this out.
(A) Conflicting with experts is not a flaw in reasoning.
(B) It does not presuppose this; the conclusion is a conditional. The students say that if the professor is right, then most experts are wrong.
(C) He doesn't need to say what the criteria are, just that they are not met.
(D) This is not a mistaken viewpoint; the traditional view is the majority view in this case.
(E) Correct. This paraphrases the predicted answer. The student believed claims were false just because there was inadequate evidence that they were true.

### 23. Question Type: Parallel Reasoning
The argument can be diagrammed as follows:

    mattress sold → mattress madness    ~mattress madness → ~mattress sold
    mattress madness → 20% off          ~20% off → ~mattress madness
    Therefore: mattress sold → 20% off  ~20%off → ~mattress sold

(A) This reasoning is not logically sound, so it is not the right answer
    F → R
    P → R
    Therefore, F → P
(B) This reasoning is not logically sound, so it is not the right answer
    R → A
    F → P
    Therefore, P
(C) Correct. This has the same structure and is logically sound, like the prompt.
    F → R
    R → P
    Therefore, F → P
(D) This reasoning is not logically sound, so it is not the right answer.
    F → R
    R → P
    Therefore, P → A
(E) This reasoning is not logically sound, so it is not the right answer.

*PrepTest 54, Section 2 (LR) Continued...*

      P → R
      P → A
      Therefore, A → R

**24. Question Type: Strengthen**
The conclusion of the argument is that cows should be given better diets to help keep methane in check. The correct answer will support this idea, while the four other answers will not.
**(A)** Correct. If cows produce more meat and milk with high quality diets, then less cows need to be around to produce meat and milk, lowering methane emissions.
(B) This does not suggest that methane emissions would be lowered, so it is not the right answer.
(C) This does not affect methane emissions, so it is not the right answer.
(D) The argument lumps meat and milk together, so separating them does not help or hurt it.
(E) This does not affect how much methane cows will emit, so it is not the correct answer.

**25. Question Type: Must be True**
The argument is that if a person acts courageously, then s/he perseveres despite the fear of dangers involved.
(A) This person could be courageous if they were facing fear in the process.
(B) This goes against the argument, which states a person must be afraid to be courageous.
(C) This person could be courageous if in addition to gaining pleasure s/he was facing fear to attain a goal.
**(D)** Correct. A person must be facing fear to act courageously, even if s/he is helping others.
(E) This person could have fear in other situations, in which case s/he could be courageous.

**26. Question Type: Assumption**
There is a missing link between the fact that the old company went out of business and the idea that the government will get new parts. It must be assumed that it will be difficult to obtain replacement parts if the old company went out of business.
(A) If public safety is enhanced by repairing the old sirens, the conclusion can still be correct, so this fails the negation test.
(B) Even if the newspaper was incorrect, the conclusion could still be correct, so this fails the negation test.
(C) If they were sold elsewhere, it could still be difficult to obtain them, in which case the conclusion could still be correct. This answer fails the negation test.
**(D)** Correct. This answer paraphrases our predicted answer. If it was not difficult to obtain replacement parts from somewhere else, the conclusion would be false, so this passes the negation test.
(E) The argument only said it would purchase new parts if replacement parts were hard to obtain, not if they were of worse quality, so this is not the correct answer.

# PrepTest 54, Section 3, Game 1

This is a straightforward grouping in/out game. There isn't initially a restriction on how many dancers must be on or off the stage at once, so we'll need to look for deductions.

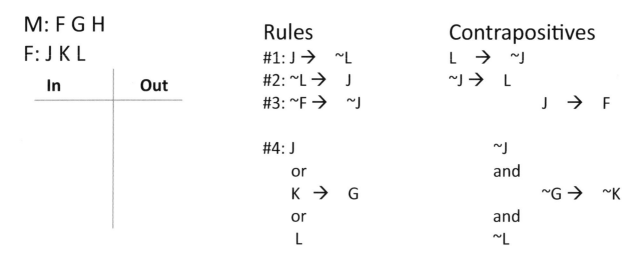

Discussion: In addition to the contrapositives, think about how the first 2 rules combine. In essence, either L or J must be in, but not both. This is very helpful; since either J or L must be in, according to Rule 4, G must be in as well!

| In | Out |
|---|---|
| G | ~L / ~J |
| L/J | |

Since either L or J must be in, we know that we'll need at least 2 dancers (with the second being G). It's not possible to have no dancers.

---

1. List question. We know that G must always be in, eliminating b). One of L/J must be in, eliminating a) and e). d) doesn't work because of the contrapositive of Rule 3 – F would also have to be on state given this configuration.
a) **Correct**.

2. Think about how the inferences above can help. d) can't be the case; we know either L or J (both women) must be on stage, so K can't be the only woman on the stage.
**d) Correct**

3. We know quite a bit when J is on stage. First, L must be off-stage as noted in the inferences. Second, according to Rule 3, F must be in as well. So we have:

| In | Out |
|---|---|
| G | ~L |
| J | |
| F | |

Since G, J, and F must be in, we can eliminate b). We know that L can be out, eliminating d). So, we need to figure out if both H and K can be out. There's no reason why not, so **e)** is correct.
**e) Correct**

4. We're asked how many dancers MUST be on stage, so we're looking for the minumum here. We know that G, a man, must be in, so we need at least 2 women. (One of those must be either J or L). So, our first guess will be that three dancers must be on stage (so we can eliminate d) and e) ).

We need to experiment to confirm. If J goes in, we'd also need F according to Rule 3, so let's put in L instead. We need more men than women, and we can't have J, so let's try K:

| In | Out |
|---|---|
| G | ~J |
| L | |
| K | |

Check through the rules. Does anything else need to be in? No. So only 3 must be in.

**c) Correct**

5. This is similar to Question 4 but without the restriction that there must be more women than men. We know that G must be in, and that one of either L or J must be in. As in Question 4, if we put J in we'll need F, so let's test whether we can have just G and F, with all other variables being out.

| In | Out |
|---|---|
| G | ~J |
| L | ~F |
|   | ~H |
|   | ~K |

Does this break any rules? No.
**c) Correct**

**PrepTest 54, Section 3, Game 2**

This is a matching game of the type more often seen on older tests. There are a couple ways to draw the diagram; some students draw a chart here, which works fine. We'll use a more traditional diagram for clarity.

With matching games it's important to chose the right "base" for a diagram. Since each rating can have multiple CDs, we'll use that as a base. (It's possible to make your base the 6 CDs with one rating for each, but that makes it a bit tougher to keep track of how many CDs get each rating.)

H I N Q R S* = 6

```
........  ........  ........  ........
_____   _____   _____   _____
  1        2        3        4
```

Rules
#1: each rating = 1 or 2 CDs

#2: | N H |

#3: | H |  or  | R |
    | I |      | I |

#4: at most 1 CD higher than Q

Discussion: Rule 2 gives us a basic sequencing inference. Since only 1 CD can be higher than Q, Q must be in 3 or 4.

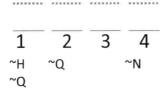

```
  1    2    3    4
 ~H   ~Q       ~N
 ~Q
```

Although it doesn't lead us to any big deductions, be aware that since each rating must have 1-2 CDs, 2 of the ratings will have 2 CDs each and 2 ratings will have 1 CD each

---

6. List question. Use rule-by-rule elimination.
   a) **Correct**
   b) Violates 4th rule
   c) Violates 3rd rule
   d) Violates 2nd rule
   e) Violates 4th rule

**64**

7. If H is the only CD in 2, we know that H must go in 1 (Rule 2). We can also infer that R and I must be together according to Rule 3, since H must be by itself and either H or R must be with I.

Where can this block of R and I go? It can't go first, because that would put 3 variables in 1. It also can't go 4th; if R and I were in 4th, there's no way to get Q in such that there is a max of one variable with a higher rating. So R and I must go in 3rd and Q would go in 4th. S can go in 1 or 4.

a) **Correct**

8. If R is with S, H must be with I according to Rule 3. We also know that H is always right before N, so we have 2 blocks to fit in:

| R | | H |
|---|---|---|
| S | | N  I |

We've considered every rule except the one regarding Q. Q can only go in 3 or 4. If Q went in 3, what would happen? We know that only one variable could go in 4 (because only one variable can be higher than Q); the only other singleton variable we have is N, but N can't go last because H and I must go after. Therefore, Q must go in 4.

d) **Correct.** The other options could each be false.

9. N and R are together in 1. Since H always goes after N, H must be in 2. We also know that H and I must be together (Rule 3, since R cannot be with I). That leaves us with S and Q, either of which can go in 3 or 4:

```
 R    I
 N    H   Q/S  Q/S
 1    2    3    4
```

e) **Correct.** None of the other options could be true.

10. You should be able to eliminate several options here from past diagrams.
a) We saw in #9 that Q can go alone in 3.
b) We saw in #9 that Q can also go alone in 4.
c) We saw in #11 that R can be the only CD in 1.
d) **Correct.** If R is by itself, H and I must go together with N directly before. That block could only fit in spaces 3 and 4, but that leaves no room for Q to go in without breaking Rule 4.
e) This would work: one star N and S, two stars I and H, three stars R, four stars Q

11. Once again if R is by itself, H and I must go together, with N coming directly before. H and I can't go together in 4 because that doesn't let us fit in Q. Therefore, H and I must go together in 3 with N in 2. Q would have to go in 4 since 3 is full.

S can go in 2 or 4.

**e) Correct.** None of the other choices could work.


12. We should be able to eliminate several choices here – anything we've seen go in 4<sup>th</sup> previously will be eliminated. That's Q and S. We know that N can't have a rating of 4 stars, but unfortunately that's not an answer choice. Eliminate quickly:
a) Works; I and R, S, N, H and Q
b) **Correct.** I can't go last because it must always be matched with either H or R. That means Q can't fit; it would have at least 2 variables rated higher, violating Rule 4.
c) Works – we've seen Q last several times.
d) Works; N, I and H, S, P and Q
e) Works – we've seen S go last previously.

# PrepTest 54, Section 3, Game 1

This is a straightforward linear game with one twist – your diagram must be vertical to easily make sense of what's "above" and "below." This is fairly rare, though there have also been at least 2 apartment/office building games on other past LSATs that required a vertical diagram.

L M O R S V* = 6

Rules

#1: ~~(R/S)~~

#2: [M / L]

#3: S ∧ O ∧ M

Discussion: Rules 2 and 3 can be neatly combined.

S ∧ O ∧ [M / L]

After doing so, we can make several basic sequencing deductions:

6 ___ ~O ~M ~L
5 ___ ~M ~L
4 ___ ~L
3 ___ ~S
2 ___ ~O ~S
1 ___ ~M ~O ~S

---

13. List question
a) **Correct**
b) Violates Rule 1
c) Violates Rule 2
d) Violates Rule 3
e) Violates Rule 4

14. We'll need to insert something between S and O; keep in mind that R still can't be adjacent to S. Process of elimination:
a) Creating a block of RV, along with our block of ML, will mean that S and O have to be together in one order or another, violating the local rule.
b) Works; (bottom up) L M O R V S.
c) Only L can go directly under M.
d) R in 2 means that L and M will have to be on top of it, respectively. This will force S and O together at the top.
e) This won't work; with R on top, S can't go 5th. If we put S in 4th, O would get pushed down to second according to our local rule. Then we can't fit in the block of LM.

15. V normally floats. Here, however, the local rules will place some restrictions on where it can go. We have a new restriction on S – it can't go on top. We know that S can only go 4, 5, or 6, so with 6 out let's play out what we have left:

```
6 ____        With S in 5th, we have some          6 ____        With S in 4th, our sequence tells us
5  S          variability. Since V is our topic,   5 ____        that O, M, and L must be under it.
4 ____        think about where it might go. If V  4  S          Since S and R can't go together, R
3 ____        is in 6, this works: L M R O S V.    3  O          must go on top and V would have
2 ____                                             2  M          to go 5th.
1 ____        If V is in 4th, it doesn't work: L, M,1  L
              and O would have to go first,
              second third, which would push S                   V could go 5th.
              and R together, violating Rule 1. We
              run into similar trouble if V goes in
              1, 2, or 3.

              V could go 6th.
```

**e) Correct.**

16. If L is third, we know that M must be directly above it in 4. We also know that O and S must then go in 5 and 6. That leaves V and R which could each go in either 1 or 2.

```
6  S
5  O
4  M
3  L
2  V/R
1  V/R
```

**b) Correct.** Each of the other options violates this arrangement.

17. Process of elimination here.
a) Doesn't work because M must be above L.
**b) Correct.** V R L M O S.
c) This won't work because it puts M on the bottom, but L must be under M.
d) L must always go directly below M, so this doesn't work.
e) S can only go 4th, 5th, or 6th.

# PrepTest 54, Section 3, Game 4

This is a linear game with a small twist – the issue of which of the bids is accepted.

H J K R S T = 6

## Rules

#1: K or R accepted in 2 or 3 (add to diagram)

#2:   H < J / K

#3: J4 → J S/T

#4: ~J4 → S/T ....< J

#5: R or S 5th (add to diagram)

Discussion: The issue of an "accepted" bid is really a fancy way of saying that either K or R will go in 2 or 3; note that it's NOT the case that they must BOTH go in one of those spaces. We could have K in 2nd and R in 5th, for example.

There's no need to do the contrapositives of 3 and 4 this one time; essentially we know what happens if J is 4 and if J is not 4. But, since those rules effectively give us limited options we should check out how they play out.

## If J4...

Then we know that T and S must go after J, so they must go 5 and 6. However, only R or S can go in 5, so S must be 5 and T 6:

```
___  [K or R]  ___   J    S    T
 1      2       3    4    5    6
```

We also know that H must be before J and K, so it can't go 3rd:

```
         [K or R]
H/    H/            J    S    T
 1     2       3    4    5    6
```

Very helpful; if J is 4, we've solved half the game.

## If ~J4...

Then J obviously goes elsewhere. But where? Well, we're assuming that Rule 4 is triggered so S and T must go before J. H must also always go before J, so the earliest J could go is 4th. But, we're postulating that J doesn't go 4th. Can it go 5th? No; only R or S can go 5th.

```
___  [K or R]  ___   ___   ___    J
 1      2       3     4     5     6
```

So if J isn't in 4th, it must be last!

Knowing that J can only go in 4 or 6 will be very helpful.

18. List question
   a) Violates Rule 1
   b) **Correct**
   c) Violates Rule 1
   d) Violates Rule 3
   e) Violates Rule 4

19. We can eliminate several choices based on other diagrams.
   a) **Correct**. If H were 4$^{th}$, J and K would have to be in 5 and 6, but only R/S can go in 5$^{th}$.
   b) As we saw in the split options, J can go 4$^{th}$.
   c) Works: H R T K S J
   d) Works: H K T R S J
   e) Works: H R K T S J

20. We know from our split options that J can only be 4$^{th}$ or 6$^{th}$. If you hadn't found that inference, you could eliminate most other answers from past diagrams.

**b) Correct.**

21. We're given that R must be in either 2 or 3 since it's the accepted bid. This means that S must be in 5 (since only R/S can go there. That's a good deduction – is it an answer choice? Yes!

**d) Correct.**

22. Process of elimination.
   a) Could be false: S H K T R J
   b) Could be false: T H K S R J
   c) **Correct.** We know that J can only go in 6$^{th}$ or 4$^{th}$. If J goes 6$^{th}$, of course K would be lower in cost. If J goes 4$^{th}$, we know from our split options that it's followed by S and T. Therefore, K would still need to be lower in cost.
   d) Could be false: H K R J S T
   e) Could be false – same as d)

23. If R is lowest in cost, that means S will have to go 5$^{th}$ (Rule 5). We also know K must be the accepted bid; since K can only go 2 or 3, and since H must go before it, H will have to go second and K third.
   a) **Correct.** J could go 4$^{th}$ instead: R H K J S T
   b) S must go 5$^{th}$ as inferred.
   c) K must go 3$^{rd}$ as inferred.
   d) H must go 2$^{nd}$ as inferred.
   e) As deduced, K must be the accepted bid because R must go first.

# PrepTest 54, Section 4 (LR)

**1. Question Type: Strengthen**
The conclusion is that the results of elections do not represent the unaltered preferences of the people. The correct answer will likely support this conclusion.
(A) This would not affect the voting process in democratic countries, so it is incorrect.
(B) This would weaken the conclusion, as it would suggest that the techniques used by political strategists were apparent to those seeing the ads.
(C) This does not strengthen the conclusion, as it makes it less likely that politicians' ads will have an effect on a large portion of the population.
(D) This weakens the conclusion, as it suggests the majority of voters will not be affected by political ads.
(E) Correct. This strengthens the conclusion that the results of elections do not represent what people believed before being affected by ads.

**2. Question Type: Method of Reasoning**
Terry responds by suggesting the comparison between the chemical industry and the cellular phone industry is a poor one. The correct answer will likely paraphrase this statement.
(A) Kris does not mention a source, so Terry could not question one.
(B) Terry does not say her evidence about the chemical industry is wrong but that it does not mean anything for the cell phone case.
(C) The problem is pollution, and Terry does not suggest that the industry is caused by the pollution.
(D) Correct. This paraphrases the predicted answer. He says her analogy to the chemical industry is a poor one.
(E) Terry makes no mention of technological progress, so this is incorrect.

**3. Question Type: Assumption**
The researcher assumes that what works in one country will work in another.
(A) Correct. This paraphrases our predicted answer. If what worked in one country did not work in another, then the conclusion would not follow, so this passes the negation test.
(B) Whether or not there are children in private schools has no bearing on what should be done in public schools.
(C) The researcher only suggests that the entire system of the better-performing nation be used, not that the best parts be pin-pointed.
(D) Even if most don't, they could begin to do so and then compare results, so this fails the negation test.
(E) This does not need to be true; if they did not target comparable grade levels, they could still decide which nation scored best and adopt that system. Therefore, this fails the negation test.

**4. Question Type: Flaw**
The argument assumes that because something happened for one reason, it cannot happen for a different reason. The correct answer will likely point this out.
(A) What happens to other cars does not matter; all that matters is why Cynthia's trunk opened.
(B) What happens to the engine does not matter; all that matters is why Cynthia's trunk opened.
(C) There is no third event to be explained, so this is not the right answer.
(D) Correct. This suggests that the trunk could have opened for one reason in the past and a different reason now.
(E) The argument attempts to prove what it is trying to claim, so it does not presume it.

**5. Question Type: Most Supported/Must be True**
(A) This is not supported; journalists seem to be concerned with what constitutes lying and then try not to lie according to those standards.
(B) While the prompt has suggested that whether or not something is a lie is questionable, it is universally accepted that lying is unacceptable.
(C) Only some journalists agree with this, so this is not supported.
(D) It is not suggested that lying is ever permissible, just that what constitutes lying is not concrete.
(E) Correct. According to the prompt, journalists disagree on whether several things constitute lying or not.

## 6. Question Type: Resolve the Paradox
The paradox is that wood-frame houses withstand earthquakes better than stone houses, but a wooden house withstood an earthquake worse than the next-door stone house.
(A) and (B) These do not explain how a house that should have withstood an earthquake failed to do so.
**(C) Correct.** This would suggest that the wooden house was weaker than most wooden houses, meaning it would withstand less than usual. This explains the paradox.
(D) It doesn't matter how expensive it was, it should not withstand more than a wooden house.
(E) This does not change the fact that a stone house withstood more than a wooden house, which is not supposed to happen.

## 7. Question Type: Assumption
The argument assumes that there is not some reason a snail would normally tense its foot when a light shined on it, regardless of whether or not the water around it shakes.
(A) The conclusion is only about this one snail, so the argument makes no assumption about snails in general.
(B) It is possible that they are usually exposed to bright lights but do not normally tense their foot, so this fails the negation test.
(C) The conclusion is only about this snail, so the argument makes no assumption about snails in general.
**(D) Correct.** If the snail would have tensed its foot normally whenever a bright light shone, there is no reason to believe that any association was made between the light and the shaking. This passes the negation test.
(E) Even if it was a learned response, the conclusion could be true, so this fails the negation test.

## 8. Question Type: Parallel Reasoning
The reasoning is that because a group has a characteristic, the individual members of that group each have that characteristic.
(A) No generalization is made from group to member, so this is incorrect.
(B) This generalization is from member to group, so it is incorrect.
**(C) Correct.** This generalization is made from group to member, so this is correct.
(D) This generalization is from member to group, so it is incorrect.
(E) This is logically sound, so it cannot be the correct answer.

## 9. Question Type: Principle
The principle must include the fact that it is not wrong to fail to do something that would be helpful and no inconvenience if you have not led the person to believe you will do it. (This question is tricky due to all the double-negatives!) It must also include the fact that it is laudable to do something that is helpful and no inconvenience.
**(A) Correct.** This includes both pieces of the principle and is thus the correct answer.
(B) and (C) These fail to mention the fact that it is not wrong to fail to help someone if you have not led them to believe you would do it.
(D) This principle does not fit the prompt, so it is incorrect.
(E) This principle is too extreme; we do not know all that much about what makes an act laudable, so the "only" goes too far.

## 10. Question Type: Weaken
(A) and (B) do not weaken Erin's argument, as they still allow for thousands of premature deaths.
(C) This does not weaken Erin's argument, as there is no reason to believe the use of automobiles will decline.
**(D) Correct.** This weakens Erin's argument, as it suggests the regulation would not help prevent thousands of premature deaths.
(E) This strengthens Erin's argument, as it suggests more regulation is needed for automobile emissions if thousands of premature deaths are to be avoided.

## 11. Question Type: Conclusion
The conclusion here is that the reason Australia has fewer mammal carnivores is the sparseness of the ecosystem. The final sentence is actually a sub-conclusion, which supports this statement.
(A) This is a statement the argument is meant to explain.
(B) This is a sub-conclusion to the main conclusion.

## PrepTest 54, Section 4 (LR) Continued...

(C) Correct. This correctly states the predicted answer. It does not support any other statements, and it is supported by other statements, so it is the conclusion.
(D) This is a premise that prove the sub-conclusion.
(E) This is worded as a premise and does not fit any of the statements in the prompt.

**12. Question Type: Most Supported/Must be true**
(A) This is too extreme; all we know is that it might not be possible to test the hypothesis.
(B) This is too extreme; all we know about hypotheses in physical science are verifiable, not whether only those hypotheses are verifiable.
(C) The argument does not suggest this hypothesis should not be seriously considered, so we have no reason to believe this.
**(D) Correct.** We are unable to verify the hypothesis, so we have no reason to believe it is either true or false.
(E) The argument does not mention what should or should not be taken seriously, so this is not the answer.

**13. Question Type: Resolve the Paradox**
The paradox is that the tallest mountains are located where erosive forces are strongest. The correct answer will have to explain how this is possible.
**(A) Correct.** The erosive forces grow stronger in response to increasing height, meaning they will always be strongest at the highest mountains.
(B) This would suggest that they should be eroded more and thus be shorter.
(C) This does not explain how the highest ones can be eroded more quickly and remain the highest.
(D) This does not alter the fact that erosion is strongest at the highest peaks, so it does not explain the paradox.
(E) This would suggest that the peaks should lower, which does not explain the paradox.

**14. Question Type: Flaw**
The argument has mistakenly assumed that an antenna only needs to be symmetrical and have a fractal structure; while those are necessary, they do not have to be sufficient – there could be another trait required for antennas to work.
(A) The term doesn't need to be defined as we know the antenna had a fractal structure. Defining the term would not affect the argument in any way.
(B) The argument does not contradict itself; it begins by describing a claim, and it ends by suggesting that claim was incorrect. It never asserted that the claim was correct.
(C) The argument does suggest the claim is false, but not on the grounds that there is insufficient evidence.
**(D) Correct.** This paraphrases the predicted answer. It is possible that something else is necessary for the antenna to work equally well.
(E) If the antenna works better below than above, it does not work equally well at all frequencies. No matter how the frequencies are split, this will be the case.

**15. Question Type: Method of Reasoning**
The statement about educating drivers is half of what the argument suggests is necessary for safety. It is one of the premises used to suggest that the city is not concerned with safety.
(A) It is never claimed that the city misunderstands; it is claimed that the city knows what would need to be done but is doing something else instead.
**(B) Correct.** This is the correct answer. It is part of the argument suggesting that the city is concerned with the appearance of safety.
(C) The statement is part of a suggestion as to what would bring about safety; it does not suggest that wearing helmets would be ineffectual.
(D) The city most likely will not take this measure, so this cannot be the right answer.
(E) This statement is not an illustration of anything; it is a suggestion of what should be done to make the roads safer for bicyclists.

**16. Question Type: Flaw**
The argument can be summarized as follows: We can build a colony on the moon, but it would cost a lot of money; meanwhile, as overcrowding on Earth gets worse, more people will want to move to the moon; therefore, we will eventually build a colony on the moon to relieve overcrowding. The argument assumes that at

some point, the need to relieve overcrowding will grow large enough that people will actually want to pay the cost to build a moon colony.
(A) Correct. This paraphrases our predicted answer.
(B) The argument does not suggest there are no other ways, just that moon colonies will be used at some point.
(C) Whether or not colonies were built to deal with severe overcrowding, they would alleviate it.
(D) It is never suggested that overcrowding will be relieved indefinitely, so it is possible that Earth could become overcrowded again.
(E) The argument only suggests that it is too costly for people to build colonies now, not that no one wants to.

### 17. Question Type: Principle
To paraphrase the principle, an act is wrong if it violates a rule that promotes general welfare; an act is right if the act is required by a rule that promotes general welfare. We should be careful, because it says nothing about rules that do not promote general welfare.
(A) This does not follow the principle. Because she broke a rule that promoted general welfare, what she did was wrong.
(B) and (C) Because the rules are not designed to promote the general welfare, the actions cannot be classified as right or wrong.
(D) In order for an action to be right, one must follow a rule that promotes general welfare.
(E) Correct. This correctly follows the principle. The rule he follows is there to promote the general welfare, so his action is right.

### 18. Question Type: Assumption
The conclusion here is the first sentence. There is a missing link between the inability to attract mass audiences and the inability to maximize profits. The answer will most likely create this link.
(A) This does not create the necessary link between mass audiences and maximizing profits. If some big budget films did not attract mass audiences, the conclusion could still be true, so this fails the negation test.
(B) If a film studio can make both big and small budget films, it is still possible that it should concentrate on big ones to maximize profits, so this fails the negation test.
(C) Correct. If a film studio could maximize profits without attracting mass audiences, the conclusion would not follow, so this passes the negation test and must be assumed by the argument.
(D) This suggests the conclusion is incorrect, so it is not the answer.
(E) The conclusion is a conditional, so the argument does not need to assume this. Whether a film's studio has profits as a primary goal or not does not affect what it should do if profits are its main goal.

### 19. Question Type: Flaw
Just because winners of the Tour de France in the past have had exceptional physiology does not mean that every winner must have an extra powerful heart or extra lung capacity; it could be that this year's winner had a third exceptional trait like powerful legs, or it could be that this year's winner broke the mold by having no remarkable traits.
(A) Even if the argument did overlook that this could be an advantage, that fact does not weaken the argument, which suggests that all winners have such physiology.
(B) Correct. This correctly paraphrases our predicted answer.
(C) This possibility is not overlooked; the argument suggests that one must have at least one, meaning it is possible to have just one and not another. The rarity of this occurrence has no bearing on the argument.
(D) Where the exceptional physiology came from does not affect the argument.
(E) Whether "exceptional" is compared against other cyclists or to non-cyclists does not affect the argument.

### 20. Question Type: Strengthen
The flaw in reasoning is that it is uncertain how many times the news station has been right. Being correct a higher proportion of the time is only helpful if the station makes predictions at least as often as its competitors. It could be that it only predicted rain twice and was correct both times; this would not be useful.
(A) Correct. This would definitely strengthen the argument, as it would mean that the station correctly predicted rain more often than its competitors, rather than simply a greater proportion of the time.
(B) This weakens the argument, as it suggests the less-popular station does not have as good a meteorology department.

(C) This does not affect the argument, as it has no bearing on whether the less popular station is more useful or not.
(D) This does not affect the argument, which only discusses predictions from the day before.
(E) Because the argument only tells us that the station is correct in predicting when there will be rain, when there won't be rain does not affect the argument.

**21. Question Type: Resolve the Paradox**
The paradox is that those who initially gave the most accurate testimony on cross-examination actually gave the least accurate testimony.
(A) How observant they were has no bearing on how accurate their memory was.
(B) This fails to explain why they had more inaccuracies with the second lawyer.
**(C)** Correct. This would mean that they should be more accurate with the first lawyer and less accurate with the second lawyer, so it explains the paradox.
(D) This would not explain either case, because they remembered better with the first lawyer.
(E) The number of details should not affect how accurate or inaccurate it was.

**22. Question Type: Assumption**
The "compelling reasons" in the conclusion comes out of nowhere, so something is needed to link it with the long-term interest.
(A) If this were not the case, the conclusion could still be correct, so this fails the negation test.
**(B)** Correct. This correctly makes a link between compelling reasons and long-term interests, and if it were false, the conclusion would have to be false. It therefore passes the negation test.
(C) If they conflicted often, it could still be the case that morally preferable acts are preferable, so this fails the negation test.
(D) Even if they seldom conflict, it could still be the case that morally preferable acts are preferable, so this fails the negation test.
(E) Even if this was usually the overriding consideration, morally preferable acts could still be preferable, so this fails the negation test.

**23. Question Type: Must be True**
(A) While studying outside of class is necessary, it is not sufficient to overcome the crisis, so this is incorrect.
**(B)** Correct. This correctly identifies studying outside of class as necessary to overcoming the crisis.
(C) The argument only states that mathematics is important, not that is more important than most others.
(D) This reverses the causation inherent to the argument, so it is not correct.
(E) Spending time outside of class is not sufficient to learning better but necessary, so this is not the correct answer.

**24. Question Type: Assumption**
It is possible that new buildings have been erected, so the argument must assume this is not the case.
(A) How evenly spread they were would not affect the conclusion, so this is not the correct answer.
(B) It does not matter how many buildings there have been in the past; the argument just says that 60 have been torn down and infers that the city is in financial trouble.
(C) The reason for tearing down the structures does not affect the fact that they were torn down, so this is not the correct answer.
(D) What buildings replaced the large buildings does not affect the argument, which stakes its claim on the fact that 60 buildings were torn down.
**(E)** Correct. This assumption is required. If more than 60 new large buildings were built, the conclusion would be incorrect, so this passes the negation test.

**25. Question Type: Parallel Reasoning**
The reasoning is as follows:
FD → E + S          ~E or ~S → ~FD
E or S → FS         ~FS → ~E and ~S
Therefore, ~(FS) → ~(FD)
It's very helpful here to have written out the contrapositives. If we know ~FS we know ~E and ~S. If

## PrepTest 54, Section 4 (LR) Continued...

those are true, according to the contrapositive of the first premise, we can infer ~FD.
(A) Because there is no "and" and also no "or", this is not similar to the reasoning.
(B) This is not similar reasoning, as it does not use the contrapositive to draw a correct conclusion.
$$ECP \to L + K$$
$$L \text{ or } K \to SBD$$
Therefore, SBD, then -(ECP)
(C) Correct. This has the same structure and uses the contrapositive to draw a correct conclusion.
(D) This is not three conditionals, so it cannot be the correct answer.
(E) This incorrectly reverses the logic, so it is not sound. Because the answer is sound, this must not be

## PrepTest 55
### PrepTest 55, Section 1 (LR)

**1. Question Type: Parallel Flaw**
The argument is an ad hominem argument, meaning it attacks a person rather than that person's argument. The argument is that if you make spelling and grammar errors, you cannot comment on others doing so. (Charges of hypocrisy are probably the most common form of an ad hominim argument).
(A) Here, the charges leveled against the newspaper are actually valid. Note that this answer doesn't claim that whatever the newspaper said isn't true, just that it can't be trusted because of past inaccuracies.
**(B) Correct.** This has both the ad hominem argument and the structure of criticizing someone for doing the same thing.
(C) There is no ad hominem argument in this one.
(D) Judging swimming practice is not the same as accepting promotional deals, so this is not the right answer.
(E) There is no ad hominem argument in this one.

**2. Question Type: Assumption**
There is a missing link between plumper beans and the quality of a dish. The correct answer will likely make a connection between the two.
**(A) Correct.** This answer creates the necessary link. Meanwhile, if plumper beans did not enhance the quality of the dish, the conclusion could not be true, so this passes the negation test.
(B) This answer is too extreme, and even if there was a dish that improved in quality with faster cooking, the conclusion could still follow. Therefore, this answer fails the negation test.
(C) Appearance had nothing to do with the argument and would not affect the conclusion.
(D) This answer is too extreme, and even if some other ingredients needed to be soaked, the conclusion could still follow. Therefore, this answer fails the negation test.
(E) Since we do not know how taste relates to quality, this is not the answer.

**3. Question Type: Method of Reasoning**
The conclusion is that direct mail advertising is annoying and immoral. The argument describes a trend (increasing use of direct mail ads), and suggests that the trend is immoral because similar behavior would be immoral in any other case.
(A) The contention that it is not immoral was never presented, so no counterexample could be given.
(B) The argument did not discuss what would happen if it became more widespread.
**(C) Correct.** This is exactly how the argument proceeds, so it describes the method of reasoning.
(D) The fact that it was annoying was only part of the conclusion, and it was never stated in a premise.
(E) The argument never said that other methods did not have moral issues, just that this one did.

**4. Question Type: Assumption**
There is a missing link between dust filtration and vacuum effectiveness. The correct answer will likely create a link.
**(A) Correct.** This creates the necessary link. Meanwhile, if the dust filtration efficiency had no effect on vacuum effectiveness, the conclusion would not follow, so this passes the negation test.
(B) Just because one can predict from filtration efficiency does not mean one cannot predict from motor power, so this is not the answer.
(C) This would actually prove the conclusion incorrect, so it cannot be the answer.
(D) Even if this was false, the conclusion could still be true, so this is not the right answer.
(E) Just because something is necessary for certain knowledge does not mean it cannot be sufficient for that knowledge.

**5. Question Type: Most Supported/Must be True**
(A) There is no reason to believe that forest environments were more hospitable than grasslands environments.
**(B) Correct.** It was suggested that this was true in both grasslands and forest environments, so this is the answer.
(C) This is never suggested; first it is suggested that this is true. Then it is suggested that it would also be

advantageous in a forest.
(D) The argument suggests there were advantages to becoming bipedal in both environments, so this is not correct.
(E) There is no reason to believe this; both are mentioned as positives to bipedalism in grasslands. Nothing suggests one is more important than the other.

### 6. Question Type: Principle
The answer choice must fit with each detail of the prompt. A choice that deviates in just one way is not the correct answer.
**(A) Correct.** This fits each part of the prompt, so it would justify the reasoning.
(B) Just because something is too abstract for certain students does not mean that only the most concrete things should be taught. This does not allow for teaching some students calculus, so it is incorrect.
(C) The prompt suggests that certain students would not lose motivation, so this is incorrect.
(D) The prompt did not suggest that only concrete application should be used, so this does not fit the prompt.
(E) The prompt involves considering whether certain students will be able to cope with a certain level of abstraction, so this does not fit the prompt.

### 7. Question Type: Weaken
The prompt has assumed that the correlation of two phenomena implies that one caused the other. The correct answer will likely suggest that this causation is incorrect.
**(A) Correct.** This supplies a different cause for the lowering of serious injury, so it weakens the causal relationship suggested in the prompt.
(B) Why injuries occurred before 1955 does not affect the conclusion, only what caused the lowering of injuries afterward.
(C) Even if the number has increased, the proportion has decreased, as stated in the prompt. Therefore, this does not suggest the legislation didn't cause the lowering proportion.
(D) What has happened outside of high-risk industries does not affect whether legislation affected the number of injuries in them.
(E) This would strengthen the argument, as it would suggest the legislation has helped in more than one industry.

### 8. Question Type: Most Supported/Must be True
(A) The argument only suggests that planting them again will help the economy, not that failing to do so will hurt it.
(B) It is not suggested that sunflowers are enough to stabilize the farming industry, just that they would provide relief. This answer is too general.
(C) The argument does not suggest anything about how Kalotopia could be better off now. It simply suggests something that could help for the future.
**(D) Correct.** The argument suggests that sunflowers, which were once grown, would benefit farmers and the economy if brought back.
(E) The argument does not say anything about other crops; it simply states that sunflowers would be good.

### 9. Question Type: Weaken
The prediction method is supposed to help local officials determine exactly when to evacuate people. Any answer that suggests the method will not give an exact time would weaken the argument.
(A) Even if scientists don't understand, the method can still be used.
(B) This strengthens the argument by suggesting it is better than previous methods.
(C) This does not affect the argument, as it has no bearing on how well the method will work.
**(D) Correct.** This answer suggests that officials will not know when to evacuate people, so it weakens the argument.
(E) This does not affect the argument, which does not rely on there being more than one station.

### 10. Question Type: Most Supported/Must be True
(A) This answer is too broad; we do not know about all machines that rely on other machines of the same type; we only know about one case.

## PrepTest 55, Section 1 (LR) Continued...

(B) Correct. This is true of the fax machine industry, so it is true of at least some industries.
(C) The term "high-tech industry" is too broad; we only know about the fax industry.
(D) This is too broad; we only know that some cooperation helped in the fax industry. We have no reason to believe it would help in every industry.
(E) The "only" in this answer is too extreme. It is possible that cooperation is beneficial in other industries. All we know is that cooperation was beneficial in this instance; we know nothing about other situations.

### 11. Question Type: Principle
No piece of the principle can be broken or ignored. The principle can be paraphrased as follows: critique helps someone do their job better as long as they are reminded that their job performance also relies on other things.
(A) As there is no mention of a critique, this is not the correct answer.
(B) Since the teachers did consider themselves to be teachers, this cannot be the correct answer.
(C) Because there is no mention of critique, this is not the correct answer.
(D) The critique did not need to come from a non-teacher to help, so this is not the correct answer.
(E) Correct. In this case, a person does better at his job by being critiqued and reminded that others on the team will also be critiqued.

### 12. Question Type: Assumption
There is a missing link between focusing on the author and becoming emotionally engaged in the imaginary world. The correct answer will likely create a link between these two.
(A) This is a restatement of the first sentence and as such is not an unstated premise.
(B) The amount a novel captures the imaginations of readers is not mentioned in the argument, so this is not the answer.
(C) Correct. This creates the link between focusing on the author and becoming emotionally engaged. If most readers could become engaged while focused on the author, the conclusion would have to be false, so this answer passes the negation test.
(D) The perspective of the author is not mentioned in the prompt, so this is not the correct answer.
(E) Even if they did serve literary purpose, they could still make it impossible for a read or engage with the imaginary world, so this fails the negation test.

### 13. Question Type: Resolve the Paradox
The paradox is that advertisers target people 25 and under even though those 46-55 spend the most money. The correct answer will have to allow both of these to be true.
(A) It cannot be that those 25 and under are the most likely to purchase everything because they do not spend as much as 46-55 year olds. This would mean that many advertisers should target older groups, which is not true according to the prompt.
(B) This is completely unrelated and fails to explain either piece of the puzzle.
(C) While this fact makes sense considering the facts in the prompt, it does not explain the problem.
(D) Correct. Advertisers only need to target those who will change their minds, so this would explain targeting only 25 and under despite the fact that older people spend more.
(E) This does not explain why they would target 25 and under on television.

### 14. Question Type: Flaw
The conclusion is that one should never attempt to acquire expensive tastes. This is supported by evidence that suggests there are potential negative consequences to doing so.
(A) No claim is restated in the conclusion, so this is not correct.
(B) The argument does not mention financial irresponsibility, so this cannot be assumed.
(C) Sensations is not inherently vague, so this is not the right answer.
(D) There is no cause of acquiring tastes that is suggested to be an effect, so this is incorrect.
(E) Correct. The argument rejects a goal due to possible negative consequences and fails to consider potential positive consequences.

### 15. Question Type: Most Supported/Must be True
One inference is that they offer half-off coffee almost every Wednesday.
(A) It is possible that there is some other day when there is always a poetry reading, which would mean it had

half-off coffee more often.
- (B) We have no idea when poetry readings are, except that most Wednesdays have them. Therefore, this answer is not supported.
- (C) This reverses the relationship between the two. All we know is that they offer half-off coffee when there's a poetry reading. Maybe they offer half-off coffee all the time on non-poetry days.
- **(D) Correct.** This restates our predicted answer.
- (E) It is possible that some Wednesdays there is no poetry reading, but this does not mean there is no half-off coffee. Therefore, this is not supported.

### 16. Question Type: Principle
The argument states when something is intentional and when something is a random event. Keep in mind that one can fall outside of both categories.
- (A) Because it was not a specific motivation, this is not intentional. However, that does not mean it is random. To be random, there must not be a normal physical process that can explain it.
- **(B) Correct.** This correctly expresses and applies the definition of intentional acts.
- (C) This confuses the definition by switching from one person to another. While the waving was intentional, getting distracted was not. Therefore, this is incorrect.
- (D) Breathing is a normal physical process, so this is incorrect.
- (E) All that means is that it was not a random event, which does not imply it was intentional.

### 17. Question Type: Assumption
The conclusion is the first sentence.
- (A) This would weaken the conclusion, so it is incorrect.
- (B) Even if they did not know it better, they could still know it, so this fails the negation test.
- (C) Even if the name can provide some information, it is possible to know something without knowing its name, so this fails the negation test.
- **(D) Correct.** This is a difficult answer. "Some" people use the fact that ancients had no name for moral rights as evidence that they didn't have the concept. The analogy of the fruit tree makes an incredibly obvious-seeming assumption that we would normally never consider – that people harvesting wild fruit conceptually know what that fruit is. See how it can be both incredibly obvious and also wildly difficult to find? If the people who harvested the fruit of the tree didn't know what they were doing, it wouldn't make the point the author wants to make.
- (E) If one did have to know what something was before naming it, then the conclusion would be true, so this fails the negation test.

### 18. Question Type: Conclusion
The main conclusion here is the third sentence. The first sentence is a sub-conclusion that combines with the last sentence to prove the third sentence. (You'll see this pattern on many of the harder conclusion questions.)
- (A), (B), (C), and (D) None of these paraphrases the third sentence.
- **(E) Correct.** This is the main conclusion, supported by each of the other statements and failing to support any of the others statements.

### 19. Question Type: Method of Reasoning
- (A) It is not attempting to refute the statement, so this is not the correct answer.
- (B) The argument does not object to the statement but qualifies it. The author agrees that some are better than others in execution but states that execution isn't everything.
- **(C) Correct.** This is the correct answer. While the author agrees with the statement, s/he suggests that execution should be understood in a different context.
- (D) The argument does not derive it from another claim.
- (E) The argument does not use it to justify an example but uses an example to justify qualifying the statement.

### 20. Question Type: Flaw
The argument assumes that because parthenogenesis has not been proven to occur in mammals, it does not occur in mammals. (This is a common pattern of a flawed argument).
- **(A) Correct.** This correctly describes our predicted answer. The argument assumes that because

## PrepTest 55, Section 1 (LR) Continued...

parthenogenesis has not been proven, it is false for that reason.
(B) The argument does not suggest that all non-mammalian vertebrates do this.
(C) Another explanation is never given, so this is incorrect.
(D) The argument does not give a necessary or sufficient condition for parthenogenesis, so it does not confuse them.
(E) The argument does not describe why the study was flawed.

### 21. Question Type: Principle
(A) This is close but not quite correct. The issue is that many people must buy advertising products, not just one. It is not the case that the show will be canceled if one person does not buy things, so this does not fit the prompt exactly.
**(B)** Correct. This essentially rephrases the end of the prompt.
(C) The advertiser only suggests that people should buy things, not that s/he should take whatever actions possible.
(D) The advertiser lists one specific action and does not suggest people should do at least some things.
(E) The argument does not suggest only those who feel most strongly should act.

### 22. Question Type: Weaken
The use of data and correlated phenomena to imply causation can be weakened. The correct answer will likely suggest that the causation is reversed or that something else is the true cause.
(A) This would actually strengthen the argument.
(B) This answer is too vague; the argument only refers to people who are easily angered, and it is not clear if the medication makes people angry or cheery.
(C) This would actually strengthen the argument.
(D) This is close but not quite right. The argument was that those who become angry more easily get high blood pressure from their anger, and high blood pressure leads to heart disease. The problem with this answer is that it skips the high blood pressure step and suggests that heart disease causes people to become more easily angered. However, this does not affect the data that shows those who are more easily angered have higher blood pressure, which could still cause heart disease.
**(E)** Correct. This suggests that there is a mitigating factor that causes both high blood pressure and ease of anger. This would mean the psychological factor did not cause the high blood pressure, so did not cause the heart disease.

### 23. Question Type: Strengthen
There is a missing link between printing an assignment and printing out entire books. The correct answer will likely establish this link.
(A) This does not strengthen the answer, as it does not support the conclusion that books on the computer will not make printed books obsolete.
**(B)** Correct. This establishes the missing link and suggests that the conclusion is correct.
(C) The prompt does not mention impaired vision, so this is not the correct answer.
(D) While this suggests the conclusion might be true, it does not make the argument stronger. There is still the logical hole of the missing link between the assignment and books.
(E) This is completely unrelated and does not support the conclusion.

### 24. Question Type: Flaw
The conclusion is that anyone who follows this diet will lose weight, but the data simply states that the group with that diet lost the most weight as a whole. This does not mean that each individual in that group lost more weight than they would have on a different diet. The correct answer will most likely point this out.
(A) The researchers are only concerned with losing weight, not with feeling full.
(B) While this makes the data less robust, it is not a logical flaw in the argument, and it is still possible that those who stay on the diet will lose weight.
(C) The study is only concerned with what will definitely cause someone to lose weight, not how much weight they will lose.
**(D)** Correct. This provides a counter-example to the generalized claims of the advertisement.
(E) The group did not overlook this possibility, as they believe it is better to eat earlier in the day.

## PrepTest 55, Section 1 (LR) Continued...

**25. Question Type: Most Supported/Must be True EXCEPT**

The argument can be diagrammed as follows:
>  Some 20th century art is great
>  Great art -> original ideas     ~original ideas -> ~great art
>  ~influential -> ~ great art     great art -> influential

Four of the answers will follow logically from this, while the correct answer will not.

(A) This follows logically because any great art is both influential and original, and since there is some great art, there must be some art that is both influential and original. Therefore, this is not the correct answer.

(B) This follows logically through the chain of conditionals. It is true of some 20th century that it is great, and it is true of all great art that it is original, so it is true of some 20th century art that it is original.

**(C)** Correct. There's nothing we can know for sure about art with original ideas – that term never appears as a sufficient condition. (Note that it would be a fallacy to infer from original art that it was great).

(D) It is necessary for art to be influential and original to be great, so this does follow logically.

(E) Some twentieth century art is great, and all great is both influential and original, so some twentieth century art must be both influential and original.

# PrepTest 55, Section 2 (RC)

**Passage 1**

Watch for words like "nevertheless" and "but." They occur several times here.

Paragraph 1 describes the problem that on the one hand, employers have an interest in preserving their trade secrets, while employees have an interest in seeking gainful employment elsewhere. Courts balance this by allowing the employee to work elsewhere, but prohibiting them from using trade secrets.

Paragraph 2 points out the problem with this: you can't unlearn something you already know. So the courts' balance does little to protect trade secrets.

Paragraph 3 further argues that the biggest problem is the way in which a former employee may use his ex-employer's trade secrets inadvertently or subconsciously. This type of behavior is difficult to prove; those difficulties are outlined. The result is that an injunction against using trade secrets has little effect beyond preventing actual transfer of documents.

So what's the main point? Basically, that attempts to protect trade secrets using the legal process have the major problem that most of a company's trade secrets are internalized by the employee—he takes them with him, in the form of general knowledge.

Based on this prediction, we can answer....

1. **(D)**. The other responses either overstate the author's point, or draw an inference that the author doesn't reach. (A) is wrong because there aren't "more effective" ways discussed – we just know that injunctions aren't particularly effective. (C) is too strong.

2. The passage describes what's basically a structural problem with using injunctions to protect trade secrets. (The passage also hints that barriers to using trade secrets don't do the employees any good either.) The author isn't arguing that the legal system is the best method (choice B) or that the legal system should be improved (choice C). So we're looking at **(A)**: trade secrets basically can't be protected by injunctions, so try keeping the employees instead.

3. The passage states that using injunctions to protect trade secrets is fundamentally flawed; so that's choice **(A)**. (D) is an inference you might draw from the passage, but it's not the author's primary purpose.

4. Again, there's a structural problem with using injunctions in this context. The phrase "no reliable way" in choice **(B)** pretty much sums that up.

5. Our author would probably agree with choices (A) or (B)—he or she certainly gives you that impression. But he or she undoubtedly would agree with choice **(E),** which is all but directly stated in the passage.

6. Answer **(E)** is the only one stated in the passage. See lines 46-51.

**Passage 2, Comparative reading**

Passage A states that purple loosestrife is spreading, has displaced native vegetation, has probably impacted wildlife, and has threatened habitats. Loosestrife hits disturbed habitat more clearly than it does undisturbed habitat. There's been little research on how to control it; the upshot appears to be that more research is needed.

Passage B begins with the word "apparently" in the first sentence (that's a clue—always look for words like that). It then discusses roughly the point of view stated by passage A—the scientific community refers to the plant as a "pollution." The author takes a different view, however. Only one bird has been shown to be damaged by the plant. Fur-bearing animals are impacted, but none that are threatened species. The author seems to think that the main impact of loosestrife has been economic rather than ecological.

## PrepTest 55, Section 2 (RC) Continued...

7. Passage A mentions furbearing animals (line 12); Passage B discusses them (line 56). So the correct answer is choice **(A)**.

8. The correct answer is **(E)**; both passages discuss wetlands.

9. Note from our discussion above that the main difference is that Passage B dismisses the seriousness of the ecological threat posed by the plants, while Passage A sees the plant as a threat. The best choice that reflects this disagreement is **(B)**.

10. The author of Passage B disagrees with Passage A: that much should be clear. So pick choice **(E)**.

11. The authors disagree on the main point. But what do they agree about? Well, Passage B grudgingly admits that some wildlife populations (canvasback, certain furry mammals) have been impacted. So **(A)** is correct.

12. What's the relationship between the two passages? Predict it before you read the answers. A good prediction would be "B disagrees with A." But that isn't here. So what do you do? Well, you know that B discusses A before disagreeing with it. So choice **(C)** is correct.

13. Author A thinks loosestrife is a problem; Author B downplays its significance. So you're looking for a piece of information that might indicate that loosestrife is a bigger problem than Author B originally thought. Choice **(A)** fits that description.

**Passage 3**

Mark up as follows:

Paragraph 1. The first sentence contains the phrase "some critics..." Look for a "but they're wrong" type argument in your future. These critics argue that Kingston's work is ex nihilo (out of nothing—i.e., completely without prior influences). But these critics ignore Chinese oral tradition—song/narratives called "talk story."

Paragraph 2 describes talk-story, and how it was imported into the US and adapted here.

Paragraph 3: Kingston adopted talk-story, believes herself to be part of that tradition.

Paragraph 4. One example of Kingston's talk-story is the book China Men. It's described.

So what's the main point? We can predict that it's something like, "Kingston's work isn't without literary influence; she's influenced by the Chinese tradition of talk-story." That answer is reflected in....

14. ...choice **(A)**. Choices (B) and (D) state things that are in the passage, but miss the main idea, which is given in paragraph 1. Choices (C) and (E) each make an inferential leap that the author never reaches.

15. What do we know about talk-story? Largely that it's a Chinese oral tradition. As an oral tradition, it's not going to be written down—that's mentioned in lines 15-16 and described in some detail in lines 29-35. So the right answer is **(D)**.

16. This question calls on your ability to detect meaning from context. So go read the context. She's describing storytelling processes which "sift and reconstruct the essential elements of personally remembered stories." Memory of stories that have been told—your basic oral tradition—is what's being referred to here. The stories themselves aren't personal. So neither (A) or (B) is correct. Instead, the answer is **(C)**.

17. Go read the part of the passage the prompt is pointing to. In a nutshell, it says that Kingston succeeds in making English sound like Chinese. Which of these choices is similar? The one that makes cotton feel like wool—choice **(B)**.

## PrepTest 55, Section 2 (RC) Continued...

18. Choice **(C)** is correct—it expresses the fact that the stories are part of an oral tradition.

19. What's the author's argument? Basically, that Kingston uses oral tradition. The author uses China Men as his example. If China Men were atypical, that would mean that Kingston's other work isn't like this. So choice **(D)** is correct. (It doesn't matter that there may be other authors or cultures that use oral tradition—the author does NOT argue that Kingston is or is not unique. So that eliminates choices (A), (B), and (C).)

20. The point is that Kingston is using those forms. **(B)** is correct.

21. This question tests your grasp of the author's tone. Usually, in such a question you can eliminate two or three responses that indicate a negative point of view where the author's is positive, or vice versa. But here, that only eliminates choice (B). There's nothing tentative about this article, so you can get rid of (C). Choice (E) states the case too strongly. So you're left with choices (A) or (D). Are the sources of talk-story really all that diverse? No, so (D) is incorrect. That leaves you with **(A)**. The article is scholarly, and the talk-story tradition is old, so it fits.

**Passage 4**

The first paragraph describes what a speculative bubble is. It states the "classic nineteenth-century account" of the Dutch tulip market. "But," we're told, Garber challenges the account of that market as a bubble. That sets up our main idea here.

Paragraph 2 describes what happened during the Dutch tulip-market rise and collapse. It describes Mackay's "bubble" analysis of the situation.

Paragraph 3 describes Garber's analysis of that situation: Garber believes that it was not a bubble because the price increases and collapses were not speculative, but were based on the actual value of the bulbs.

22. The main point can be predicted to be that contrary to popular opinion, the famed tulip bust was not a bubble. That's choice **(A)**.

23. Why, according to the author, did the price of tulip bulbs collapse? Because once a variety of tulips becomes established, it's easy to reproduce many copies of the formerly new bulbs. See lines 44-47. This is most like **(D)**, a publisher buying a manuscript of a book and then selling cheap copies.

24. Garber believes that, contrary to popular opinion, the prices of tulips could be explained rationally. His rational explanation is best given by **(B)**; see lines 47-56. So that's your choice.

25. Mackay is the one who described the tulip market as a speculative bubble (lines 9-12). So choice **(B)** is correct.

26. Look at your markup (see above). Choice (C) best encompasses what's going on in this paragraph. (A) is somewhat close—the paragraph does contain some facts. But notice that paragraph 2 also contains Mackay's inferences from the facts, with which Garber disagrees. So **(C)** has to be the answer.

27. Read the context. Here, this pricing pattern is described as occurring for new types of flowers. So, that's "standard" as in "typical," not as in "regulated" or "ideal." That's choice **(D)**.

# PrepTest 55, Section 3 (LR)

**1. Question Type: Resolve the Paradox**
The paradox is that Socrates was portrayed one way when he was in his forties and another after he was dead.
(A) While this description could be true, it does not explain either piece of the puzzle.
**(B)** Correct. This would explain the difference between his portrayals in his forties and after his death.
(C), (D), and (E) While these may be true, they do not explain either piece of the puzzle.

**2. Question Type: Flaw**
The conclusion does not logically follow from the premises. The agreement was that the work would not contain material that hurt the foundation's reputation. Just because the work did not mention the foundation's laudable achievements does not mean it broke this agreement.
(A) Intellectual value has no bearing on the argument.
(B) The argument does not confuse these; to get the grant, an agreement was reached.
**(C)** Correct. This correctly labels the assumption that would make the argument sound. This fact would fill the hole mentioned in the predicted answer.
(D) It does not matter what usually happens, only what happened in this instance.
(E) Whether there was more to the agreement and whether it was broken or not does not affect this argument, which suggests that this portion of the agreement was broken.

**3. Question Type: Strengthen**
The argument states that when breaking habits, immediate concerns are more motivating than long-term concerns. This only means that cigarette smokers will more likely quit from social pressure if social pressure is immediate and health concerns are not. The argument states that social pressure is immediate, so the correct answer will likely state that health concerns are not immediate.
(A) This fails to make the argument sound, as it does not suggest health concerns are not immediate.
**(B)** Correct. This paraphrases our predicted answer.
(C) This answer is too vague – we don't know what the courses of action are or how they relate to whether health concerns are immediate or not.
(D) This is completely unrelated.
(E) Even if this were true, it would not suggest that health concerns were not a motivating factor.

**4. Question Type: Weaken**
The answer will most likely weaken the assumption that it will be difficult to find new agents.
**(A)** Correct. This would weaken Melvin's position quite a bit, and it paraphrases our predicted answer.
(B) This would not make his argument any weaker, so it cannot be the right answer.
(C) Melvin's argument is that it is not feasible, not that it is undesirable, so this does not weaken his argument.
(D) This would not weaken his argument, as it simply suggests an alternative to doing something he says is impossible.
(E) This strengthens his position, so it cannot counter his argument.

**5. Question Type: Most Supported/Must be True**
**(A)** Correct. If the mole detects electric fields to catch worms and insects, it follows that worms and insects must produce electric fields.
(B) and (C) The argument only says it uses its nose to find food, not that it doesn't use anything else, so these are not supported.
(D) This is too extreme; the "only" is not supported by the argument. All we know is that one animal that hunts has tentacles on its nose.
(E) This is not supported, as the prompt does not include any information about whether or not the mole has an electric field.

**6. Question Type: Principle EXCEPT**
Four answers will fit the prompt, and the correct answer will not.
(A) This fits the prompt.
(B) This fits the prompt. The child misbehaves, and the parent's reaction to misbehavior affects the child's behavior in the future.
(C) A parent who simply wants their child to be quiet can inadvertently reinforce misbehaving by giving in.

# PrepTest 55, Section 3 (LR) Continued...

(D) Correct. This is nothing like what happened in the prompt, so it is not a generalization from the prompt. This means it is the correct answer.
(E) This fits the prompt.

### 7. Question Type: Method of Reasoning
The statement in question is mentioned as the only evidence for a proposition (that chemical R is safe for humans) that the argument will oppose.
(A) The argument does not suggest there is evidence against that conclusion, just that this evidence is not proof of that conclusion.
(B) It is not used to support that statement; it is used in conjunction with that statement to say something else.
(C) It does not illustrate this claim, as it does not suggest any of the claim is true.
(D) It is not used as evidence for such a claim, so this is not correct.
(E) Correct. This paraphrases our predicted answer.

### 8. Question Type: Assumption
The argument suggests that offering free gift wrapping is a bad idea because if most people want it or if few people want it there are negative consequences either way. However, the argument fails to consider that there is a middle ground between these two that could have positive consequences. The correct answer will likely point this out.
(A) This is not required; even if gift-wrapping were not more expensive than in previous years, there could still be no reason to offer free gift-wrapping, so this fails the negation test.
(B) Even if this were not true, it could still be that there was no reason to offer gift-wrapping, so this fails the negation test.
(C) This doesn't affect the argument – the past history of patients is not at issue.
(D) Even if this were not expensive, the conclusion could still be true, so this fails the negation test.
(E) Correct. If a moderate number of people want gift wrap, it may make sense to offer it.

### 9. Question Type: Weaken
The argument suggests that correlated phenomena are causally related. It assumes that because those who use behavior modification tend to fall asleep sooner, behavior modification is the reason they fell asleep sooner. The correct answer will likely suggest that this causal link is incorrect.
(A) Total sleeping time has no bearing on the argument, which is about the length of time it takes to fall asleep.
(B) This would have no bearing on the conclusion, which simply compares two groups of people who do have trouble falling asleep.
(C) This would not weaken the argument, and it could strengthen it.
(D) Correct. This answer suggests that the causal link is incorrect, as we suggested in our predicted answer. This would make the conclusion false, so it weakens the argument most.
(E) Why people chose one over the other has no bearing on whether one worked better than the other, so this does not weaken the argument.

### 10. Question Type: Assumption
The argument seems to assume that testimony should not be included if one cannot identify both people involved in an assault. The correct answer will likely paraphrase this.
(A) This is a mistaken negation of the assumption.
(B) Whether there are other witnesses has no bearing on whether or not this witness's testimony should be thrown out.
(C) Even if it was possible to determine this, the conclusion could still follow, so this fails the negation test.
(D) Correct. This paraphrases the contrapositive of our predicted answer.
(E) This has no bearing on the argument, though it does seem like the argument is implying this. Remember, an assumption on the LSAT is an unstated premise that is required to make the argument sound. Since this would not make the argument sound, it is not an assumption.

### 11. Question Type: Flaw
The argument assumes that because other animals adapted in different ways, humans could not have adapted in a certain way. The correct answer will likely mention this assumption.

*PrepTest 55, Section 3 (LR) Continued...*

(A) The argument states it was not sufficient or necessary, so this is incorrect.
(B) Correct. This paraphrases our predicted answer.
(C) No similar change was made in other animals, so this is not correct.
(D) The argument does not suggest that there were greater difficulties for humans, so this is not correct.
(E) It does not take this for granted, because it suggests that it is not true.

### 12. Question Type: Most Supported/Must be True
(A) This is not supported, as sales have increased since television was first available. There is no reason to believe that television is responsible for the slowing of the rate of increase or the decline in library circulation.
(B) This is not supported, as we only know that library use has declined in recent years and have no information regarding any other time period.
(C) This is not supported, as the number is still increasing, even if the rate is slowing.
(D) Correct. This is supported, as the early days of television did not cause a decline.
(E) This is not supported, as there is no reason to believe that there was a causal relationship between the rise in book sales and the spread of television.

### 13. Question Type: Conclusion
The main conclusion is that the belief is mistaken. Every other sentence supports this sentence, and this sentence does not support any others.
(A) This is never stated, so it is not the conclusion.
(B) While this is suggested by the prompt, it supports the conclusion that people shouldn't believe they are dangerous, so this is not the conclusion.
(C) This is not the conclusion, as it is used to support the main conclusion.
(D) Correct. This paraphrases our predicted answer.
(E) While this is suggested, this is used to support the conclusion that people should not believe they are dangerous.

### 14. Question Type: Strengthen
There is a leap from suggesting that most buildings with one type of stone were human dwellings and concluding that a building with more than one type of stone was not a human dwelling. The correct answer will likely draw a connection that allows this conclusion to be drawn properly.
(A) This fails to make an adequate connection. This does not suggest that the conclusion is correct, as the building in question is made in part of limestone.
(B) Correct. This suggests that the conclusion is correct by drawing the connection referred to in the predicted answer.
(C) This would have no bearing on whether or not a building was a dwelling, so this does not support the conclusion.
(D) This does not affect whether or not a particular building was a dwelling, so this is not the right answer.
(E) This knowledge does not suggest that the building is not a dwelling, so it does not strengthen the argument.

### 15. Question Type: Parallel Reasoning
The argument can be diagrammed as follows:         Contrapositives
    TR on time → accountant and ~(add. Doc.)    add. Doc or ~accountant → ~TR on time
        accountant → add. Doc.                    ~add. Doc → ~accountant
        Therefore, ~(TR on time)

This argument is logically sound, so any answer that is not logically sound must be incorrect. The argument is sound because Theodore only files on time if he has an accountant and no additional documents are needed. But we know that if he has an accountant, he'll need additional documents. Therefore, he either needs additional documents or doesn't have an accountant, but in either case he won't file on time according to the contrapositive of the4 first rule. Note that you'll be able to visualize how the argument flows better if you write out the contrapositives.
(A) This argument can be diagrammed as:
        next free evening → Friday

*PrepTest 55, Section 3 (LR) Continued...*

        next free evening → probably at home
        Therefore, he will probably be at home on Friday
Because there is no "and" in either conditional, this is not parallel to the reasoning in the main argument.
(B) This argument can be diagrammed as:
        away on business → cannot attend concert
        misses concert → no opportunity to see concert this month
        She will be away on business
        Therefore, no concert this month
Because there is no "and" in either conditional, this is not parallel to the reasoning in the main argument.
(C) This argument is not logically sound, so it is not the correct answer.
(D) This argument can be diagrammed as:
        ~(FC) → BC
        ~(FC)
        Therefore, BC
Because there is only one conditional, and it does not include an "and", this is not parallel.
**(E)** Correct. This can be diagrammed as:
        relaxing vacation → children behave and ~(susp. Misch.)
        children behave → susp. Misch.
        Therefore, ~(relaxing vacation)
This follows the argument's structure exactly, saying that two things are necessary for something to be true and then suggesting it is impossible for both things to occur at the same time.

**16. Question Type: Most Supported/Must be True**
(A) This is not supported, as there is no reason to believe that the government is likely to act on what people estimate to be the greatest threats.
(B) This is not supported by the prompt.
**(C)** Correct. This is suggested by the prompt, which states that people estimate risk based on prominence in the news and that the news tends to ignore common risks except in the most outrageous cases. This suggests that people will estimate higher risks for things that are uncommon.
(D) The prompt makes no mention of focusing on risks in terms of timeline, so this is not supported.
(E) The prompt does not say anything about how resources are spent, so this is not supported.

**17. Question Type: Principle**
**(A)** Correct. This is a near-paraphrase of the argument in the prompt.
(B) The prompt only suggests that a seller should keep someone from believing they will receive an appliance with their purchase if they will not receive it. It says nothing about whether a potential buyer thinks something is a permanent fixture or not.
(C) This does not fit the prompt, which does not say what a seller should do if s/he fails to meet the moral obligation stated.
(D) This does not fit the prompt because no one is misleading anyone; people are making an assumption that this argument suggests a seller should try to avoid.
(E) This does not fit the prompt, which refers to all cases of selling homes, not just to those in which a seller indicates a large appliance comes with the home.

**18. Question Type: Flaw**
There is a missing link between a child's creativity/resourcefulness and his/her cognitive development. The correct answer will likely point this out.
(A) The argument suggests that something is not conducive to a goal, so this does not describe the argument or a flaw in it.
(B) Whether or not a child enjoys playtime has nothing to do with that child's cognitive development, so this is not the answer.
(C) The argument suggests that something will not enhance a child's creativity, so it does not list any sufficient or necessary conditions, nor does it confuse them.
(D) Regardless, creativity and resourcefulness would still be necessary, so this is not the answer.
**(E)** Correct. This correctly exposes the missing link mentioned in our predicted answer.

*PrepTest 55, Section 3 (LR) Continued...*

**19. Question Type: Assumption**
The argument assumes that problems that do not fit into current regulations will constantly arise. The correct answer will likely paraphrase this.
(A) This would not suggest that the bureaucracy will continue to stack on more and more regulations, so this is not the answer.
(B) Even if this were not true, it could still be the case that the regulations will grow indefinitely, so this fails the negation test.
**(C) Correct.** This paraphrases our predicted answer. If an ideal bureaucracy were without complaints not covered, no new regulations would come about, and the conclusion would have to be false.
(D) If this were not true, the conclusion could still be true, so this fails the negation test.
(E) Even if some complaints could be dealt with according to existing regulations, regulations could still grow from other complaints.

**20. Question Type: Conclusion**
The main conclusion is the last part of the final sentence. This is supported by the rest of the prompt, and it is not used to support any other part of the argument.
(A) This is a claim that the argument mentions some other people believe, so it is not the conclusion.
**(B) Correct.** This paraphrases the final part of the final sentence, which we identified as the conclusion.
(C) This is never actually stated, as the diversity was used to conclude that generalizations should not be made from one type of bacteria to all types of bacteria. Therefore, this is not the conclusion.
(D) This is a premise because it is used to support the conclusion.
(E) This is never suggested by the argument, so this is not the conclusion.

**21. Question Type: Assumption**
There is a missing link between failing to complete all reading assignments and failing to receive a high grade. The correct answer will likely establish this link.
**(A) Correct.** This creates a link, and the link serves to prove the conclusion. If students who did not do all the reading received high grades, the conclusion would be incorrect, so this passes the negation test.
(B) and (C) would not prove the conclusion, as they still allow students who did not do all of the work to get high grades, which the conclusion says is not true. Therefore, these are not the assumption.
(D) Even if highly motivated students did not do all of their work when required to hand in homework, the conclusion could still be true, so this fails the negation test.
(E) Even if no highly motivated student earned high grades in a course with written homework, the conclusion could still be true, so this fails the negation test.

**22. Question Type: Weaken**
There are two assumptions in this question. The first is a leap from seeing that one diet is more effective than the other to claiming that that diet is more effective than any other diet. The second involves the use of the term body fat in the conclusion, which wasn't mentioned elsewhere. It is assumed that the weight lost is body fat. The correct answer will likely expose one of these assumptions and suggest it is incorrect.
**(A) Correct.** This exposes the second assumption and suggests it is incorrect, so it weakens the argument most effectively.
(B) Because this answer does not include information on how much carbohydrates these people eat, it does not weaken the argument, which requires that people shun carbohydrates.
(C) This would still lower body fat, the claim in the conclusion, so this does not weaken the claim.
(D) This would strengthen the argument because the low-carb diet would have done better even though the high-carb dieters participated in this exercise.
(E) This strengthens the argument by suggesting stopping the diet results in weight gain, which makes it more likely that the diet was the cause of weight loss.

**23. Question Type: Parallel Flaw**
The argument attributes a quality to an object (a computer), then suggests that something else (a human mind) is that object because it also has that quality.
(A) This argument suggests that there is a biological basis for something because it exists in all animals. This argument is very different from that in the prompt.

# PrepTest 55, Section 3 (LR) Continued...

(B) This argument suggests that two objects having the same quality means that that quality cannot be used to distinguish one from the other. This is different from the prompt.

(C) Correct. This argument attributes a quality to an object (an organism), then suggests that something else (a community) is that object because it also has that quality. This is just like the prompt, so it is the correct answer.

(D) This argument involves conditionals, so this is not similar to that in the prompt (which had no conditionals).

(E) While a quality is attributed to two different things, it is not used to suggest that one of those things is really the other thing. Therefore, this is not the same as the prompt.

### 24. Question Type: Assumption

The term "objective evaluation" is introduced in the conclusion, so there is a missing link between it and one of the premises. It is assumed that if aesthetic value cannot be discussed, a poem cannot be evaluated objectively.

(A) Even if they could judge a poem's aesthetic value without agreeing on the same meaning, the conclusion could be true, so this fails the negation test.

(B) This does not establish the necessary link between aesthetic value and objective evaluation. Additionally, even if two readers agreeing did not mean an objective evaluation could be reached, the conclusion could still be correct, so this fails the negation test.

(C) This would not make the argument logically sound, as it still does not suggest anything about whether or not a poem can be objectively evaluated. Therefore, this is not the assumption.

(D) Correct. This is the contrapositive of our predicted answer. It establishes the necessary link, and if it were negated, the conclusion could not be true. Therefore, it passes the negation test.

(E) This is pretty off topic, as it is about literature and not poetry. It would not make the argument sound, so it is not the assumption.

### 25. Question Type: Flaw

The argument suggests that a view is incorrect (that math professors should teach statistics courses) on the basis that one thing that supports this view (that there is some math in statistics) is insufficient to prove that view to be correct. The correct answer will likely paraphrase this.

(A) Teaching the subject well did not come up in the argument, so this is not the answer.

(B) Correct. This describes the argument correctly and points out the flaw in reasoning.

(C) The argument does not assume anything about students' knowledge of math or history, so this is not the correct answer.

(D) While the argument does fail to do this, this is not a flaw in the argument's reasoning. The argument did not rely on whether math professors could teach statistics effectively or not, so failing to mention this does not weaken the argument.

(E) This is not assumed; an analogy is drawn between math and history, but no mention of history courses is made. Instead, the argument refers to courses with historical perspectives, which are not necessarily history courses. Therefore, this is not the answer.

# PrepTest 55, Section 4, Game 1

This is a straightforward grouping game. There are 6 law students and 6 spots for them, each going exactly once. Note that the diagram could have been oriented differently (with O and F on the y-axis, for example) without affecting the usefulness of the diagram.

GLMRSV=6

```
___  ___
___  ___
___  ___
 O    F
```

Rules

#1: (MG) OR (MV)

#2: L gives an opening (insert into diagram)

#3: G_final or R_final but not both. (Inference: either G or R opens).

Discussion: Note that it doesn't matter in what order the teams are arranged; there is no linear factor in the game. (Team 1 does not "go before" Team 2). Since either G or R gives a final but not both, whichever of those 2 doesn't give a final must give an opening. This is helpful to insert as a space holder. (We can't insert a space holder in the Final column because G/R may or may not go with L.

```
  L    ___
 G/R   ___
  O     F
```

---

1. List question.
a) Violates rule 3 (G and R BOTH give a final)
b) Violates rule 2
c) Violates rule 1
d) **Correct**
e) Violates rule 3 (neither G nor R give a final)

2. M and G make up a team. Since G gives a final argument, we know from Rule 3 that R must give an opening argument. We also know that L must give an opening argument, so L will be on the third team.

```
 M    G
 L   S/V
 R   S/V
 O    F
```

a) V must give a final argument
b) S must give a final argument
c) **Correct** – this could be true.
d) S and V must be on different teams
e) S and V must be on different teams

3. Here we have a pure trial-and-error question.
a) **Correct**. Example: 1: R, G  2: M V  3: L S
b) If G and V are together Rule 1 will be violated since neither can go with M.
c) Little cannot give the final argument.
d) M must go with G or V.
e) M must go with G or V.

4. If R and V are together, M must be with G (because it must be with either G or V). Therefore, L and S are together as the only 2 left. What do we know about who gives which argument? We know only that L must give an opening, so S must give a closing. We don't know the order of the other 2 teams. **b), two, is correct.**

5. L is teamed with R. What other rules do we have that involve L or R? We know L must open, so R must give the final. We also know that G or R but not both must give a final. Since R gives the final, G cannot. Is there an answer choice that reflects this inference? Yes – **E is correct.** All the other choices could be true but they do not have to be true.

6. Here S opens. We know L always opens, and one of either G or R must open. Note that we've now filled the Open column, so M,V, and either G/R must all give the finals. (Knowing when you have filled a column can be a major advantage).
a) If G were with L, M would have to go with V, and there's not an open space since S, L, and G/R must open.
b) Similarly, this forces MV, which doesn't work here.
c) **Correct**. LV, GM, SR
d) Same as above – MV doesn't work here.
e) No space for RV.

# PrepTest 55, Section 4, Game 2

This game has a surprising amount of variability and will take some more work to set up since we don't know how many total messages will be delivered or how many will be sent by each associate. There are also key rules in the setup (before the indented rules) that you should write down).

HJL

= 1 J

___  ___  ___  — — — —
 1    2    3
L

**Rules**
(1-2 from each associate)
(Only one message each day)
#1: 1st =|= L (insert into diagram)
#2: 1st message = last message
#3: HJ exactly once
#4: Of first 3 exactly 1 J (insert into diagram)

Discussion: We have diagrammed the final 3 spaces with dashes; we don't know exactly how many spaces need to be filled. Further, since we don't know we have left the labels off to avoid confusion. There are several ways we can upgrade the diagram with inferences. First, Rule 2 gives us more surety on our numbers; if the first must also be last, at least one variable must go twice. Further, we know by Rule 1 that L can't be first, so either H or J will have to be first; therefore, either H or J will have to be last by Rule 2.

= 1 J

H/J ___ ___ ___ ___ H/J
 1   2   3   4   5   6

It's then worth thinking about our limited options with the first and last space, H and J. (Whenever you have two choices that significantly define the game, it's worth seeing how they play out.)

H    J    L    J/L   J/L   H
1    2    3

If H goes first, it must also go last. J must go second to fit in the HJ block. L must go third because H has already gone twice overall, and J can only go once within the first 3. The remaining optional spaces could each be J or L (but not H since H has already gone twice.)

J    H/L   H/L   H/L   H    J
1    2     3

If J goes first, it must also go last. H must go second to last to fit in the HJ block. The rest of the spaces would be H/L, though we don't know exactly how many.

---

7. List question.
    a) Violates Rule 1
    b) Violates Rule 3
    c) Violates Rule 2
    d) **Correct**
    e) Violates Rules 3 and 4.

8. We know we are dealing with the second option with J going first because the question is asking about situations where J's first message is before H's first message. We want to create the maximum number of spaces between J and the first H. We know J can't go 2 or 3 because it can only go once in the first 3. We can therefore put L's in 2 and 3 before we would need an H in 4 (because we've run out of L's). The answer is **two, c)**.

9. If there are exactly 4 messages, we know that two associates will go once and one will go twice. We also know that whoever goes first must also go last (Rule 2), so that's the associate who will go twice here. Is there an answer choice which expresses this deduction?
a) **Correct**. We've ruled out L going twice.

B) through E) could be true false.

10. What restrictions do we have on L? Well, we know it can't go first, and therefore can't go last. Is this deduction expressed in an answer choice? Yes!
e) **Correct.** L cannot be 6th (last).

L could be in 2,3,4, or in 5 if there is a 6th message.

11. If there are 6 messages, we know each associate goes twice. If L goes 5th, according to our limited options we know that it must be H who goes first and last. (If J goes first and last, H would have to be 5th). When H is first and last, we have already determined spaces 2 and 3. according to our limited options diagram.

$$\underset{1}{H} \quad \underset{2}{J} \quad \underset{3}{L} \quad \underset{4}{J/L} \quad \underset{5}{L} \quad \underset{6}{H}$$

Since we now have 2 Ls and 2 Hs, the fourth space must be J and we've completed our diagram.

**d) must be true.**

12. This scenario fits into either of our limited options but turns out the same answer. (Copied from limited options diagrams on previous page).

$$\underset{1}{H} \quad \underset{2}{J} \quad \underset{3}{L} \quad \underset{4}{J/L} \quad \underset{5}{J/L} \quad \underset{6}{H} \qquad \underset{1}{J} \quad \underset{2}{H/L} \quad \underset{3}{H/L} \quad \underset{4}{H/L} \quad \underset{5}{H} \quad \underset{6}{J}$$

In the first option, L must go 3; it can also go 5, for one space. In the second option, L could go 2 and also 4, again for one space.

**b) must be true.** One space is the maximum.

This is a straightforward linear sequencing game to set up. There's the additional wrinkle of who is on the night crew, but that only comes into action in a few of the questions.

FGHRST= 6

G and T night OR S and H night

___  ___  ___  ___  ___  ___
 1    2    3    4    5    6

**Rules**
#1: F < G
#2: R < S
#3: R < T
#4: S < H
#5: G < T

Discussion: Many of the rules can be combined.

F < G < T (rules 1 and 5).

R < S / T     (rules 2 and 3)

Then, combine again to create one final diagram incorporating each rule (and, fortunately, every variable). Note that if it's less confusing for you to leave the rules at the previous stage, that's totally fine).

```
                  → H
          R <  S
               T
       F< G ←
```

We can then be aggressive with our exclusion rules. We also find the important inferences that only R or F can go first and only H or T can go last.

|  R/F |     |     |     |     | H/T |
|------|-----|-----|-----|-----|-----|
|  1   |  2  |  3  |  4  |  5  |  6  |
|      | ~H  | ~T  | ~F  | ~F  |     |
|      | ~T  |     | ~R  | ~R  |     |

Note that for simplicity's sake it is not necessary to list exclusion rules under 1 and 6 because we have already noted the only variables which *could* go there.

13. List question.
   a) Violates Rule 3
   b) Violates Rule 4
   c) Violates Rule 1
   d) **Correct**
   e) Violates Rule 2

14. If F is third, R must be first because only R or F can go first. From here we can do quick process of elimination.
   a) G must go after F.
   b) **Correct**; e.g. R S F H G T
   c) R must be first
   d) If S is in 4$^{th}$, there is not room to fit G, T, and H all in the remaining 2 spots.
   e) G must go between F and T.

15. Look at our exclusion rules. What do we know can't be ranked 5$^{th}$? R or F.

**c) is correct.**

If you had not made this inference, you could solve the problem by eliminating based what we placed in 5th in past diagrams, then process of elimination.

16. This will be process of elimination.

**c) is correct.** If H is 3$^{rd}$, R must be first and S must be second (because S is before H and R is before S). We then need to fit in our sequence F < G < T, but that's easy since there are only 3 spaces left.

17. Do a quick split option diagram here. GT and SH are our options for night crews; luckily, within each of those pairings we know their order from other rules.

```
              G   T                            S   H
___ ___ ___ ___ ___ ___        ___ ___ ___ ___ ___ ___
 1   2   3   4   5   6          1   2   3   4   5   6
```

From here, you will need to do some quick process of elimination, trying each option in both diagrams.

a) In diagram 1 G obviously is not 4$^{th}$. In Diagram 2, we know that T must follow G, so it still can't be 4$^{th}$.
b) H clearly does not rank 5$^{th}$ in either option.
c) **Correct**. In diagram 1, it could go F G R S G T. It works in Diagram 2 as well: F G R T S H
d) In diagram 1 S cannot be 4$^{th}$ because there isn't room for H after it. It clearly can't go 4$^{th}$ in diagram 2.
e) T clearly cannot rank 5$^{th}$ in either option.

18. Look back at your initial inferences. Only T cannot be ranked third.

**e) is correct.**

# PrepTest 55, Section 4, Game 4

This is a challenging advanced linear game. There are 4 stops. For each, we must know where the shuttle stops and who gets off. Everyone who has not yet gotten off is still on the van.

Stops: F L M S

People: G J R V

```
     L/    L/
    ___   ___   ___   ___
     1     2     3     4
    ~J                 ~V
```

## Rules

#1: L is 1st or 2nd (insert into diagram)
#2: R on at M
#3: V < J
#4: J on at F → G on at S    ~G on at S → ~J on at F
    ~J on at F → ~ G on at S    G on at S → J on at F

Discussion: Make sure to note the contrapositives of the two conditional rules within Rule 4. There aren't key inferences to this game, so move on to the questions. It's a bit confusing to wrap your head around the idea of being "on the van when..". Essentially, people are on the van up to and including the space in which they get off.

---

19. List question.
a) Violates Rule 4
b) Violates Rule 1
c) Violates Rule 3
d) Violates Rule 2
e) **Correct**

20. If M is the first stop, L must be the second stop. We can easily exclude J, as J can never get off first; that eliminates E. Do we have any reason to exclude anyone else? No; R is on at M, we dealt with Rule 3, and the 4th rule doesn't really come into play because everyone is on at the first stop.

**d) is correct; only J can not get off first.**

21. If F is the first stop, L must be the second. Start going through the rules for deductions. We know Rule 4 is in effect here; J is definitely on at F, so G must be on at S. This is very helpful, because S could only go 3rd or 4th, so we can eliminate A and C which have G getting off too early. We can also eliminate B; Rosa must be on at M, so she can't get off first. We can eliminate E for the same reason. This leaves us with only D as the correct answer.

**d) is correct.**

22. If G is second off the van and still on board at S, then L/S must be first/second, but we do not yet know what order. We know that R is on at Mineola, so she can't get off first. J can't get off first because it must always get off after V. Therefore, only V can go first. Does this get us to an answer?
a) V gets off first but we don't know if first is Simcoe or Los Altos, so this does not have to be true.
b) Same thinking as A; we don't know if 1 is Los Altos or Simcoe.
c) **Correct**. Whether Simcoe is 1 or 2, we know that R will still be on because she must go 3rd or 4th.
d) R could go 3 or 4 and Fundy could be 3 or 4, so we don't know for sure.
e) Same as d), we have no information about the last 2 stops.

23. Make sure you have your contrapositives written out! If ~G on at S → ~J on at F (meaning Jasmine gets off before Fundy). Can we link this with other rules? We know that Vijay is always before Jasmine, so he also must get off before Fundy. Are either of these inferences the answer?

**d) Is correct.** It must be false that Vijay is on at Fundy.

# PrepTest 56
## PrepTest 56, Section 1, Game 1

This is a straightforward linear game. There are, however, several ways to save time via inference.

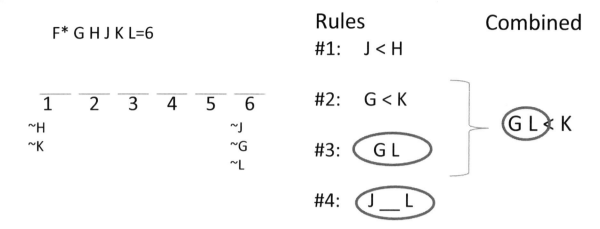

Discussion: Rules 2 and 3 can be easily combined into the "Combined" rule above right; we know we'll have to do so since G appears in both rules.

L also appears in two rules; what can be done with that? Since the block of J__L can go either way (J__L or L__J), we should try out all the options. There are only 4 ways rules 3 and 4 can fit together, and it makes sense to list them all out.

```
J __ G L
J G L
L G J
G L __ J
```

1. List question.
   a) Violates Rule 3
   b) Violates Rule 2
   c) Violates Rule 4
   d) Violates Rule 1
   e) **Correct**

2. Scan the options to see if any of our inferences come into play. They do.

   **b) Correct.** We know from combining Rules 2 and 3 that L must be before K. The other options could be true.

3. Looking back at our rules, we know that K must go after G and L. There aren't any other constraints on K. If you like, you could put this into the diagram to make sure 3rd works, e.g. G L K J F H. Once you see that K works in 3, you have your answer.

   **c) Correct.**

4. You'll have to do some quick process of elimination here, so draw a diagram quickly.

a) There are any number of configurations with H in 4.
b) We can see from our limited options that if J goes in 1, there are multiple options.
c) **Correct.** If J goes 5th, H must go in 6th (Rule 1). We know L must go in third because it has to have one intermediate space, and L can't go later than J here. Since K has to go after G/L, K must go in 4th. We then know G must go in second, because it must be next to L. That leaves F to go in first place. There is only one configuration if J goes 5th.
d) If L goes first we know from our limited options that G and J must follow, but then H, K, and F can go in any order.
e) If L goes second there are many options, such as G in 1 or F in 1.

5. There's quite a bit of process of elimination here as well, as the restriction on F going first doesn't lead to any clear inferences. Work each of these out quickly.

a) **Correct.** E.g. J F G L K H
b) If G goes 5th, we know that K would have to go 6th and L would have to go 4th. Then, J would have to go 2nd to create one space before L.
   ___  J  ___  L  G  K
   Then we run into a problem. H has to follow J, so it must go third, leaving F in first – which is exactly what this question asked us to avoid.

c) If H is third, we know J must come before it. That means that our block of G/L must go 4/5, and K would have to go after in 6th. However when we try to fit in J __ L we have a problem. L can't go 5th because that would force J into 3rd, and H is there already. So L would go 4th and J 2nd, but again that places F in 1st, which we were trying to avoid.
   ___  ___  H  L/G  G/L  K

d) If J goes second, every variable except F would have to go after it, which is not tenable since F cannot go first for this question.
e) If J is 5th, H is 6 and L is 3rd. K must go after L so it goes 4th. G therefore has to go 2nd to be next to L, again putting F in first.

6. Again, this is mostly quick process of elimination. Re-draw your diagram and put each option in. Remember that the right answer must be true and the 4 wrong answers could be false (but also could be true). Therefore, you want to try to falsify each of these choices.

a) Could be false; F J H L G K
b) We test by placing H in 2nd. J goes 1st, then we can easily complete: J H G L F K
c) Review your diagram for 5; H can go in 6.
d) Our quick diagram for choice A here demonstrates that K can go last.
e) **Correct.** If L went 5th, K would be 6 and G would be 4th. Rule 4 demands that J go second, but we can't do that because J has to be before H and there are no spaces left after J.

# PrepTest 56, Section 1, Game 2

This is a basic grouping game, but it involves some conditionals that can be tricky to diagram.

G H J M = 4

**Rules**
(Each person moves at least one piece)

R __ __
S __ __
T __ __

#1: Gs ←→ Hr    ~Gs ←→ ~Hr

#2: Jt → Mr    ~Mr → ~Jt

#3: ~(G J) [circled, crossed out]

Discussion: The first rule seems tricky. Not only does it use the "only if" formulation, but also uses "if *but* only if," as opposed to the much more common "if *and* only if." Just treat them the same here. Remember that the "only if" operator essentially reverses the direction of the relationship. If we say "if Gs then Hr" we get Gs → Hr. If instead we say "*Only if* Gs, Hr" we get Hr → Gs. Since here we have "if but only if," the relationship is bi-directional. If these relationships are new to you, you must find a good long-form explanation of LSAT conditional logic.

Other than that tricky conditional there aren't important inferences to be made.

---

7. List question.
a) **Correct**
b) Violates Rule 3
c) Violates Rule 2
d) Violates Rule 1
e) Violates Rule 1

8. This is straightforward as long as you listed out your contrapositives. Since the recliner is moved by J and M, it cannot be moved by H. We know that if ~Hr then ~Gs according to the first rule. If G doesn't move the sofa and clearly can't move the recliner, G must move the table. Scan your answer choices.

d) **Correct**. Grace must move the table. All other answers could be false.

9. If H moves each piece, H certainly moves the recliner. If Hr → Gs. We still need to have J and M move a piece, but don't know exactly where they go:

R H J/M
S H G
T H J/M

b) **Correct**. Maria could move the recliner. All the other choices must be false.

10. Quick process of elimination is effective here. We know that if 2 people move both the recliner and the table together, the remaining 2 people will have to move the sofa since each person must move at least one item.
   a) G and J can never go together.
   b) **Correct.** H and J would then move the sofa, which works.
   c) If J moves the table, we know from rule 3 that M would have to move the recliner, which is not the case here.
   d) This would force G and J together to move the sofa, violating rule 3.
   e) This forces G and H into the sofa. Rule 1 tells us that if G moves the sofa, H must move the recliner, which is not the case.

11. If J and M move the sofa, we know that G does not move the sofa. Rule 1 tells us that if ~Gs → ~Hr. If H doesn't move the recliner and doesn't move the sofa, it must move the table. Address the answer choices with this inference.
   a) We know ~Hr
   b) Again, ~Hr
   c) H must move the table, so this won't work
   d) Same as c)
   e) **Correct.** H must move the table. If M also moves the table, T and G could move the recliner.

# PrepTest 56, Section 1, Game 3

This is a grouping game with some key inferences that will make it straightforward (if you find them).

M O S T = 4

G  M ___ ___ ___
L ___ ___ ___ ___

### Rules
#1: Each park = 3 (use to create your diagram)

#2: [MS (at least once)]

#3: O → T        ~T → ~O

#4: M in G (insert into diagram)

Discussion: Think about what your options are here for getting the block of MS into the diagram. Below are the three options.

| MS in G | MS in L | MS in G and L |

G  M  S ___        G  M ___ ___        G  M  S ___
L ___ ___ ___      L  M  S ___         L  M  S ___

Now, think about how the rest of the diagram can be filled in each case. We have O and T left, and they have a very specific relationship: if O goes in, T goes in as well. That leads us to a huge inference; whatever park has both M and G must have T; the reason is that those parks need a third tree, and if we insert O, we also have to insert T, giving that park 4 trees. Therefore the options are:

| MS in G | MS in L | MS in G and L |

G  M  S  T         G  M ___ ___        G  M  S  T
L ___ ___ ___      L  M  S  T          L  M  S  T

Finally, consider what happens when we try to fill the blanks in the first two options. The contrapositive of Rule 3 is that if ~T → ~O, a key inference. Think about a blank park, like Landing in the first option. If T isn't in there, O can't be there; further, we only have M and G left, so we're left with only 2 trees! *We deduce that every park must have T!*

| MS in G | MS in L | MS in G and L |

G  M  S  T         G  M  *T* ___       G  M  S  T
L  *T* ___ ___     L  M  S  T          L  M  S  T

12. List question.
a) Violates Rule 3
b) Violates Rule 2
c) Violates Rule 3
d) **Correct**
e) Violates Rule 4

13. We've figured out enough of the game that the questions should be easy.

c) Correct. Landing must be planted with T. Everything else could be false.

14. We have a couple options for planting both parks with S, so w can move to quick trial and error.
a) **Correct.**

$$\boxed{\text{MS in G}}$$

G  $\underline{\text{M}}$  $\underline{\text{S}}$  $\underline{\text{T}}$
L  $\underline{\textit{S}}$  $\underline{\textit{O}}$  $\underline{\textit{T}}$

b) By definition this can't be true – both parks have S according to the question, and there are only .
c) Examining our limited options, there is no way both parks can be planted with oaks.
d) Again looking at our options, G is always planted with M, as per the question will be planted with S, must always be planted with T.
e) Landing must always have T, so if it also has M and O it can't be planted with S as per the question.

15. Make use of your inferences here.
a) **Correct.** Whichever park is planted with M and S must also be planted with T and thus can't also have O. At least one park must be without O.

b) Through e) could be true.

16.
a) As we've seen previously, any park with O also has T, so there wouldn't be room for the M S block.
b) Both parks cannot have O and at least one park must have S by rule.
c) We know that both parks must have T.
d) Again, both parks must have T.
e) **Correct.** We see from the third possibility that both parks could have M S T.

# PrepTest 56, Section 1, Game 4

This is a hybrid game; there is a linear aspect as well as grouping. The difficulty is enhanced by the uncertainty we have around how many executives visit each site.

execs: Q R S T V

visits: F H M

```
        ......  ......  ......
        ......  ......  ......
        ~R              ~Q
        ~T
        ____  ____  ____
         1     2     3
        ~H          ~F
```

## Rules

(Each site visited by at least 1 exec)
(Each exec visits at least 1 site)

#1: F < H
#2: F = 1 exec
#3:
$$Q < \begin{matrix} R \\ \cdots \\ T \end{matrix}$$

#4: S can't be after V

Discussion: There is little in the rules to provide certainty about this game, and there are no major inferences. Make sure you understand Rule 4; S can't be *after* V, but it could be at the same visit as V. Therefore we can't establish any exclusion rules in our diagram as S and V could both go first, and they could both go last.

We do know that since Farmington only has one executive visit, H and M must have either 1 and 3 visits *or* 2 and 2 visits to get all the executives in.

Incidentally, this game also has one of the most frustrating LSAT challenges — a lack of room to do a proper diagram. This sort of challenge can and will appear on test day as well, so make sure you get used to doing diagrams in the very limited space LSAC provides for this game.

---

17. List question.
    a) **Correct**
    b) Violates Rule 4
    c) Violates Rule 3
    d) Violates Rule 1
    e) Violates Rule 2

18. If visit 2 includes both T and R, we can get 2 inferences. First, Q must go in the first visit because Q is always before R and T. Second, the second visit cannot be Farmington because Farmington only has one executive. Since Farmington can't be last, it must be first.
    a) **Correct.**

b) through E could each be false.

19. We know that both R and T will go after the Q/S visit. We aren't sure about V; we know that S is not after V. We'll need to do some elimination.

a) F can only have one executive, so if it's first it can't have Q and S. Since V must be tied or after S and R/T have to be after, this won't work; there's no way to put just one executive first here.
b) If H is second, it forces F to be first. For the same reason as a), that won't work.
c) **Correct.**

```
 Q    R/T
 S     V    R/T
 M     F     H
```

d) Similar to a) and b), this won't work. If S is second, we know that R and T must go third. V could go second or third, but either way it would leave the first visit empty.
e) If the second site includes two visits, we know a number of things. First, Farmington must be the first visit. Second, we know that R/T will have to be third (because Q and S can't to go together in Farmington; Farmington can only have one visitor). Therefore we're left without a place for V; it can't go first because it can't go before S.

20.
a) Could be true: S visits F, Q V visit H, R T visit M
b) Could be true; S visits F, Q V visit M, RT visit H
c) Could be true: Q visits F, R S visit H, R V visit M
d) **Correct.** Can't be true; if Q S and V go together, both R and T must go after. That would work if we didn't have the additional constraint that Q S and V are in Homestead; since Homestead can go 2nd at the earliest, this would force R and T to go after and leave no on to go in first (which would be Farmington).
e) Could be true: Q visits F, R S T visit H, V visits M.

21. We are given that Q and V are in Morningside. R and T must go after this block.
a) R must go after the block that includes Q. However, S cannot go after that block because it can't go after V.
b) If 3 executives fit in the second visit, it would have to be Q V and S (since R and T go after). However this wouldn't work because we'd leave no one for the first visit (which incidentally would have to be Farmington).
c) If the last visit has 3 it would have to be R T and S since we already have a block of Q and V. This doesn't work because it puts S after V.
d) This would necessitate an order of Farmington, Homestead, Morningside since F is always before H. This won't work because it puts the QV block last, and we know that R and T must follow Q.
e) **Correct,** could be true. This requires the order of visits to be M < F < H:

```
 S
 Q
 S    R/T   R/T
 M     F     H
```

22. We are given that Q and V are in Morningside. R and T must go after this block.
a) See past diagrams where M can go before F. (#21)
b) V and R could easily be tied as long as they stay after S and Q, e.g. Q, ST, VR
c) S can go last as long as V does as well, e.g. Q, RT, SV
d) See past diagrams
e) **Correct.** We know that Farmington cannot be last because of Rule 1, and we know that Farmington has only one visitor according to Rule 2.

23. If S is the lone visitor to F by rule, we know that the sequence of Q< RT will have to be split up. While Q can then go either in 1st or 2nd depending on where S is placed, TR will definitely have to go last.

**b) Correct.** All other answers could be false.

# PrepTest 56, Section 2 (LR)

**1. Question Type: Flaw**
The argument assumes that because more shark attacks occur during the day, it is more dangerous during the day. However, because people are much more likely to swim during the day, the number of attacks during the day is increased and at night decreased.
(A) Even if some sharks were nocturnal hunters, it could still be more dangerous to swim during the day, so this is not a vulnerability of the argument.
(B) No source is given, so we have no reason to believe it is unreliable.
(C) Though the argument does not specifically mention this, this is not a flaw. Excluding this possibility does not mean the conclusion is not properly drawn.
(D) The argument does not presume this, so this is not the correct answer.
(E) Correct. This paraphrases our predicted answer and points out the flawed logic of the argument.

**2. Question Type: Most Supported/Must be True**
(A) Correct. According to their statements, each would agree with this, so this is the answer.
(B) Neither has suggested this, so this cannot be the correct answer.
(C) Reshmi would not agree with this statement, so this cannot be the correct answer.
(D) Neither suggests this, so this cannot be the correct answer.
(E) Reshmi would not agree with this, so this is not the correct answer.

**3. Question Type: Weaken**
The argument assumes that someone working at an entry-level position is unskilled. The correct answer will likely point this out.
(A) This does not weaken the reasoning, as it merely suggests that more high-level employees began as entry-level workers.
(B) Correct. This points out the possibility that entry-level workers can be skilled, meaning the argument is not sound. Therefore, this weakens the argument.
(C) This has no effect on the argument, as it has no bearing on whether or not unskilled workers have advancement opportunities.
(D) This does not suggest that she was or was not unskilled when she began working, so this does not affect the argument.
(E) This does not mean that the entry-level workers are or are not unskilled, so it has no effect on the argument.

**4. Question Type: Assumption**
The conclusion is that yellow warblers have no competition for their food supply when molting. This is incorrectly drawn because the argument fails to consider competitors that are not yellow warblers. The argument assumes that yellow warblers only compete with each other for food.
(A) Whether there is enough food or not does not affect whether there is competition or not.
(B) Even if this were false, the conclusion could still be true, so this answer fails the negation test.
(C) Correct. This paraphrases our predicted answer. If there were other birds that competed, the conclusion would not follow, so this passes the negation test and must be assumed.
(D) Even if warblers did not share their territory, the conclusion could still be true, so this fails the negation test.
(E) Even if the areas were different, the conclusion could still be true, so this fails the negation test.

**5. Question Type: Flaw**
Lana suggests that Chinh's comparison between producer and painter is not a good analogy and offers one that she thinks is better.
(A) Lana does not suggest Chinh's argument was circular, so this is not the answer.
(B) Lana does not suggest there is any sampling bias, so this is not the answer.
(C) Lana makes no mention of the effects of an action, so this is not the answer.
(D) The argument did consider this but suggests it is not the case; Lana does not suggest the argument didn't consider this.
(E) Correct. This is exactly what Lana suggested, and it is a paraphrase of our predicted answer.

## PrepTest 56, Section 2 (LR) Continued...

#### 6. Question Type: Assumption
The conclusion is that people should eat fresh fruits and vegetables rather than frozen ones. This only follows from the premises if canned and frozen fruits and vegetables have less potassium than fresh ones. Therefore, the argument assumes this is true.
- (A) Even if they did not have more potassium than sodium, the conclusion could still be true, so this fails the negation test.
- (B) Even if food processors did not add sodium, the conclusion could still be true, so this fails the negation test.
- (C) Even if there are other minerals, the conclusion could still be true, so this fails the negation test.
- (D) Even if it did have negative side effects, the conclusion could still be true, so this fails the negation test.
- **(E)** Correct. This paraphrases our predicted answer. If they did not contain more potassium, the conclusion could not follow, so this passes the negation test.

#### 7. Question Type: Parallel Reasoning
Someone (Dana) did something on purpose (watered the plant every other day), and that caused an effect (the plant died because of it). The argument concludes that the person must have caused the effect on purpose.
- (A) While the reasoning here is flawed as well, it is not similar to the reasoning in the prompt. In this case, someone (Jack) did something (took money), then did something else (gambled the money). The argument concludes that the person took the won amount, not the gambled amount. This is very different from the reasoning in the prompt.
- (B) Someone (Celeste) knows one thing, and she knows another thing, so she should know a final thing. This is very different from the reasoning in the prompt.
- **(C)** Correct. Someone (a restaurant owner) did something on purpose (took an item off the menu), and that caused an effect (it disappointed Jerry). The argument concludes that the person must have cause the effect on purpose. This is exactly like the prompt, so it is the correct answer.
- (D) and (E) There is no intentionality mentioned in either answer, so neither is similar to the prompt.

#### 8. Question Type: Weaken
The argument assumes that the glacier could have brought a volcanic rock southward with it. The correct answer will likely suggest this was not the case.
- (A) It is possible that 100 miles would be enough to bring a volcanic rock to the site, so this does not weaken the conclusion.
- (B) There could be a different source to the North; even if it is further away, that does not mean the glacier could not carry it.
- (C) This does not undermine the conclusion in any way, as it suggests that the conclusion is entirely possible.
- **(D)** Correct. This suggest the assumption mention in our predicted answer is incorrect, so this is the correct answer. If there is no source of volcanic rock to the north, then southward-moving glaciers could not have deposited the volcanic rock at the site.
- (E) This does not affect whether this rock was carried to the site by a glacier or not, so it is not the correct answer.

#### 9. Question Type: Method of Reasoning
R says there is no need to stop because that would only be necessary if they were lost. She therefore assumes that they are not lost. C says they do need to stop because they are lost. Therefore, he denies an assumption of R's to come to the opposite conclusion.
- (A) This is incorrect because he does give a reason.
- **(B)** Correct. R's assumption is an implicit premise (one this is not stated explicitly but that is implied by her reasoning). C says this assumption is incorrect and thus arrives at a different conclusion.
- (C) C does not accept the truth of her premises, as he believes they are lost, which she does not.
- (D) C does not have a counterexample, so this is incorrect.
- (E) C says the conclusion is wrong, so this cannot be the answer.

#### 10. Question Type: Assumption
The conclusion is the last sentence. For this to follow from the premises, it must be assumed that characters do not change over time in romance and satirical literature.

## PrepTest 56, Section 2 (LR) Continued...

(A) Even if all are debased or idealized, it is still possible that tragedy and comedy cannot be classified as satirical or romance. Therefore, this fails the negation test.
(B) If this were the case, the characters would also change, and the conclusion could not follow. Therefore, this cannot be the assumption.
(C) Even if this were not the case, the conclusion could still be true, so this fails the negation test.
(D) **Correct.** This paraphrases our predicted answer. If they did change during the course of the action, the conclusion would not follow, so this passes the negation test.
(E) What happens with minor characters has no bearing on the argument, which only talks about major characters. Therefore, this is not the assumption made in the argument.

### 11. Question Type: Method of Reasoning
Frank suggests that Lance's argument leads to a contradiction, which would mean that it is not correct.
(A) Frank does not suggest this, so this is not the answer.
(B) **Correct.** This paraphrases our predicted answer and describes how Frank counters Lance's argument.
(C) Frank does not show this; he shows that suggesting that every general rule has an exception leads to a contradiction and thus cannot be true. This does not mean that no general rule has an exception.
(D) Frank does not suggest anything about what experience teaches us, so this is not the right answer.
(E) Frank does not show this; his argument has nothing to do with real cases.

### 12. Question Type: Flaw
The conclusion is the final sentence. This does not follow from the premises, as it is possible that many rural areas did gain access to electricity (just because many did not receive electricity does not mean that none did or even that most did not). The correct answer will most likely point this out.
(A) This is not suggested by the argument; the argument merely suggests that the subsidy has not achieved its goal. It has not suggested anything about whether the goal could have been reached without the subsidy.
(B) This is not the reasoning used in the argument. The argument suggests that the subsidy helped those unintended and did not help many of those intended. These two facts together are used to suggest the conclusion.
(C) This is not presumed, as the argument seems to suggest the subsidy's intended purpose did not include other people.
(D) This is not overlooked, as it suggests that the subsidy did help many urban dwellers get electricity.
(E) **Correct.** This paraphrases our predicted answer. It points out that the intended purpose may have been reached despite the facts given. Therefore, this describes a flaw in the argument's reasoning.

### 13. Question Type: Resolve the Paradox
The paradox is that even retirees who no longer have to work are more likely to have heart attacks on Mondays. The correct answer will explain why they would be more likely to have heart attacks on Monday.
(A) **Correct.** This would explain the phenomenon, so it is the correct answer.
(B) This does not explain the phenomenon, as the argument only refers to unemployed retired people, who still have a greater chance of heart attack on Monday.
(C), (D) and (E) These do not explain the greater likelihood on Mondays, so none of these is the correct answer.

### 14. Question Type: Strengthen
The conclusion is the last sentence.
(A) This does not strengthen the conclusion, so it is not the correct answer.
(B) Whether or not some had calculated the odds does not affect whether they were overconfident or not, so this does not strengthen the conclusion.
(C) This does not affect whether or not overconfidence led to starting businesses.
(D) **Correct.** This would mean that the overconfidence among business managers also followed the pattern in the conclusion, thus strengthening it.
(E) This does not strengthen the conclusion, as it merely suggests what those who were overconfident were overconfident about, which does not affect the conclusion.

## PrepTest 56, Section 2 (LR) Continued...

**15. Question Type: Flaw**
The information about Immanuel's proposal is all distracting. The flaw in reasoning here is that the director's support is necessary for approval, but that does not mean it is sufficient for approval. The argument assumes it is sufficient for approval. The correct answer will likely point this out.
(A) The fact that the argument presumes this does not weaken it; there is no problem with this assumption, and it does not affect whether or not the conclusion is properly drawn.
**(B)** Correct. This paraphrases out predicted answer. While it is necessary for the director to support a proposal, it is possible for the proposal to be rejected despite this support.
(C) This is not presumed, so this cannot be the correct answer.
(D) Whether Immanuel wants to move to a bigger lab or not does not affect whether the conclusion is properly drawn, so this is not a flaw in reasoning.
(E) This does not accurately describe the flaw. Whether or not this fact was justified, the conclusion would not follow from the premises. Therefore, the flaw must be something else.

**16. Question Type: Principle**
The correct answer must fit the prompt exactly; if one piece does not agree, the answer will be incorrect.
(A) This does not fit the prompt, which states that the incentives are an unethical business practice, not the act of exploiting personal relationships.
(B) This makes no mention of the second half of the last sentence, where the bulk of the reasoning is. This cannot be the answer for this reason.
(C) This does not fit the prompt, which states that it is unethical due to the risk of harming relationships, not the actual harming of relationships.
**(D)** Correct. If it is unethical to encourage people to damage their relationships, and if as the prompt states asking customers to give their friend's emails would "risk the integrity" of relationships, it's unethical for the sports company to use this strategy.
(E) This makes no mention of something being unethical, so it cannot be the correct answer.

**17. Question Type: Point at Issue**
(A) This is too general and is not supported. Neither of the passages suggests that the speaker believes or does not believe this.
(B) G most likely believes this, but S does not suggest that she agrees or disagrees.
(C) S believes this, but G does not suggest that he agrees or disagrees.
(D) G believes this, but S does not suggest that he agrees or disagrees.
**(E)** Correct. G says this is true, and S disagrees, so they disagree about this.

**18. Question Type: Principle**
The principle in this case is that something should almost never be done if it will be more costly in the long run, even if it will help in the short run.
(A) The principle in this argument has nothing to do with long run consequences, so this is not the correct answer.
(B) The principle in this argument does not discuss long-term consequences, so this is not the correct answer.
**(C)** Correct. The principle in this argument suggests that an action should not be taken if it will be more costly in the long run, despite the fact that it will help in the short run. This is just like the principle in the prompt.
(D) This principle suggests the opposite of the principle in the prompt, so this is not the correct answer.
(E) This principle does not suggest anything about long-term costs versus short-term benefits, so it is not the correct answer.

**19. Question Type: Most Supported/Must be True**
**(A)** Correct. If none who take physics take lit, but some who take physics take art, then some who take art must not take lit (those who take physics).
(B) This is not supported; those who are in art and physics will not take lit, but it is perfectly possible that there are kids taking art who are not taking physics and thus are able to take lit.
(C) There is no reason to believe this is true; students taking lit aren't taking physics, and students taking rhetoric are not taking physics. This leaves the possibility open that no students are taking rhetoric but not lit.

## PrepTest 56, Section 2 (LR) Continued...

(D) There is no reason to believe this is true; students taking lit aren't taking physics, and students taking rhetoric are not taking physics. This leaves the possibility open that some students are taking both rhetoric and lit.

(E) This is not supported; nothing suggests that a student taking art or lit will or will not take the other. This means that it is perfectly possible that no students will take both.

### 20. Question Type: Assumption

There is a missing link between the fact that psychotherapy will probably not be high-quality and that it should not be done. The correct answer will likely establish this link.

(A) Even if it were sometimes appropriate, it could still be the case that they should not provide services on talk shows, so this fails the negation test.

(B) Even if context did not have a greater impact, it could still be the case that psychotherapy was not high-quality due to being entertaining and for this reason should not have been done. Thus, this fails the negation test.

(C) This answer is too general, though it does establish a link similar to the one we were looking for in our predicted answer. This argument is specific to talk shows, though, so this is not the assumption made.

(D) What viewers want has no effect on the argument, so this is not the assumption that would make the conclusion properly drawn.

(E) Correct. This draws the connection we were looking for, and it also fits the prompt exactly. If sometimes psychotherapists should attempt to provide help in a way that was unlikely to be of high quality, the conclusion would not be properly drawn. This therefore passes the negation test.

### 21. Question Type: Point at Issue

The correct answer will be a statement that one of the speakers clearly disagrees with while the other clearly agrees with.

(A) While M certainly believes this, there is no reason to believe that T does not also believe this.

(B) Correct. T believes this, while M disagrees with this.

(C) Both would disagree with this statement.

(D) Both seem to agree with this.

(E) Neither suggests that this is true.

### 22. Question Type: Resolve the Paradox

The paradox is that judges generally try to avoid writing decisions of high literary quality because such writing is easily misinterpreted, but dissenting judges often include pieces of high literary quality in their opinions.

(A) and (B) These do not explain why there is writing of high literary quality in dissenting opinions, so they do not resolve the paradox.

(C) Correct. This means that judges do not have to worry about being misinterpreted in their dissenting opinions, so they can include writing that could be misinterpreted. This explains why such writing is in dissenting opinions but not decisions, so this resolves the paradox.

(D) and (E) These do not explain why there is writing of high literary quality in dissenting opinions, so they do not resolve the paradox.

### 23. Question Type: Most Supported/Must be True

The first two sentences can be diagrammed as follows:

~intervention → extinction    ~extinction → intervention
preserved → ~extinction       extinction → ~preserved

The contrapositives of these statements allow for several inferences. The correct answer is likely to be one of these.

(A) This is not supported by the argument, as there could be other areas, plentiful in fruit and insects, that would also help squirrel monkeys survive if preserved.

(B) The argument states that without intervention, they will go extinct. This does mean that if there is intervention, they will survive (this would be a mistaken negation). Therefore, this is not implied.

(C) This is not implied by the argument, as it is possible that there are other areas that could be preserved that have different fruits and insects but where they would nonetheless survive.

(D) This was mentioned in B; it is a mistaken negation and is not implied by the prompt.

## PrepTest 56, Section 2 (LR) Continued...

**(E) Correct.** (E)'s argument can be written as:
~intervention → ~preserved          preserved → intervention

Then note the first premise and the contrapositive of the second: if ~intervention we know extinction, and if extinction we know ~preserved.

### 24. Question Type: Strengthen

The assumption in this argument is very well-hidden. However, the argument assumes that letters were opened in the same period. If they were not, we have no reason to believe that the seals were recast, as we only know that they were likely to be recast during that period. The correct answer will likely suggest that this assumption is true.

**(A) Correct.** This suggests that the assumption mentioned in the predicted answer is correct, so it strengthens the argument.
(B) The documents don't have to have been destroyed, as they could be somewhere but not discovered yet.
(C) Whether this is true or not has no bearing on whether the conclusion is true or not, so this does not strengthen the answer.
(D) and (E) While these do not suggest the conclusion is incorrect, they fail to strengthen the conclusion.

### 25. Question Type: Method of Reasoning

This statement is used to support the conclusion, and it is a claim about what will happen if a particular action is taken. The conclusion is the first sentence.
(A) The statement is not a conclusion, so this is not the answer.
**(B) Correct.** It is an effect of another action, so a causal explanation is provided. Meanwhile, it supports the conclusion, and there is only one. Therefore, this is the correct answer.
(C) It is not a conclusion, so this is not the answer.
(D) There is no intermediary conclusion, so this is not the answer.
(E) The main conclusion does not offer a causal explanation, so this is not the correct answer.

# PrepTest 56, Section 3 (LR)

**1. Question Type: Flaw**
W's argument suggests that A is incorrect because her source was not reliable. This is a sort of indirect ad hominem argument, and as such is flawed. The fact that Pliny had some incorrect views does not invalidate his other views.
(A) W does not distort A's conclusion, so this is not the answer.
(B) W does not suggest P was in bad faith but that P could not be trusted because of this opinion.
**(C)** Correct. This correctly identifies the issue with W's argument that we predicted.
(D) W does not accept the views of an ancient scholar, so this is incorrect.
(E) W does not suggest that P's views are outdated but rather that they must all be wrong because some were wrong.

**2. Question Type: Most Supported/Must be True**
(A) The argument implies that it would be a mistake to remove funds from existing operations, not that they will need more funds.
(B) The argument only suggests that pharmaceuticals would be less risky, not that it would require no funds from other operations.
(C) The argument only suggests that it is risky to enter the food industry, not that they will certainly lose money if they do so.
(D) Pharmaceuticals are less risky than the food industry, but that does not mean they are the only way to increase profits.
**(E)** Correct. The fact that the food industry is more risky implies this, so this is supported by the prompt.

**3. Question Type: Principle**
The reason the argument suggests Adam should not judge the contest is that he has no experience, so the principle must justify this reasoning.
(A) This does not justify the argument, as it does not suggest A should not judge the contest.
**(B)** Correct. This justifies the argument, as it suggests A should not be a judge because he does not have experience.
(C) This does not justify the argument, as it suggests that A could judge the contest.
(D) This does not justify the argument, as it does not suggest A should not judge the contest.
(E) This is not the reasoning used, so this is not the correct answer.

**4. Question Type: Flaw**
The argument assumes that if neither part of a product causes something, that product cannot cause it. The correct answer will likely point this out.
**(A)** Correct. This paraphrases our predicted answer; it is possible that the whole could help where neither part does.
(B) The argument does not suggest that one thing causes another, so this is not the answer.
(C) There is no reason to believe there would be any bias in the sample, as the study was about smokers, and smokers were the test subjects.
(D) Even though this is possible, it does not affect the reasoning used in the argument, which only makes a statement about the product's ability to reduce cravings.
(E) The argument does not suggest that there was a bias, so this is not the correct answer.

**5. Question Type: Conclusion**
The main conclusion is that the researchers' advice is premature. It is supported by each of the other statements, and it does not support any other statement.
(A) This is not the main conclusion, as it is a premise used with the final sentence to support the conclusion.
(B) This is merely a premise, used to support the conclusion.
(C) This is not the conclusion; it is a claim that is countered to come to the conclusion.
**(D)** Correct. This correctly restates the conclusion. It restates the researchers advice, but this does not mean that it is not the correct answer.
(E) This is not suggested by the argument, which suggests that weeds can reduce caterpillar presence, though they may have unintended negative consequences on the garden.

# PrepTest 56, Section 3 (LR) Continued...

**6. Question Type: Method of Reasoning**
The argument discusses two phenomena (response to website and response to print ads), one of which it has direct information about (website), and one that it does not have direct information about (print). It uses the information it has to come to a conclusion about the phenomenon for which it had no information.
(A) The argument does not discuss the cause of consumer response, so this is incorrect.
(B) The argument does not discuss the frequency of any event, so this is incorrect.
(C) No statistical inference is drawn, so this is incorrect.
**(D) Correct.** This paraphrases the predicted answer. It includes the lack of direct information about one case and the use of direct information from a different case to make a conclusion about the case without information.
(E) The argument does not predict future events.

**7. Question Type: Resolve the Paradox**
Authorities removed coyotes from an island because part of their diet, the plover, were dying out. This ended up quickening the extinction of the plover on the island.
(A) This would not explain why getting rid of coyotes would hasten their demise.
(B) We don't know anything about the wild cat population, so this cannot be the answer.
(C) and (D) do not explain why the plover population plummeted after the coyotes were removed, so they cannot be correct.
**(E) Correct.** This explains the plummet in plover population. If there are fewer coyotes, then there are fewer predators of wild cats. This means the wild cat population will increase. This in turn means the wild cats, as a group, will eat more plover, driving the plover population down.

**8. Question Type: Strengthen**
The argument assumes that companies are more likely to take the action that will lower morale less, in this case firing an employee. The correct answer will likely suggest that this assumption is correct.
**(A) Correct.** This paraphrases the assumption in our predicted answer. This statement makes the conclusion properly drawn from the premises, which it was not before. Thus, this strengthens the argument.
(B) This does not affect the argument, which is about choosing between a pay decrease and firing someone.
(C) Whether or not companies are able to make a profit during recession does not affect the argument, so this is not the correct answer.
(D) and (E) These do not strengthen the argument, as neither clearly suggests whether companies would be more likely to cut employees or wages.

**9. Question Type: Assumption**
The conclusion is that the success of chains has hurt book consumers. This only follows if it is assumed that having less variety hurts consumers.
**(A) Correct.** This is just the inversion of our predicted answer; if less variety hurts consumers or more variety is good for consumers, the conclusion is properly drawn. Therefore, this is an assumption of the argument.
(B) If independent bookstores did sell the kinds of books that were typically available in chain bookstores, it could still be the case that the success of chains has hurt consumers, so this fails the negation test.
(C) and (D) Size does not necessarily mean anything about variety, so these would neither help nor harm the argument if assumed. Therefore, these are not the assumption.
(E) This might hurt the conclusion, and it definitely does not help the conclusion, so it is not the correct answer.

**10. Question Type: Flaw**
The conclusion is that the critics are mistaken. This is based on the sales of memorabilia. However, just because it has better sales than other series does not mean it is popular; those series could be unpopular. If something is more popular than something that's not popular, the first thing might still not be objectively popular.
(A) No emotional considerations are mentioned, so this is not the answer.
(B) The argument only implies that memorabilia sales is the most important, not the sole consideration.
**(C) Correct.** This is the flaw mentioned in our predicted answer.
(D) The argument states that they are similar, so we have no reason to believe that they are dissimilar.
(E) While the argument does this, it does not affect the argument, which is about the concert series as a whole

## PrepTest 56, Section 3 (LR) Continued...

and not individual concerts within the series.

### 11. Question Type: Most Supported/Must be True
(A) No information is given about the portion of people who wear sunscreen, so this is not supported.
(B) This is not supported, as until 10 years ago, sunscreen did not protect against wrinkling rays. That means people who have premature wrinkles could have worn sunscreen every time they went outside, as long as they spent time in the sun before 10 years ago.
(C) There is no support for this answer, as we are given no indication of why sunscreen did not protect against UVA rays.
(D) This is not supported, as there is no difference in terms of protection from sunburn between before and after 10 years ago.
(E) Correct. This is supported, as until 10 years ago, sunscreen did not protect against premature wrinkling. This means people wearing sunscreen would be damaged just as much by those rays as were people who did not wear sunscreen.

### 12. Question Type: Principle
The correct answer will need to fit each portion of the prompt. It should be noted that the conclusion says "sports activity," not "competitive sports." This means the principle will need to support this generalization from competitive sports to all sports activity.
(A) Correct. This correctly states that stressed people should not participate in sports, and it justifies the reasoning used to go from competitive sports to sports activity.
(B) This does not justify the argument, as competitive sports have been the basis of a study, but they should not be participated in while stressed.
(C) This principle does not justify the argument, as the argument referred to people who were stressed and says nothing about those who are not stressed.
(D) This principle states the opposite of the reasoning in the argument, so it must be incorrect.
(E) The argument makes no mention of whether people have had sports injuries in the past, so this is too specific to justify the argument.

### 13. Question Type: Strengthen
The conclusion here is that tent caterpillars are communal foragers. This is only true if the tracks left behind while foraging are used by other caterpillars to find food. The correct answer will likely suggest that this is true.
(A) Correct. This suggests that the assumption mentioned in the predicted answer is correct. It therefore supports the conclusion.
(B) This does not support the conclusion, as it would only communicate where other caterpillars have gone, not whether there was food there or not.
(C) and (D) These do not affect the reasoning or the conclusion, so they do not support the argument.
(E) This has no bearing on whether or not tent caterpillars communicate where food is, so this is not the correct answer.

### 14. Question Type: Parallel Reasoning
Because the reasoning is flawed, an argument that is not flawed cannot be the correct answer. The argument assumes that because one thing (well-known actors) is generally sufficient for a particular outcome (doing well at the box office), that thing is generally necessary for the outcome.
(A) This reasoning has no flaw, so it cannot be the correct answer.
(B) Correct. The argument assumes that because one thing (bee palm) is generally sufficient for a particular outcome (abundant crops), that thing is generally necessary for the outcome. This is just like the original argument.
(C) This reasoning is not flawed, so it cannot be the correct answer.
(D) The argument assumes that because one thing facilitates something else, its absence will make that thing harder. This is not the same as the reasoning in the prompt, so this is not the answer.
(E) This argument assumes that because one thing (perspective) is necessary for another (being a great painter), it is also sufficient for that thing. This is the reverse of the reasoning in the argument. Meanwhile, this answer is more extreme. The prompt only said many, while this says all.

## PrepTest 56, Section 3 (LR) Continued...

**15. Question Type: Most Supported/Must be True**
(A) The issue isn't studying these things but making them the emphasis, so this is not supported.
(B) This is not supported, as the argument only states that overarching trends are often overlooked, not always. This means that the trends are still discerned sometimes while emphasizing the details.
(C) We have no evidence that there is no other emphasis that would be even better; we simply know that the current emphasis is supposedly worse than the one that came before it.
**(D)** Correct. This is supported by the prompt.
(E) The argument does not suggest that they should be treated equally, just that the current emphasis is hurting our ability to learn from history.

**16. Question Type: Assumption**
The conclusion is that trusting is essential to happiness. This is only true if feeling isolated means one will not feel happy.
**(A)** Correct. This paraphrases our predicted answer. If some who felt isolated were happy, the conclusion would be incorrect, so this passes the negation test.
(B) Even if some could not be happy, trust could still be essential to happiness, so this fails the negation test.
(C) While this is implied by the argument, it does not help the argument, so it is not the assumption.
(D) Even if no people who did not feel isolated were happy, it could still be the case that trust is essential to happiness, so this fails the negation test.
(E) This is a mistaken reversal of one of the premises and does not help the argument. Even if it were not true, the conclusion could still be true, so it fails the negation test.

**17. Question Type: Flaw**
The argument assumes that because one thing (the epic poem) has two characters (it has survived a long time and it is performed in a unique way), one of those characters caused the other (singing caused longevity). The correct answer will likely point this out.
(A) The evidence could be corroborated, so this is not the correct answer.
(B) No source is listed, so this is not the correct answer.
**(C)** Correct. This paraphrases our predicted answer. The poem's characters are correlated, and it is suggested that one caused the other.
(D) There is no reason to believe that what is mentioned is mere popular opinion.
(E) There is no conditional reasoning, so this is not the correct answer.

**18. Question Type: Assumption**
The conclusion is the final sentence. There is a missing link between the emotional connection and the amount donated. The correct answer will likely provide such a link.
(A) Even if this was not the most effective way, it is possible that it could increase donations, so this fails the negation test.
(B) Even if most charities that have raised donations did not do this, it is still possible that it could increase donations, so this fails the negation test.
(C) This merely corroborates a stated premise, so it cannot make the conclusion properly drawn.
(D) Even if most potential donors were willing to do this, it is possible that giving the right to vote would increase donations, so this fails the negation test.
**(E)** Correct. This establishes the link in our predicted answer. If this was not the case, the conclusion would have to be false, so this passes the negation test.

**19. Question Type: Conclusion**
L's main conclusion is that E's behavior is irrational. Everything else she says is used to support this assertion, and this assertion is not used to support anything else.
(A) This is not the conclusion, as it is used to support the fact that his behavior is irrational.
(B) L never says this; she merely states that his behavior is irrational.
(C) L does not suggest that it has no value but that it is not valuable enough to risk his life for.
(D) L's conclusion is not that he can be convinced but simply that his behavior is irrational. She gives no evidence to suggest that he can be convinced, and her entire argument is instead meant to prove that his behavior is irrational.

(E) Correct. This paraphrases our predicted answer.

### 20. Question Type: Weaken
The conclusion is the first sentence. The only evidence given is regarding heart disease; it is possible that vitamin C is harmful in other areas of health. This would weaken the argument.
(A) This does not affect the argument, which only makes a claim about supplements.
(B) Even if other things can also make people healthier, that does not change the fact that vitamin c supplements can make people healthier, so it does not weaken the argument.
(C) This does not suggest that the conclusion is incorrect, so it is not the correct answer.
(D) Correct. This would weaken the argument, as suggested in our predicted answer. Despite the fact that the supplements helped with heart health, overall health might not be better than average if resistance to common diseases is lowered.
(E) This would strengthen the conclusion, so it is not the correct answer.

### 21. Question Type: Flaw
B needs to explain why ballroom dancing is so popular now, which confused G because it was not popular in the 80s and early 90s.
(A) B does not suggest this, so it is not the correct answer.
(B) This does not need to be explained, so it is not a flaw.
(C) The relationship to other forms of dance does not need to be explained, so this is not a flaw.
(D) Correct. B simply pushes the question back a few years; he suggests it is popular now because it became more popular in 1995. However, B does not explain why it became more popular in 1995.
(E) This does not need to be demonstrated, so it is not a flaw in the argument.

### 22. Question Type: Could be True EXCEPT
The correct answer must be false. The four incorrect answers are all possible, though they are not necessarily true.
(A) This is supported by the prompt, so it could be true. That means it is not the correct answer.
(B) Correct. This must not be true. The argument states that the two must have faced the same daily challenges, and it states that they are in different environments. That means that different environments must be able to have the same daily challenges, so this answer cannot be true.
(C) This is possible, as nothing in the prompt suggests it is incorrect.
(D) This is possible and partially supported by the prompt. While it is not definitely true, it could be true, so it is not the correct answer.
(E) There is support for this statement, so it is not the case that this must be false.

### 23. Question Type: Principle
The two statements can be diagrammed as:
intermittent wind and below 84 → pleasant
high humidity and (above 84 or no wind) → oppressive
(A) Because there was no wind, this cannot be labeled pleasant.
(B) Because the day does not have high humidity, it cannot be labeled oppressive.
(C) Because the temperature was not below 84, it cannot be labeled pleasant.
(D) Because there was wind and the temperature was below 84, the day cannot be labeled oppressive.
(E) Correct. Because there was no wind and there was high humidity, the day can correctly be labeled oppressive.

### 24. Question Type: Parallel Reasoning
The reasoning here is that because something was one way in the past, it will likely be that way in the future. This is supported by the fact that the station has not tried to change its ratings through any traditional channels.
(A) This generalizes from a subset of a population to the entire population. This reasoning is not similar to that in the prompt.
(B) While this generalizes from earlier to later, it is generalizing about something that is purely determined by chance. The rating of the radio station depends upon the actions of thousands of people deciding what

station they will listen to, which is not determined by chance.
(C) The reasoning here is that because all members of a population are something, a member of that population is something. This is not similar to the reasoning in the prompt.
(D) Correct. This generalizes from the past to the future. Meanwhile, it is generalizing about something that is determined not by chance but by a large group of people acting in real-time. The prompt generalizes about a similar phenomenon, so this is the correct answer.
(E) The reasoning here is that if one thing is necessary for something else, than anyone who is that something else must have that necessary character. This is not similar to the reasoning in the argument.

**25. Question Type: Assumption**
The conclusion is that he can skip the first step. This only follows from the premises if he bought the mussels for his recipe at a seafood market. Therefore, this is assumed by the argument.
(A) Whether or not this was the case does not affect the reasoning of the argument, so this is not the answer.
(B) Since the first step is not designed to remove contaminants but simply sand, this is irrelevant to the argument.
(C) The taste of the mussels has no bearing on the argument, so this is not the answer.
(D) Even if there were farm-raised mussels when the recipe was written, it would still be possible that the chef could skip the first step, so this fails the negation test.
(E) Correct. This paraphrases our predicted answer. If he did not get them from a seafood market, the conclusion would not follow, so this passes the negation test.

# PrepTest 56, Section 4 (RC)

**Passage 1**

Mark the passage. There are a few reversals in the first paragraph, so be careful to get the right main idea—which isn't actually stated directly in the first paragraph. Paragraph 1 mentions that many critics praised Tutuola as giving a fresh approach to the novel. It mentions, however, that many others noted that he merely rewrote local tales. Our author, however, seems to be preparing to say they're both wrong, because critics failed to grasp that Tutuola wasn't necessarily writing novels.

Paragraph 2 elaborates: Tutuola is, instead, a teller of folktales. Different expectations are made of that genre than of novels.

Paragraph 3: A foktale is common property: known to most, but capable of elaboration and change by each teller.

Paragraph 4: specifics of how Tutola's works are like folktales.

So what's the main idea? Basically, something like this: Critics misunderstand Tutuola's work, because he wrote not novels but folktales. That's ….

1. … choice **(B)**.

2. Read that last paragraph closely, if you need to: from your markup you know that it tells you what Tutuola's technique is. Since we're asked to extrapolate that technique for an Irish writer, we'll need something like Tutuola. He sometimes transplants folklore into modern settings (see 45-47). Choice C is a little off, since the stories themselves aren't modernized. So you want choice **(D)**.

3. Choice **(A)** is the only one that reflects the author's concern with Tutuola as a folklorist rather than a novelist. The other choices make inferences that aren't supported by the passage.

4. The criticism was that his works weren't original (lines 9-11). That's reflected in choice **(D)**.

5. Remember that when you see an EXCEPT, you should mentally flip the question on its head. So, we're being asked, Which of the following is NOT attributed to Tutuola? The whole point of the passage is that Tutuola did NOT write novels. So choice **(E)** is the right one.

6. You're pointed to a particular part of the question. In that situation, always read the context—at least the whole sentence where it appears. This is a long sentence—it starts all the way up on line 21. What's the point of the sentence? Well, it's that novels are supposed to be original, but folklore draws from "the corpus of traditional lore." We're contrasting the two genres. So choice **(A)** reflects that.

7. The purpose of the passage—what does that mean? Look at the main idea again, and try to put it in abstract terms. You'll get something like choice **(C)**.

**Passage 2**

This one's wordy, but not all that complicated. The real problem here is that the paragraphs are too long—each contains more than one main idea.

Paragraph 1: Why do animals learn to recognize their kin? One response is inclusive fitness: evolution favors the survival of not just the individual but his gene pool—therefore, of his close relatives. This theory explains honeybee behavior (one example).

Paragraph 2. Inclusive fitness explains new findings about cannibalism. Tadpoles will eat other tadpoles, but not ones that are related to them. It's not a perfect explanation, though: look at that last sentence.

# PrepTest 56, Section 4 (RC)

Paragraph 3. "But there may be other reasons why organisms recognize kin. " Salamander larvae do it to avoid eating harmful bacteria when they eat each other. So that means that it's just self-preservation again.

What's the point of all that? Well, that inclusive fitness might be one good reason why kin recognition occurs, but might not be the only reason. Let's see if one of the choices matches that prediction.

8. Choice (A) looks pretty close to our prediction.

9. Choice (C) is in the passage (line 34-37); the others are not. Note that choice (E) is implied (sort of) by the passage, but you're asked to find something that's stated, i.e., in there directly.

10. Kin recognition is explained by inclusive fitness for the toads, but not for the salamanders, so choice (D) fits closely with what the passage says.

11. Read the sentence you're directed to—and, for good measure, the sentence before it. We're told that we have "at least a partial answer." Why the equivocation? Well, "interestingly," it's because of the tidbit in the last sentence. So that last sentence is there to point out one wrinkle that the neat theory of paragraph 2 doesn't explain. So, choice (A) is correct. Choice (D) is wrong, because it overstates the problem.

12. How does kin recognition work in tadpoles? With "nipping" (line 41). So choice (A) is correct.

13. Choice (B) is stated directly (lines 4-6) and is correct.

14. Honeybees, according to our notes, are an example of inclusive fitness (a modification of evolutionary theory) explaining a species' behavior. So that's choice (E).

15. The right choice is (C), because it gives a plausible alternate reason why salamanders recognize their kin—and thereby weakens the author's evaluation.

**Passage 3, Comparative reading**

Passage A states that terms like "nation," "people," and "minority" have vague definitions in international law. This problem is especially acute for the Roma people, since they fit so few of the common conceptions for such terms.

Passage B focuses on one particular definition of a minority: fewer in number, non-dominant, ethnically or culturally distinct, and desirous of preserving their culture. The Roma are problematic for citizenship reasons, but still fulfill those criteria.

16. The main point of Passage A—take a look at the notes—is given by choice (E). It's the only one that says that there are problems for all definitions of minorities, but especially for the Roma.

17. Most of these choices are close. But which one is dead-on? Choice (C): "Problematic" here means "creating problems." Note that (D) is very close – but in context it's clear that they aren't talking about solving the problem – only that problems exist.

18. Choice (D) is correct. The first passage does not mention the Roma's population.

19. Choice (E) is correct. Be careful here: several of the choices sound good, but get the relationship between the two passages backwards.

20. Don't be distracted by the gimmick: this question asks you to take the relationship between the two passages and apply it to a different context (in all cases, "is welding a technical job?") Passage A says, "Problems with definitions make it difficult to classify [Roma] as [a minority]." Passage B says, "Based on one definition, [Roma] are [a minority]." Plug "welding" and "a technical job" into the brackets, and what do you get? Choice (A).

## PrepTest 56, Section 4 (RC)

21. Definitions for Roma are apparently "problematic," according to the authors. They wouldn't be if they didn't create difficulties. So both passages assume that failure to be recognized as a minority group might cause problems. That's choice **(B)**.

**Passage 4**

Paragraph 1: "One recent observer" is your clue that the author is likely to disagree with this person. Watch for the "however," which occurs in line 11. So, contrary to recent opinion, legislators proposed two egalitarian reforms during the revolutionary period.

Paragraph 2 describes those two approaches: (1) founded on education as a public good: public, single-sex schools for both girls and boys—girls only through age 8. (2) founded on education as an equal right: coed schools, but continued to define women in terms of domestic role.

Paragraph 3: Neither proposal was perfect; "nevertheless," they influenced policy a century later.

22. The 1880 reform is described in the last paragraph; reread it. Choice **(C)** describes what it says there.

23. Just look at your mark-up. Choice **(E)** is the best answer. Note that choice (C) is close, but not quite right—did the eventual reform require "less of a break with tradition"? No.

24. If you look back at what you've marked, you'll see that the first proposal was for public schools, and the second was for equal treatment of the sexes in school. That's most like choice **(A)**.

25. The big point in the second proposal was that it be coed. That's choice **(B)**.

26. Choice **(E)** is correct. Look at lines 11-15, which state the answer directly. (You don't have to go reread it though: you should remember reading the word "egalitarian" in the passage).

27. The author seems to think that at least in historical context, the proposals were laudable. The best description of that is in choice **(C)**. Choice (D) is wrong, because it seems like the author has little difficulty understanding why the proposals failed.

# PrepTest 57

## PrepTest 57, Section 1, Game 1

This is a straightforward linear game.

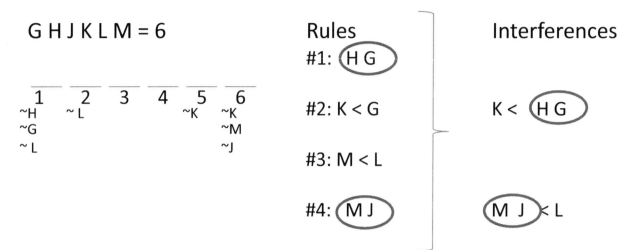

Discussion: The rule combinations are straightforward; G is used in rules 1 and 2 which should be combined, and M is used in rules 3 and 4 which should be combined. No variables are unrestricted. Exclusion rules are helpful here. As you work through the questions, keep in mind that the primary challenge is fitting in the two blocks (HG and MJ) quickly into new diagrams.

---

1. List question.
a) Violates Rule 4
b) Violates Rule 2
c) Violates Rule 3
d) **Correct**
e) Violates Rule 1

2. We don't have an exclusion rule yet for 3, so we'll have to use quick process of elimination.
a) Could work, e.g. K H G J M L
b) **Correct,** H cannot be third. If H is 3, G is 4th. The next step is fitting in the other block of JM, It would have to go 5th and 6th, but that leaves no room for L after JM.
c) Could work, e.g. K M J H G L
d) Could work, e.g. J M K H G L
e) Could work, e.g. K J M L H G

3. Again, this is about quick elimination of options in a new diagram.
a) Could work, e.g. J M K H G L
b) Could work, e.g. K H G J M L
c) **Correct.** If K is second, there's nothing to go in first since HG have to be after K and there's not room for the JM block.
d) Could work, e.g. J M L K H G
e) Could work, e.g. J M L K H G

4. Again, this is about quick elimination of options in a new diagram.
a) Could work, e.g. J M K H G L
b) Could work, e.g. J M L K H G
c) Could work, e.g. K H G M J L
d) **Correct,** L cannot go 5th. IF L goes 5th, nothing can go 6th since there's not room there to fit in the block of H and G.
e) Could work, e.g. K H G J M L

5. On rule change questions you'll have to first disaggregate the relevant rule you combined. It's still the case that J and M must appear together; we're asked to think about what new rule would keep L after both J and M.

a) This doesn't work; the initial rule allowed for L to be third, so it does not need to be in the last 3.
b) This creates a block of either [M J L] or [J M]. Since this allows L to be before J and M, it doesn't work the same way as the original rule.
c) **Correct.** If we say that L must go after J, we still get the same rule combination we made before: J (M) L
d) The original rule did not link H and L so there's no reason to do so here.
e) Putting L before J is actually the opposite of the original rule!

## PrepTest 57, Section 1, Game 2

This game is essentially an advanced linear game; while there are some grouping aspects, a good linear diagram will help us organize effectively.

O1, O2, G1, G2, R1, R2 = 6

```
 W    Th    F     S
~R1         ~O1
```

Rules
(At least one audition per day)
#1: O1 < R1
#2: ⎡G⎤
    ⎣R⎦
#3: At least one Thurs/Sat

Discussion: It really helps to disaggregate the variables here; O's first visit has distinct conditions from O's second visit, so we should use the notation O1, O2, etc.

We haven't notated that every one of the second auditions cannot go on Wednesday, but you can do so if you like. It is good to know that R1 cannot go first (because it must go after O1) and that O1 cannot go on Friday; that would put R1 on Saturday which can't happen because it does not leave room for R2.

---

6. List question. This is a bit trickier; after doing a simple rule-by-rule elimination, many students are left with B and D. When this happens, put each of the options into a diagram on your page; you will quickly see the problem with D.
   a) Violates Rule 3
   b) **Correct.**
   c) Violates Rule 1
   d) When you insert this into the diagram, it becomes quickly clear that there is no one to go on Friday. While it's certainly possible to see this without the diagram, students often miss this the first time through. When that happens it's much quicker to eliminate with a visual aid.

```
         O1   R1        O2
         G1   G2        R2
e) Violates Rule 1
         W    Th    F    S
```

7. If O auditions on Thursday and Saturday, we know that R will audition on Friday and Saturday. This is because R1 must be after O1, so if O1 is on Thursday R must go the last 2 days. We now have only G1 and G2 to place; G1 will have to go on Wednesday because no one else goes there. Finally, G2 will have to go with R1 or R2 to satisfy Rule 2.

```
                        G2/
                  G2/   O2
         G1  O1   R1    R2
         W   Th   F     S
```

b) **Correct.** G definitely goes on Wednesday and can go on Friday. All other answers must be false.

8. Scan the answer choices for one of the inferences made in the setup. If you don't find anything initially, rely on quick trial-and-error.

e) **Correct.** Since O1 must go before R1 and R1 must go before R2, the earliest R2 can go is Thursday.

9. We can very quickly work through process of elimination here in a diagram.
d) **Correct.** If O is Thursday and Friday, we know that R will have to go Friday and Saturday. Since no one is on Wednesday yet, G1 will have to be Wednesday. This won't work because no matter where we place G2, no variable goes both Thursday and Saturday as per rule 3.

10.
a) We know that R1 can't go on Wednesday because it must go after O1.
b) If all 3 audition on Friday, no one will be able to go on both Thursday and Saturday (Rule 3) since they can each only go twice.
c) **Correct.**

```
                              G2
              O1              O2
         R1        G1         R2
    ___  ___  ___  ___
     W   Th    F    S
```

d) O1 can't go on Friday since we need two spaces behind it for R 1 and R2.
e) R1 cannot go first.

11. If G auditions Wednesday and Saturday, we can deduce that R2 must go on Saturday. We have to have G with R at least once, and we know that R cannot go on Wednesday:

```
                              G2
         G1                   R2
    ___  ___  ___  ___
     W   Th    F    S
```

After this point we have some variability, so we can move to the answer choices.
a) If O is Wednesday and Thursday, that forces R1 into Friday since it's the only variable left to go in an otherwise empty Friday. However that violates Rule 3 as no one is going Thursday/Saturday.
b) **Correct.** If O goes Wednesday/Friday, R1 would go in Thursday, which works.
c) This leaves Thursday and Friday both empty with only R1 left to place.
d) R1 can never go on Wednesday
e) We already established by inference that R2 must go on Saturday.

## PrepTest 57, Section 1, Game 3

The dinosaur game is a famously challenging game. It is a hybrid of grouping and matching aspects, which is relatively rare; most hybrid games combine linearity with matching or grouping. The game is incredibly hard if you don't find one relatively minor insight, which guides your process on each question.

ILPSTUV = 7 dinos
GMRY = 4 colors

```
   S  __ __ __
   __ __ __ __
   R  M  M
```

## Rules

#1. Exactly 2 M (insert into diagram)

#2:  | S |
     | R |   (Insert into diagram)

#3: I →  | I |
         | G |

#4: P →  | P |
         | Y |

#5: V → ~U       (the contrapositive of this rule is  U → ~V; they can be combined into one easier-to-use rule:)
             V ←|→ U

#6: L
    and  →  at least one note M
    U

(The contrapositive isn't very useful, if Lm and Um then ~L or ~U doesn't make very much sense, although it's technically true.)

Discussion: What variables appear multiple times? Mauve appears in rules 1 and 6, but in reality, it also appears in rules 2, 3, and 4, all of which limit which dinosaurs can be mauve. We know we'll always have to get 2 M's into our diagram from among L, T, U, and V; S, I, and P cannot be mauve. Further, there are limitations on how L and U can go in, and we can't have both V and U at the same time.

There aren't "inferences" per se, but if you begin each question thinking about how to work the most restrictive part of this game (as usual), the game will not be too hard.

12. List question. Simple rule-by-rule elimination often leaves students with B and C as options.
a) Violates Rule 5
b) **Correct.**
c) As soon as you put this configuration into a diagram and layer on the colors, you're left with L and U to be your 2 mauves, which violates Rule 6.
d) Violates Rule 1
e) Violates Rule 5

13. When T is ruled out in this question we are alerted that our selection of mauves is even more limited to just L, U, and V. Which of these can go in together as our 2 mauves? We know that U and V can't go together; we also know that it can't be L and U since they would both be mauve, violating Rule 6. Only L and V can be our mauves.

| S | L | V | | |
|---|---|---|---|---|
| R | M | M | | |

What can go in those last 2 spaces? Out of our original 7 dinosaurs we have ruled out the 3 that already used, U by inference above, and T by rule for this question. That means we have only I and P left, and we know which color each of those will be:

| S | L | V | I | P |
|---|---|---|---|---|
| R | M | M | G | Y |

**d) Correct.**

14. Again, we'll be evaluating based on what we can do with the mauve spaces.
a) **Correct.** We are given V as a mauve. What else can be mauve of the 3 other candidates (L, T, and U)? L is already used and U cannot be in with V, so it would have to be T. This meets all the rules.
b) Without L or T as mauve possibilities we are left with just U and V, which cannot go in together.
c) Similarly, with L and U being non-mauve we would need T and V to be mauve, but V and U cannot exist together (Rule 5).
d) Again, with T and U out of the mauve running we're left with L and V; U and V cannot both be included.
e) With T and V out of the mauve running we have L and U; U and V again conflict.

15. This setup will look very familiar after doing #13. With T out of the running for M, we only have L, U, and V as options. Just like #13, with L U and V as options the only workable configuration is L and V.

| S | L | V | T | |
|---|---|---|---|---|
| R | M | M | Y | |

**e) Correct.** We must have a mauve velociraptor. a), b), and c) could be true but could be false, while D is definitely false.

16. U is definitely in, but we aren't sure what color it is. We have L, V, and T as options. V is out because U and V cannot coexist. L is an option, but we know that either L or U must not be mauve if they are both included. This lets us deduce that T will definitely be a mauve, and either U or L will be the other. (U is definitely included regardless of color, but L does not have to be).

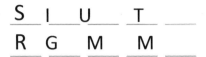 OR

Either way, we know that T will be included and will be mauve.

a) **Correct.**

17. What toys are there that could be green? We have I, L, T, U, and V. We also need to make sure we have our 2 mauves, as usual. P is out because we've filled all our colors and P always has to be yellow if it's in.

S _____ _____ _____ _____
R  M    M    G    G

How could this play out? Well, we have 4 spaces to fill with 5 variables. How do they interact? We know that 2 of the variables can't coexist – U and V. So, in effect we have 4 spaces to fill: 3 for which we know the variable, and 1 of which will be either U or V. Of course, we know that I will have to be green.

S _____ _____ I _____
R  M    M    G    G

Starting here we have some uncertainty about what colors L, T, and U/V could be, so we move to the answer choices.

a) There can't be yellow toys.
b) **Correct**, could be true:

S  L    V    I    T
R  M    M    G    G

c) L has to be in, though V could be out.
d) T must be in.
e) Either U or V must be in.

PrepTest 57, Section 1, Game 4

This is essentially an advanced linear game with some grouping aspects. The quarters certainly go in order, and we need to fill each quarter with one or more awards.

MTWY = 4

```
                W
___   ___   ___   ___
 1     2     3     4
~W          ~W
```

Rules
(One or more grants awarded each quarter)
#1: Grants awarded in all 4 areas
#2: 6 awards max
#3: no same quarter or consecutive awards
#4: =2 M
#5: W in 2 (insert into diagram)

Discussion: There are few inferences to be made here, other than that there can't be W in 1st or 3rd due to Rule 3 and Rule 5.

Give some thought to what will be challenging in this game. One challenge will be getting in our 2 M's given that they can't be consecutive. That means there will have to be at least one space between our M and M.

Again, LSAC has given you the minimum amount of space to draw diagrams on this game, so be neat.

18. List question. Again, simple rule-by-rule elimination often leaves students with B and C as options.
a) Violates Rule 4
b) Violates Rule 5
c) **Correct**
d) Violates Rule 3
e) Violates Rule 2

19. Process of elimination here.
a) The Ms can easily be by themselves in 1 and 3 or 1 and 4.
b) This works with M in 1 and 3 and Y anywhere.
c) This works with multiple configurations, such as M in 1 and 4 and T anywhere.
d) **Correct,** cannot be true. The math doesn't work here. There are always 2 M's so if there are also 2 W's, 2 Y's, and the minimum of one T that adds up to 7, violating Rule 2.
e) M, Y, and T could all easily be in 4.

20. If Y and W are together, where could they be? They could be in 2, where we know W always is; they could also go 4th, the only other place where W can be.

```
                W                              W
        W       Y                              Y
___  ___  ___  ___      OR     ___  ___  ___  ___
 1    2    3    4               1    2    3    4
```

e) **Correct.** Y can't be in 3rd because that would put it next to the Y in 2, violating Rule 3.


21. The local information limits us to 5 total grants. Think about how this works. This is 3 grants going once, and one grant going twice. Which grant has to go twice? That's right, M has to go twice by rule and can thus be the only variable that goes twice in this question.
a) This can't work since only M can go twice.
b) **Correct:**

```
              M
       T   W   Y   M
      ___ ___ ___ ___
       1   2   3   4
```

c) This makes W go twice (2nd and 4th)
d) This leaves a quarter without any award. W is 2nd, but that leaves 3 and 4 for our 2 M's. That doesn't work since the 2 M's can't go together.
e) Similar to D, this leaves us our 2 M's for the 3rd and 4th quarters, which can't work.

22. Remember to eliminate based on past questions.
a) This works, e.g.

```
              T
              Y
       M   W   M   Y
      ___ ___ ___ ___
       1   2   3   4
```

b) We've seen this configuration before; M is a great place to start as you work through.
c) We've seen this configuration before in the list question correct answer, so we can eliminate.
d) **Correct.** If nothing but T can be in 1st or 4th, that means our 2 M's have to go in 2 and 3, which doesn't work (Rule 3).
e) This works with M in 1 and 3 and Y/T in 1,2, or 3.

23. This is process of elimination; work through each option and stop to eliminate when you get to multiple possibilities.

e) **Correct.** If three grants are in the 3rd quarter, we know they must be Y, T, and M since Y is already in 2. from there, we know the other M must go in 1ist. We also know that W must go in 4, since we need something in 4 and none of the options in 3 can go 4th as well. We've reached 6, our limit.

# PrepTest 57, Section 2 (LR)

**1. Question Type: Principle**
The correct answer will have to justify the conclusion, which is the last sentence. It also cannot contradict any of the prompt.
(A) Correct. This closely paraphrases the prompt.
(B) This does not justify the conclusion, and it also contradicts the claim in the prompt that there is no positive effect on the patient.
(C) This would suggest the conclusion could be incorrect, so it does not fit the prompt.
(D) The prompt does not discuss any case in which a doctor is unsure of the effect a treatment will have, so this does not pertain to the prompt.
(E) The argument does not suggest that the patient claims a treatment will help, so this does not fir the prompt.

**2. Question Type: Complete the Argument**
The correct answer will likely suggest that associative runners don't want to run the day before a race, as this would leave them mentally exhausted for the next day. The first half of the last sentence opens with "since", suggesting that it will explain the part of the sentence we are filling in.
(A) Correct. This paraphrases our predicted answer, and it finishes the sentence with something that is explained by the first half of the sentence.
(B), (C), (D) and (E) are not explained by the first half of the sentence, so they cannot be the answer.

**3. Question Type: Resolve the Paradox**
The paradox is that the payment plan suggested the bank should be getting more money each payment, but by the end of the payment plan, the bank was receiving less money.
(A) This would not affect the amount of money received as payments for these 10 loans, so this cannot be the answer.
(B) and (C) Neither explains why these 10 businesses are paying less money at the end of the payment plan.
(D) Correct. This explains the bank receiving less money at the end of the payment plan; if the largest borrowers finished paying early, only the smaller borrowers would be left paying at the end.
(E) This does not explain the situation with these ten borrowers, none of whom had such a payment plan.

**4. Question Type: Flaw**
The argument draws a conclusion about all universities from one talk at a particular university. The correct answer will likely point out that the conclusion is drawn from too little data.
(A) The professor's opinion is not given, so this cannot be the answer.
(B) The argument does not advocate tolerance, so this is not the answer.
(C) It does not rely on an emotional appeal; it relies on the anecdote provided.
(D) Correct. This paraphrases our predicted answer. The problem with the argument is how little supporting data there is.
(E) Because the argument is about the behavior of students, it is okay that it focuses on students' behavior.

**5. Question Type: Strengthen**
(A) If people believed this, then health experts would not need to emphasize this.
(B) The prompt already suggests this, so this does not add anything to the argument. Hence, it does not strengthen it.
(C) Whether they have been moderately successful or not does not affect whether they would be more successful if they focused on flavor, so this does not strengthen the argument.
(D) This would suggest that people do not think of wholesome food as flavorful, which would mean that they probably would not eat more wholesome food.
(E) Correct. This suggests that people would be likely to have more wholesome foods if they were told that they were flavorful, so it adds support to the conclusion.

**6. Question Type: Flaw**
The argument cites statistics that shows that three pairs of phenomena are correlated, but the argument assumes that one causes the other in each case. The correct answer will likely point this out.
(A) The argument does not suggest that anything is always true, so this is not the answer.
(B) The argument does not suggest that this is more important, only a way that this could be achieved at a

# PrepTest 57, Section 2 (LR) Continued...

business school.
- **(C) Correct.**
- **(D)** The argument makes no mention of what is morally wrong, only of when people have ethical principles and what kind of people are more likely to break those ethical principles.
- **(E)** The conclusion is the last sentence, and it does not restate any of the premises, so this is not the correct answer.

### 7. Question Type: Assumption

The conclusion is that one must reject L's claims if imagist poems are considered legitimate. The evidence cited is that imagist poems are merely collections of disparate images, and literature must consist of words that represent actions or events occurring in sequence. The assumption here is that collections of images cannot be events occurring in sequence.

- **(A) Correct.** This paraphrases our predicted answer. If an amalgam of disparate images could represent a sequence of events or actions, the conclusion would have to be false, so this passes the negation test.
- **(B)** The argument's conclusion is a conditional; a conditional statement can be true even if the sufficient condition is false (for example, "if unicorns are real then I am a liar" is a true statement, even though unicorns are not real). This means that this answer fails the negation test.
- **(C)** Even if Lessing was aware of this character of Imagist poetry, he could still have made the same argument; maybe he didn't think imagist poetry was legitimate.
- **(D)** Even if some art did not represent something, the conclusion could still be true, so this fails the negation test.
- **(E)** Lessing's claim is only about what art is legitimate, so this answer is too extreme.

### 8. Question Type: Parallel Reasoning

Someone (a psychiatrist) suggested that something (multiple personality disorder) did not exist because s/he never encountered it.

- **(A)** This answer is not extreme enough. In the prompt, the person suggested something never occurs because s/he had not seen it; in this answer, the person only suggests it only seldom occurs.
- **(B)** This is different from the reasoning because it relies on a large group of people, rather than one person's experiences.
- **(C)** The reasoning here is different because it uses the fact that something rarely happens as its evidence, while the argument in the prompt uses the fact that a person has never encountered something as evidence.
- **(D)** T argues that because something happened in the past, it is likely to continue into the future. This is very different from the reasoning in the prompt.
- **(E) Correct.** Someone (J) suggested that something (deer in his area) did not exist because he never encountered one. This is exactly like the reasoning in the prompt.

### 9. Question Type: Weaken

This is a mere statement of fact, so the correct answer will likely suggest that this fact is incorrect.

- **(A)** This would suggest that hunger is caused by something that abstaining from meat would not alleviate, strengthening the argument.
- **(B)** This does not suggest that the argument is incorrect, so it does not weaken the argument.
- **(C) Correct.** This suggests that the argument is incorrect; if this answer is true, then it seems that excluding meat would help alleviate world hunger.
- **(D)** This suggests that hunger can be caused by something that abstaining from meat would not alleviate, strengthening the argument.
- **(E)** This suggests that severe episodes of world hunger had nothing to do with whether people ate meat or not, strengthening the argument.

### 10. Question Type: Principle

The prompt suggests a couple of things. The company is concerned with environmental conditions and profits, and some improvements to the environmental conditions can have a positive impact on profits as well. The correct answer will fit each of these parts of the prompt.

- **(A)** The argument does not suggest anything about knowledge of milk production physiology, so this is not illustrated by the prompt.

## PrepTest 57, Section 2 (LR) Continued...

(B) Correct. This fits each of the three parts of the prompt, so it is the correct answer.
(C) The argument makes no mention of other farm animals, so this is not illustrated by the prompt.
(D) The argument makes no mention of the quality of the product, so this is not illustrated by the prompt.
(E) The argument does not suggest that the concern is the reason for the maximized profits; it only suggests that it was able to do something that benefited both. Therefore, this is not illustrated by the prompt.

### 11. Question Type: Point at Issue
There will be clear evidence that one person agrees and one person disagrees with the correct answer.
(A) While there is evidence that P believes this, there is no reason to believe that A disagrees.
(B) There is no evidence that either P or A believes or disagrees.
(C) Correct. P clearly believes this, and A clearly does not, so this is the correct answer.
(D) There is no evidence that either P or A believes or disagrees.
(E) While P definitely agrees with this, there is no reason to believe A agrees or disagrees.

### 12. Question Type: Assumption
There's a disconnect here; criminal organizations want to generate profit, but it's a leap to say that because they have that goal they will necessarily get involved in any new profitable enterprise. The assumption should reflect this disjuncture.
(A) This reverses the sufficient and necessary conditions of the correct answer.
(B) This is not extreme enough; the prompt suggests that all criminal organizations will try to become more involved, not just some.
(C) Even if they were not involved in some, it could still be that they are going to try to become involved in this one, so this fails the negation test.
(D) Correct. This paraphrases our predicted answer. The fact that it is slightly more specific is fine because in this case, the argument only refers to technological revolutions. If this was false, the conclusion could not follow, so this passes the negation test.
(E) Remember that the definition of assumption on the LSAT is a bit different than that of every day usage; an assumption here is an unstated premise that would make the conclusion properly drawn. It may seem like this is assumed, but it does not make the argument logically sound, so it is not the answer.

### 13. Question Type: Method of Reasoning
The conclusion is that this statement is false. Therefore, this is a premise that the rest of the argument is meant to counter.
(A) It is presented as the only explanation for why teachers fear computers, so it is not presented as a possible explanation of this.
(B) It is not a problem, and it is not supposed to be solved by the argument.
(C) Correct. This paraphrases our predicted answer.
(D) It does not support the main conclusion; the main conclusion states that it is not true.
(E) It is not the main conclusion, as it is not supported by any premises.

### 14. Question Type: Weaken
The conclusion is that foraging leads to increased brain size. This only follows if it is assumed that the correlation between foragers and brain size is a causal link. The correct answer will likely suggest that one does not cause the other.
(A) The argument does not require brains to continue growing, only that they grow larger from learning to forage, so this does not weaken the argument.
(B) The argument does not require brains to grow smaller once foraging stops, so this does not weaken the argument.
(C) The argument does not suggest there is a link between forage distance and brain size, so this does not weaken the argument.
(D) Even a small increase in brain size is an increase, so this does not weaken the argument.
(E) Correct. This suggests that there is no causation between the two; if foraging caused brain size increases, then bees that never foraged should not have increased brain sizes. This suggests the difference in size is due to age instead.

*PrepTest 57, Section 2 (LR) Continued...*

**15. Question Type: Flaw**
Carla suggests that professors should get paid leaves of absence because it will increase knowledge and improve their teaching. David suggests that the increase in knowledge is not enough.
**(A)** Correct. David ignores C's assertion that it would improve professors' teaching, which would answer his question.
(B) David does not take this for granted, as he suggests professors also do research.
(C) D did not mention tax money, so this is not the answer.
(D) D does not assume that research is the only function; he simply replies to C as though that is the only suggestion she has made. This does not mean he believes there is no other function.
(E) D does not assume this, so this cannot be the answer.

**16. Question Type: Method of Reasoning**
This is the argument's conclusion. Each of the other sentences supports this statement, and this statement does not support any of the other sentences.
(A) It is the only conclusion, so this is not the answer.
**(B)** Correct. This is correct. It is a conclusion, and there is no other conclusion, so it is the only conclusion.
(C) There are no other conclusions, so this is not the answer.
(D) It does not support any other statement, so this is not the answer.
(E) There is no intermediate conclusion, so this is not the answer.

**17. Question Type: Weaken**
The conclusion is the second to last sentence. The argument draws an analogy between the brick wall review and another poetry anthology. The correct answer will likely suggest that this is a poor analogy.
(A) This suggests the analogy is strong, so it does not weaken the argument.
(B) This suggests the other poetry anthology is more prestigious than the brick wall, which has no real bearing on whether the analogy is strong or not.
(C) How poets are compensated does not affect the strength of the analogy, and it does not weaken the argument, so this is not the answer.
(D) Where the brick wall gets money for its operating costs from does not affect the analogy, since we do not know how the other journal gets money for its operating costs.
**(E)** Correct. This suggests that the analogy is not a good one, as it suggests the Brick Wall anthology will have more sales due to the celebrity poets, which the new magazine might not have access to; it's a particular property of the Brick Wall anthology that made it successful. Therefore, it weakens the argument.

**18. Question Type: Complete the Argument**
The sentence is drawing an analogy. In the first sentence, a person does not rely on the average person to get medical treatment. For this reason, the rest of the sentence will probably suggest that the public servant will not rely on the average person.
(A) The analogy merely suggests that a public servant should not rely on the average person, not that s/he should not be concerned at all with what they think.
(B) We have no reason to believe that the public servant knows any better, only that s/he will look for someone who knows better.
(C) The first sentence does not suggest that people should know more about medicine, so this would not fit the analogy.
**(D)** Correct. This fits the analogy.
(E) The public servant doesn't need to be more knowledgeable as long as s/he gets advice from someone who is more knowledgeable, as was the case in the first sentence.

**19. Question Type: Parallel Reasoning**
The reasoning can be diagrammed as follows:
        win → willing to cooperate    ~cooperate → ~win
        willing to cooperate → motivated    ~motivated → ~cooperate
        Therefore, ~motivated → ~win
This is logically sound; the conclusion is the contrapositive of the combination of the first two conditionals.
(A) This can be diagrammed as follows:

# PrepTest 57, Section 2 (LR) Continued...

        healthy → exercise
        exercise → risk injury
        Therefore, desire health → ~exercise

This is pretty different from the reasoning in the prompt, so it is not the answer.
(B) This is not logically sound, so it cannot be the correct answer.
**(C) Correct.** This can be diagrammed as follows:
        retain status → raise money
        raise money → increase campaigning
        Therefore, ~increase campaigning → ~retain status

This is exactly the same reasoning as that in the prompt, so it is the correct answer. Note again that you must consider the contrapositives to see how the logic works.
(D) This is not logically sound, so it is not the correct answer.
(E) This is not logically sound, so it is not the correct answer.

### 20. Question Type: Weaken
The argument assumes that a correlation between two phenomena (lowering rates of accidents and setting a speed limit) implies causation between the two. The correct answer will likely suggest this is incorrect.
(A) This does not weaken the argument, as it suggests the speed limit could have been effective at reducing speed and thus accident rate.
(B) This does not suggest the conclusion is incorrect or that the reasoning is incorrect, so this does not weaken the argument.
(C) It is possible that the limit still reduced the average speed and accident rate, so this does not weaken the argument.
**(D) Correct.** This supplies a different cause for the lowering accident rate, so it suggests the conclusion is incorrect. Therefore, it weakens the argument.
(E) The argument is about accident rate, not harm to passengers, so this does not weaken the argument.

### 21. Question Type: Method of Reasoning
The conclusion is that the criticism is misplaced. The sentence in question supports this statement. Therefore, it is used to suggest the reasoning behind a statement is flawed.
(A) It supports the conclusion, so this is not correct.
(B) The argument suggests that most social critics do not know this fact, so it cannot have misled them.
(C) It is not the conclusion, so this is incorrect.
(D) This refutes the false assumption, so this is not the correct answer.
**(E) Correct.** This correctly states the sentence's use in the argument; it suggests the reasoning behind the sentiment in the first statement is faulty.

### 22. Question Type: Strengthen
The argument assumes that the spearheads were made in Siberia first, then brought to North America, so the correct answer will likely support this assumption.
**(A) Correct.** This supports the assumption mentioned in the predicted answer. This suggests that the spearheads were first made in Siberia, then brought to North America.
(B) This does not support the assumption mentioned in the predicted answer. If this is true, then it is unclear where they were made first. It suggests that they were made before the land bridge disappeared, which would mean that we hadn't found the oldest Clovis points and thus did not know where they were made first.
(C), (D) and (E) These do not suggest anything about where it was made first, so they do not strengthen the answer.

### 23. Question Type: Least Supported
(A) This is supported by the prompt, as taxi drivers who need more money will likely set higher targets.
**(B) Correct.** This is not supported, and it is in fact suggested to be wrong. Taxi drivers work shorter hours on busy days, when their effective hourly wage is higher. This directly contradicts with this answer, so this answer is not supported.
(C) This is not supported, but it is not contradicted in any way either as (B) is.

## PrepTest 57, Section 2 (LR) Continued...

(D) This is supported by the prompt, as taxi drivers set goals that might require them to work long hours to maintain their standards of living.

(E) As in C, this isn't supported but neither s it contradicted.

**24. Question Type: Assumption**

The second sentence is the conclusion. The argument assumes that if someone believes something is expressed in a poem, then that sentiment was intended by the author.

(A) Even if readers didn't tend to disagree, the conclusion could still follow, so this fails the negation test.

(B) Even if poets sometimes intend to express more than one idea, the conclusion could still follow, so this fails the negation test.

(C) Even if people do sometimes agree about this despite disagreeing about intention, the conclusion could still follow, so this fails the negation test.

(D) Even if some people could not discern the all of the author's intentions, the conclusion could still follow, so this fails the negation test.

(E) Correct. This paraphrases our predicted answer. If this was not true, the conclusion could not follow, so this passes the negation test.

**25. Question Type: Most Supported/Must be True**

(A) It could be that nonresidents who were also former residents made such contributions, since they would not have to report them. Therefore, it is not the case that this must be true.

(B) There is no reason to believe that any contributions were registered with the council, as every contributor did not fit in the category or people who need to register. Therefore, this is not supported.

(C) Correct. This is the correct answer. A contribution only needs to be registered if a nonresident who was not a former resident made the contribution (and it was in excess of 100 dollars), but all of the contributors were residents or former residents. Therefore, this must be true.

(D) We do not have any information about what contributions were registered, so this is not supported by the prompt.

(E) All we know is that the law did not require any contributions to be registered; this does not mean that no contributions were registered, so this is not supported.

**26. Question Type: Flaw**

It is not clear that being the subject of satirical plays mean that one was disliked, so this inference is questionable.

(A) The argument only suggests that a large number of plays being satirical mean he was disliked; whether or not a large percentage were about him does not affect this suggestion.

(B) Correct. This paraphrases our predicted answer, suggesting that the inference is questionable.

(C) Evidence is provided – he removed state funding from them.

(D) The argument does not suggest they were successful; in fact, they might not have been, considering the number of plays written about him.

(E) This has no bearing on the argument, so it is not a flaw not to consider it.

# PrepTest 57, Section 3 (LR)

**1. Question Type: Resolve the Paradox**
Those who did best had job, morning class, and limited social life. Those who did worst had no job, morning class, and active social life. It must be explained that those who had a job and no social life did better than those with no job but an active social life.
**(A)** Correct. This would explain why those with jobs but no social lives did well, and it explains why those with no jobs but active social lives did poorly.
(B) This would not explain their good performance, nor would it explain the poor performance of those with no jobs.
(C) This would not explain the differences in performance among those in an early morning class.
(D) This does not mean that those with jobs should do better than those with social lives, so it does not explain the findings.
(E) This would suggest that those with full-time jobs should have done poorly, but they were among the best, so this does not explain the findings.

**2. Question Type: Flaw**
The argument is essentially ad hominem; it suggests that people should not have believed an argument because the person arguing it did not act in the way argued for. (Charges of hypocrisy are classic ad hominem arguments).
(A) This is not why it says the argument was defective, so it is not the answer.
(B) It does not rely on any testimony, so this I not the answer.
**(C)** Correct. This paraphrases our predicted answer and points out the ad hominem character of the argument.
(D) The prompt does not suggest the argument was inadequate but that regardless of how strong the argument was, it should not have been listened to because the person arguing for it did not act in the way argued for.
(E) It does not rely on public opinion to reject the argument, so this is not the answer.

**3. Question Type: Conclusion**
The conclusion is that specialization carries risks. This is supported by each of the statements following it, and it does not support any other statement.
**(A)** Correct. This paraphrases our predicted answer.
(B) and (C) These are used to support the idea that specialization is risky, so neither is the conclusion.
(D) This is used in conjunction with the statements that follow to support the idea that specialization is risky, so this is not the conclusion.
(E) This is merely a premise of the argument, which the conclusion states is risky.

**4. Question Type: Resolve the Paradox**
The paradox is that the group that was told they could win a prize wrote worse stories than the group that believed there was no prize for writing well.
(A) This does not explain why the group would do worse, so it is not the answer.
**(B)** Correct. This suggests that those who were told there was a prize would produce worse writing than those who did not believe there would be a prize.
(C) The topic was given to both groups, so this does not explain one group writing better than the other.
(D) There is no reason the group with no prize would write more realistically.
(E) This would not explain why one group did so much better than the other group.

**5. Question Type: Method of Reasoning**
H responds to G by changing an earlier premise to be more limited – instead of referring to all cars, he changed it to only those cars subjected to normal use.
**(A)** Correct. This paraphrases our predicted answer.
(B) He does not criticize any salespeople, so this cannot be the answer.
(C) He does not suggest that G's evidence is incorrect, so this must not be the answer.
(D) H does not bring up this topic; G does. Therefore, this does not describe H's response.
(E) H does not suggest that any phrase used by G was ambiguous, so this is not the answer.

# PrepTest 57, Section 3 (LR) Continued...

**6. Question Type: Weaken**
- **(A) Correct.** If this were true, then businesses would simply raise prices to make up for the new wages paid, rather than firing employees and raising the unemployment rate. Therefore, this would weaken the argument by suggesting the conclusion was incorrect.
- (B) The argument made no mention of skilled versus non-skilled workers, so this does not weaken the argument.
- (C) The argument does not rely on the fact that increasing unemployment is right or wrong, so this does not weaken the argument.
- (D) The argument only refers to those jobs that are paid minimum wage, so this does not weaken the argument.
- (E) The argument does not depend on the way unemployment has changed in recent years, so this is not the answer.

**7. Question Type: Resolve the Paradox**
The paradox is that all viruses were removed from seawater, but this reduced the population of the plankton inside.
- (A) This would suggest that removing the viruses would allow the plankton to reach their maximum level, so it is not the correct answer.
- (B) This would suggest that removing the viruses would allow the plankton to grow faster, so this cannot be the right answer.
- **(C) Correct.** This would suggest that removing the viruses would lower the nutrient supply of the plankton, reducing the plankton's population.
- (D) This answer is too general; it would only explain the prompt if it stated the bacteria harmed plankton.
- (E) This would not explain the drop in plankton population, so it is not the correct answer.

**8. Question Type: Flaw**
The conclusion is the final sentence. This only follows if it is true that granting the first exception will lead to many other, undeserved exceptions. While this is suggested, no support is given. The correct answer will likely point out this presumption.
- (A) The prompt does not distort any argument, so this is not the correct answer.
- (B) The source of a claim is not discussed, so this is not the correct answer.
- **(C) Correct.** This paraphrases our predicted answer.
- (D) No premises contradict one another, so this is not the correct answer.
- (E) The argument does make this distinction but suggests that granting a deserved exception will lead to undeserved exceptions.

**9. Question Type: Strengthen**
The argument assumes that every ulcer case in each country is treated with a prescription for ulcer medication. The correct answer will likely suggest that this is true.
- (A) This does not affect whether the ulcer rate in the third country is lower than the others, so this is not the answer.
- (B) This would weaken the argument, as it would suggest the assumption in our predicted answer was incorrect.
- (C) This does not affect whether the country has a lower ulcer rate than the two countries mentioned.
- **(D) Correct.** This paraphrases our predicted answer. If this is true, then the conclusion is properly drawn.
- (E) This would suggest that the data from the other two countries could not be trusted, thus weakening the hypothesis that one country has fewer ulcers than the other two.

**10. Question Type: Flaw**
The argument assumes that there is no overlap between the two causal factors listed. The correct answer will likely point out this assumption.
- (A) The argument does provide justification for this idea, so this is not the answer.
- (B) The argument does not mention a correlation, so this cannot be the answer.
- **(C) Correct.** The argument acts as though there is only one cause for each accident; if this were not true, the conclusion would not follow from the premises. Therefore, this expresses the flaw in the argument.

## PrepTest 57, Section 3 (LR) Continued...

(D) The argument does not need to cite its source in order to be logically correct.
(E) The argument does not make any claims about the severity of injuries, so this is not a flaw.

### 11. Question Type: Weaken

The doctor's claim is in the final sentence, and it suggests that the immunity will be permanent, which is not supported by the rest of the prompt. The correct answer will likely suggest that the immunity is not permanent.

**(A)** Correct. This would prove that the immunity was not permanent, so it effectively counters the doctors' claim that the immunity is permanent.
(B) This has no bearing on the doctors' claim about the vaccine made for humans, so it does not counter the argument.
(C) and (D) This has no bearing on the doctors' claim about the E vaccine, so it does not counter it.
(E) This would actually strengthen the argument, as it would suggest that immunity can be permanent. Therefore, it does not counter the claim.

### 12. Question Type: Assumption

The argument assumes that because there is no international police force, there is no effective enforcement mechanism for international law. It is possible that something else could enforce international law. The correct answer will likely point out this assumption.

(A) This is not required, as the argument does not say how many people must obey a law for it to be called effective. Even if some obeyed a law without a mechanism, the law might still not be effective, and international law might not be effective. Therefore, this fails the negation test.
(B) The argument assumes that a police force is necessary, which means it would need to be on the "then" side of the conditional. This is a reversal of the assumption.
(C) Other differences could exist, and international law might still not be effective; therefore, this fails the negation test.
(D) Even if this is not the primary purpose, a police force could still enforce laws and make them effective, and international law could still be categorized as no effective. Therefore, this fails the negation test.
**(E)** Correct. This paraphrases our predicted answer. If something other than an international police force could enforce international law, then the conclusion could not follow from the premises, so this passes the negation test.

### 13. Question Type: Most Supported/Must Be True

(A) The argument only suggests that there is less control in these, which does not imply that they are only good for reflection, so this statement is not supported.
(B) The argument does not suggest these are the only ways but simply that they are ways, so this answer is not supported.
(C) The argument makes no statements about non-representational painting, so this is not supported.
**(D)** Correct. This is supported by the prompt, which suggests that still life paintings are better for self-expression because these are done. This means they must be done in still-life painting and not in the genres it is compared to.
(E) The argument only suggests that this is done more in still-life, not that this is rarely done in other genres, so this is not supported.

### 14. Question Type: Principle

(A) We aren't concerned with foods that are not labeled nonfat.
(B) and (C) Since there do not contain fat, and they usually would, they are allowed to have the nonfat label. Therefore, these do not violate the principle.
**(D)** Correct. Since the food is normally nonfat and people generally know this, it is not allowed to be labeled nonfat. Therefore, this violates the principle.
(E) Since people mistakenly think salsas contain fat, this product can be labeled nonfat.

### 15. Question Type: Parallel Flaw

The argument can be diagrammed as follows:
(reasonable chance) + (extreme symptoms) → acceptable to offer

## PrepTest 57, Section 3 (LR) Continued...

Therefore, -(extreme symptoms) → -(acceptable to offer)

This assumes that part of the sufficient condition (extreme symptoms) is necessary.

(A) This argument suggests that someone who is very knowledgeable about something can lose money at it, so those with less expertise should expect to lose money sometimes as well. This is very different from the reasoning in the prompt, so it is not the answer.

(B) This can be diagrammed as follows:

test-driven → good judge

Therefore, -(good judge) → -(test-driven)

This logic is not flawed, so it cannot be the answer.

(C) Correct. This can be diagrammed as follows:

(born and raised) + (lived abroad) → exceptionally qualified

Therefore, -(born and raised) → -(qualified)

This follows the same flawed pattern of reasoning, assuming a sufficient condition (born and raised) to be necessary. In this case and in the prompt, someone is not the best qualified to make a judgment, so it is assumed that that person is not qualified at all to make a judgment.

(D) Only the conclusion has a conditional, so this cannot be the answer.

(E) There is no conditional reasoning here, so this cannot be the answer.

### 16. Question Type: Principle

(A) The argument only suggests that the fast pace makes us feel like we can't achieve things, not that we actually can't. Therefore, this does not fit the prompt.

(B) The prompt did not suggest anything about advantages or disadvantages, so this does not fit the prompt.

(C) Correct. The prompt lists some technological changes, then suggests how those changes have affected people's feelings. Therefore, this fits the prompt.

(D) The prompt never suggested that it was more difficult, just that people might not know what they want. It gives us no information about if this was the case in the past. Therefore, this does not fit the prompt.

(E) This does not fit the prompt, which suggests that technology can affect people's feelings, not that people's feelings justify technological advance. Therefore, this does not fit the prompt.

### 17. Question Type: Assumption

The argument can be diagrammed as follows:

(buy watch) + (only use correctly) + (stops working next day) → return

(buy watch) + (stops working next day) → return

This makes it clear that the argument must be assuming that the person only used the watch in the way it was intended to be used. The correct answer will likely paraphrase this statement.

(A) The argument is not about when one should sell things but when one should give a refund, so this is not the necessary assumption. Even if this was not true, the conclusion could still follow, so this fails the negation test.

(B) The argument is only about the case when the watch stops on the next day, so this is not the correct answer. Even if one was longer, the conclusion could still follow, so this fails the negation test.

(C) This is very different reasoning from the argument, and even if this was not the case, the conclusion could still follow, so this fails the negation test.

(D) Correct. This paraphrases our predicted answer. If the person did use the watch in some other way, the conclusion could not follow from the premises, so this passes the negation test.

(E) Whether or not the watch was used has no bearing on the argument.

### 18. Question Type: Flaw

The argument assumes that a correlation implies causation. The correct answer will point out this assumption.

(A) The argument states that they used different techniques, so this is not a flaw.

(B) Correct. If this were the case, it would be the type of patient, not the treatment, that led to the better results. So the conclusion would be incorrect.

(C) The argument does not presume this; it only makes statements about those practicing the experimental and traditional therapies. Therefore, this is not the flaw.

(D) It does not ignore this possibility; it suggests that there is something about those with the experimental treatment that makes them more effective. It does not say that this is not the reason. Therefore, this is not

*PrepTest 57, Section 3 (LR) Continued...*

the flaw.
(E) It does not presume this; it could be that the experimental therapists are better at developing rapport, and that is why they are more effective. Therefore, this is not the flaw.

**19. Question Type: Principle**
The conclusion is the last sentence. The reasoning is that extreme freedom will lead to people making poor choices, which could lead them to establish totalitarian political regimes.
(A) This answer is too extreme; the prompt merely says it is possible, not that it is inevitable.
(B) This would justify the premises but not the conclusion, so this principle does not justify the reasoning from premises to conclusion.
(C) The prompt only suggests when a political system should not be supported, so this does not fit the prompt
**(D) Correct.** This answer fits the prompt. It justifies the conclusion on the basis of the premises.
(E) This answer is too general; we only know about those that give people extreme freedom.

**20. Question Type: Parallel Reasoning**
This can be diagrammed as follows:
        moral action → keeping agreement
        keeping agreement → securing mutual benefit
        sometimes keeping agreements are not moral actions
        Therefore, sometimes securing mutual benefits is not a moral action

Sometimes on parallel reasoning questions with lots of words and several steps it can be easier to generalize it:
A → B
B → C
Sometimes B aren't A
Therefore sometimes C not A
Taking this step will let us easily generalize each answer choice and compare against this structure.

(A) This can be diagrammed as follows:
        Calculator → Computer
        Computer → Automated Reasoning
        Sometimes automated reasoning not calculator
        Therefore, sometimes automated reasoning not computer
    Note that the third argument here would be "sometimes C aren't A," different from the prompt.
(B) This can be diagrammed as follows:
        exercise → beneficial
        beneficial → promote health
        sometimes beneficial not exercise
        Therefore, some exercise does not promote health.
    The conclusion is "sometimes A isn't C", the reverse of the conclusion in the prompt.
(C) This can be diagrammed as follows:
        metaphor → comparison
        some comparisons are not surprising
        Therefore, some comparisons not metaphors
    There are only 3 arguments here instead of 4 as in the prompt, so it can't be the correct answer.
(D) This can be diagrammed as follows:
        architecture → design
        design → art
        Sometimes design is not architecture
        Therefore, some art is not design
    The conclusion here is "sometimes C is not B" which is different from the prompt.
**(E) Correct.** This can be diagrammed as follows:
        Book → Text
        Text → Document
        Some texts are not bookstores

### *PrepTest 57, Section 3 (LR) Continued...*

Therefore, some documents not books
This follows the prompt's reasoning exactly, so it is the correct answer.

**21. Question Type: Method of Reasoning**
The sentence in question is used to explain why the first sentence would be true.
(A) This is not a conclusion, as it is a premise meant to explain the statement in the first sentence.
**(B)** Correct. This paraphrases our predicted answer.
(C) This does not support that statement, so this cannot be the answer.
(D) The argument did not claim anything about how difficult it is to adjust to innovations, so this cannot be the correct answer.
(E) It is not an example, so this cannot be the answer.

**22. Question Type: Flaw**
The conclusion is that the belief that candidates will compromise their views is false. However, the last sentence refers to political parties rather than candidates; some candidates could change their views to be more in line with those of a political party.
(A) Whether or not this is the primary function, this could still negate the influence, so this is not the flaw.
**(B)** Correct. The argument fails to consider this, meaning it fails to consider our predicted answer (that candidates change their views to be more in line with political parties).
(C) Whether or not this is true does not affect how the influence of wealth could be negated in countries where elections are not fully subsidized, so this is not a flaw in the argument.
(D) The argument is only about how much pandering to wealthy patrons alters candidates' viewpoints, so whether or not this is true does not affect the argument. Therefore, this is not the flaw.
(E) The argument is not meant to describe all of the possible flaws of a democracy but rather to explore the possibility of a single flaw. Therefore, this is not the flaw.

**23. Question Type: Most Supported/Must be True**
(A) The mitters are easier on cars' finishes, but the finishes are also more easily scratched. We do not know which effect is greater, so this answer is not supported.
(B) Nothing in the prompt suggests why the new car washes were introduced, so this is not supported.
**(C)** Correct. This is supported. Because the new mitters are easier on finishes and older cars had finishes that were less easily scratched, it is much less likely for older cars to get scratched by the new car washes.
(D) The prompt does not suggest that one is more effective than the other, so this is not supported.
(E) The prompt does not suggest how many older and newer cars there are, so this is not supported.

**24. Question Type: Assumption**
The argument assumes that the contracting vessel is a heart because it looks like a heart and act similarly to a heart.
(A) Even if some animals that did not have contracting vessels had hearts, it is still possible that the lancelet has a heart, so this fails the negation test.
(B) Even if no other primitive animals had hearts, lancelets could still have hearts, so this fails the negation test.
**(C)** Correct. This paraphrases our predicted answer. If a vessel with those characteristics was not a heart, the conclusion could not follow, so this passes the negation test.
(D) Even if muscular contraction was not necessary, lancelets could still have hearts, so this fails the negation test.
(E) Even if some animals that had hearts lacked arteries, the conclusion could still follow, so this fails the negation test.

**25. Question Type: Most Supported/Must be True**
(A) This is not supported, as the prompt states it is not as flexible and easy to use.
(B) This is a possible generalization, but we do not have conclusive evidence that this is the case. There is no logical support for this to be inferred from the prompt.
(C) There is no reason to believe that the new software lacks some capability that the old software had, so this is not supported.

*PrepTest 57, Section 3 (LR) Continued...*

(D) The idea behind the new software is that everyone will be able to use it more easily than the old software, so this is not supported.

(E) Correct. This is supported by the prompt. The manager draws an analogy to other companies, where most employees are sticking to the old software despite the flexibility of the new one. The manager therefore concludes that they do not need to switch software. This suggests that many at the manager's company would stick with the old software.

# PrepTest 57, Section 4 (RC)

**Passage 1**

The passage discusses an event that changed the way the FCC approached citizen input into licensing decisions. Initially, it was a closed world (paragraph 1). This changed when a church group challenged a segregationist radio station's license renewal (paragraph 2). A court case, after some procedural ins and outs, revoked the station's license (paragraph 3). This set a precedent for future public involvement in FCC license renewals (paragraph 4).

1. The historical development described above is best encapsulated in choice **(A)**. (C) is wrong because it's not the history of the FCC but the history of citizen group organization that's at issue. (E) is true; it doesn't capture the main point as well for two reasons: first, it doesn't specifically address the church groups, and second it only discusses opening the hearings to the public, whereas the real story here is that the FCC actually has to consider public input (as opposed to simply letting the public into the meeting).

2. The passage is a "that was then, and this is now" sort of thing. So the description of topics now covered at FCC hearings show what has changed as a result of the events described. So that's choice **(A)**.

3. Choice **(D)** is stated directly in the passage, thus is correct. See lines 9-11. Choice (B) is close, but there's no statement in the passage that the advice came from broadcasters. Choice (E) might be appealing, but it overstates the point.

4. This one is best approached by process of elimination. Choices (B), (D), and (E) are phrased categorically, and make claims far beyond anything the author states. Choice (A) is incorrect, because the station's policies had already been drawn to the FCC's attention (by the church) before the church went to court (see lines 18-20). That leaves **(C)**.

5. What did the case do? Predict the answer before you read the choices: The case opened FCC hearings to the public. That's choice **(E)**. Choice (D) is incorrect because it goes too far: The FCC is not required to obtain public input; it is only required to listen if the public decides to weigh in.

**Passage 2**

The structure is as follows:

Paragraph 1. A synthesis between science and humanities is needed—the two disciplines are separated by misunderstandings. (For once, the main idea is actually contained in the first sentence.)

Paragraph 2. Humanists see scientists as mechanical, unfeeling and cold.

Paragraph 3. Scientists see humanists as flaky and undisciplined.

Paragraph 4. Clearly, each discipline has something to teach the other, since both fields are really only interested in better understanding our world. Science can be tempered by things other than data, and humanities can benefit from greater rigor. "Scientific humanism" is therefore advocated.

The main idea is that science and the humanities should reconcile their differences and combine forces in some way.

6. **(E)** restates our prediction best. None of the other choices really get close.

7. The author claims that humanists incorrectly see scientists as exclusively rational and unfeeling. That point of view is given by choice **(C)**.

8. The author wants humanists to think like scientists, and vice versa. So you're not looking at (B), (C), or (E). Choice (A) is wrong because it's an incorrect description of scientific humanism. Choice (D)—the idea that

## PrepTest 57, Section 4 (RC) Continued...

humanities have benefited when they've adopted scientific methods—is in line with the author's point of view.

9. The separation is caused by misunderstanding; that's choice **(B)**, which is correct. Choices (D) and (E) are mentioned within the passage, but not as the primary cause of the separation.

10. What's the last paragraph doing? It's stating that science and the humanities should view each other as having valuable things to teach. In other words, it's an alternative to the misconceptions listed in the previous two paragraphs. So that's choice **(D)**. Choice (B) is problematic, because the author disagrees with the points of view in paragraphs 2 and 3.

11. The author wants humanists and scientists to adopt each other's methods and stances as a means of enriching their studies. So he would want a humanist to be more scientific (and vice versa). So that's choice **(C)**.

12. Read the context given (start at line 25 and keep going to line 30 or so). Scientists, according to the author, see humanists as being insufficiently grounded in practicalities. That's choice **(B)**. Out of context, the phrase might seem to suggest (E), but the context of the passage does not accuse scientists of believing that humanists are illogical.

**Passage 3, Comparative reading**

Passage A states that Cather was influenced by Turgenev, according to Wilson. How? Choice of details that show emotions, rather than overloading with details or directly describing emotions. Turgenev anticipated Cather, who called the psychological element "the thing not named." Importance of mood also mentioned.

Passage B: Cather stated that her work was narrative rather than a novel. This anticipated French critics who created narratology. This rejected the realistic novel, focusing instead on narrative. Critics who expect a novel miss the point of Cather's work, which relies on the bold, simple, and stylized.

Passage B has a rather different explanation of Cather's work than Passage A does. They don't explicitly agree on much, but they also don't have points of explicit disagreement.

13. So where's that point of agreement here? It's in choice **(E)**. Author A states that Cather used psychology to pick telling details. Author B states that she chose simple and stylized details. (E) suggests how those two points can easily be reconciled.

14. Which of these choices is implied in Passage B? Well, not (A), since the author does not actually state that the narratologists had read Cather, much less singled her out as a good example. Not choice (D), which is straight out of Passage A but is missing in Passage B. Not choice (B), which is nowhere to be found in either passage. And not choice (E), since we don't have any statements about "most" critics. We're left with choice **(C)**, which is implied in lines 32-34.

15. According to both authors, Cather carefully chooses a few external details to show (rather than tell) about her characters. That's like choice **(C)**.

16. The main point of Passage B is that Cather's works are best thought about as narratives, not as traditional novels. That's choice **(A)**. It's true that choice (B) gives something that's contained in the passage. But it's used as just support for the main idea.

17. We're looking for a statement supported by both passages. Choice **(A)** isn't supported at all—stream-of-consciousness isn't mentioned in either passage. (B) and (C) are only in the second passage. (D) is only in the first passage. So we're left with choice (E). Note that "impressionistic" is a bit of an inference from both passages, but it's not a real big inference.

18. Once again, you're looking for a point of agreement between both passages. One describes how Cather essentially uses external details to limn a character's psychology. The other describes Cather as essentially

## PrepTest 57, Section 4 (RC) Continued...

interested in narrative. Neither type of writing would have any room for direct description of characters' thoughts. So that's **(E)**.

19. Both passages describe Cather's techniques. That's choice **(B)**.

**Passage 4**

Paragraph 1 describes fractals, and describes how the Koch curve (a significant example) is constructed.

Paragraph 2. Self-similarity is built into fractals, in theory; but in practice, this cannot be actually drawn or displayed. However, the attraction is the complex patterns that can be constructed from simple processes.

Paragraph 3. Fractal geometers have been attracted by the new language for describing complex forms. Other mathematicians have reservations about the lack of rigor or success in proving new theorems.

The main idea should reflect that fractal geometry is an exciting new theory, but according to Paragraph 3 traditional mathematicians have doubts as to its usefulness.

20. The answer is **(B)**, which captures both the promise of fractal geometry and its critics. Each of the other answers discusses the promise of fractals but doesn't mention the anti-fractal crowd.

21. You're directed to define a specific passage in context. So read the context. It says that the rules are fully explicit; in context, that means "spelled out." This is best expressed by choice **(C)**.

22. The definition of self-similarity is given in paragraph 1 (lines 4-8). It's where at smaller scale, a part of the object looks the same as the object as a whole. The only choice that isn't like this is choice **(D)**.

23. You should have noted that the Koch curve was an example. Of what? Not a natural form, so that rules out choice B. You're left with choice **(D)** – illustrating the concept of self-similarity.

24. You're asked to find something that is "presented" (i.e., stated directly) in the passage. Take a look at **(E)**, which is directly stated in lines 35-36. The other choices either require an inference from the passage, or are not supported at all.

25. You need to have understood how the Koch curve is constructed: one-third of the line is removed and replaced with a triangle. The one choice that's inconsistent with that process is **(A)**: no matter how long the starting line, there will always be one protrusion per stage of the construction.

26. Read the context. In the same sentence you're referred to, the potential for fractals to describe clouds is discussed. That's a natural form. Choice **(E)** is correct.

27. When asked for a statement that is best supported by a passage, you're looking for something either directly stated, or one that can be very easily inferred. In this case, that's choice **(D)**. We know that fractals have applications (see lines 43-47). We know that they don't have precise definitions (see line 3). So choice **(D)** must be true.

# PrepTest 58
## PrepTest 58, Section 1 (LR)

**1. Question Type: Assumption**
The conclusion is the last sentence. This only follows from the premises if the water supply is not increased enough to meet the increasing need. The correct answer will likely paraphrase this.
(A) The wasteful use of other resources and the way humans would react to restrictions do not affect the argument, so this is not the answer.
(B) What has happened in recent years has no bearing on whether we will need restrictions in the future.
(C) Correct. This paraphrases our predicted answer. If the freshwater supply did increase, then we would not need to have restrictions, so this passes the negation test.
(D) Even if some attempts did have appreciable effects, it is possible that the effect will not be enough, so this conclusion could still be true. This fails the negation test.
(E) How previous water conservation attempts went has no bearing on the argument.

**2. Question Type: Principle**
The best way to achieve something is by thinking about something else, and this is because the more one tries to achieve the first thing, the less likely s/he is to do so.
(A) This does not follow the same principle because happiness is not the same thing as wealth and fame.
(B) and (C) These are incorrect because of the reasoning in the second half of each answer, which does not follow the same principle as in the prompt.
(D) Correct. This follows each piece of the prompt, so it follows the same principle.
(E) This does not follow the same principle because turning to those with greater hardship is different from thinking about something else entirely.

**3. Question Type: Strengthen**
(A) What happened with other departments has no bearing on whether this department is doing the same job but spending more money.
(B) Even if it has reduced its spending on overtime pay, it still has a much larger budget, so it is still possible that the department is doing the same job but spending more money.
(C) It does not matter what happened in some years; the budget did increase 5-fold, and it is possible that the department does the same job spending more money now.
(D) If they were adjusted for inflation, then the 5-fold increase is completely accurate, which would weaken the argument.
(E) Correct. This would mean that the department now does more stuff, so it cannot be doing the same job for more money; it has increased duties.

**4. Question Type: Principle**
(A) Whether it is more precise or not does not affect whether the jury makes the same decision as the judge, so this is not illustrated.
(B) This would mean that the judge should have the same influence in both cases, which would not explain the difference between the two groups.
(C) If it was not an effective means, how could it be that the judge communicated with jury members through nonverbal communication?
(D) Real trials were not mentioned, so this cannot have been illustrated by the prompt.
(E) Correct. When the judge instructed two different ways, the verdicts were different between the groups, so this is illustrated by the prompt.

**5. Question Type: Weaken**
(A) Correct. This would mean that doctors would give less effective treatments to people with serious illnesses, which would prove harmful to them, violating the doctor's principle. Therefore, this weakens the argument.
(B) How they are marketed does not affect the argument, so this is not the answer.
(C) What things patients have allergic reactions to does not affect the argument, so this is not the answer.
(D) What they are driven by has no bearing on the argument, so this is not the argument.

# PrepTest 58, Section 1 (LR) Continued...

(E) It does not matter where the benefits came from but that the benefits were there.

### 6. Question Type: Method of Reasoning
The argument draws an analogy to suggest that a set of rights can and should be limited in some cases.
**(A)** Correct. This paraphrases our predicted answer.
(B) The argument does not say anything about observed facts, so this is not the answer.
(C) No experimental results were given, so this is not the answer.
(D) The argument does not describe any particular instance, so this cannot be its method of reasoning.
(E) No empirical generalization is mentioned, so this cannot be the answer.

### 7. Question Type: Parallel Flaw
The conclusion is that negative advertising actually benefits its targets. The argument is flawed by a correlation/causation problem. The targets of negative advertising win elections, but there's no reason to believe this is because they are the targets of negative advertising.
(A) This reasoning is not parallel because achieving better health is different from ending up winning an election.
**(B)** Correct. This argument has a similar correlation/causation problem.
(C) This argument is valid because it makes a much more modest causal claim – that studying in fact contributes to academic achievement. (There's an element of common-sense in this question; we know that studying contributes to academic success).
(D) This reasoning is logically sound, so it cannot be the right answer.
(E) The prompt does not include any idea of things being acceptable, so this is not the correct answer.

### 8. Question Type: Resolve the Paradox EXCEPT
People from S live farther away from their workplaces, but there are fewer bus routes in S. Four of the answers will explain this, and the correct answer will not.
(A) This would explain the difference because only one route would be needed for ¾ of the population.
(B) This would explain the difference because if there were more cars, there would be less of a need for public transit.
(C) This would explain the difference, as the railways would make up for the bus routes.
(D) This would explain the difference because fewer bus routes would be needed.
**(E)** Correct. This would not explain the difference. In fact, this could suggest that there should be more bus routes in S.

### 9. Question Type: Flaw
The conclusion is that N5 is of no use to people who want to reduce their fat and calorie intakes.
(A) and (B) These do not affect the conclusion or the reasoning, so they are not the correct answer.
(C) and (D) These do not apply, as the argument was only about those who were using N5 because of its fewer calories.
**(E)** Correct. This is a flaw in the argument. Since the people were concerned with lowering both fat and caloric intake, lowering one of these means that N5 would have some use for them, even if it did not help them achieve all of what they wanted.

### 10. Question Type: Most Supported/Must be True
(A) The argument does not say these are not valuable but that they are not superb.
**(B)** Correct. The beneficial consequences were the creation of superb recordings and compactness in subsequent live playing.
(C) This answer is too extreme; the always superior is not supported by the prompt.
(D) The prompt does not suggest the following generation is of lower overall quality, just that it was not as short as that of early bebop.
(E) This takes a sufficient condition from the prompt (difficult recording conditions) and makes it a necessary one. Therefore, this is not supported by the prompt.

### 11. Question Type: Flaw
There's a clear flaw here – just because there are counter-examples doesn't mean that there are definitively no

causal factors – only that they are not absolute.
- (A) Correct. This would mean that those who had a damaged chromosome and did not get schizophrenia could have had a different kind of damage from those who had damage and developed the condition.
- (B) The argument does not presume that this is the only cause, so this cannot be the answer.
- (C) There is no reason to believe that the sample is unrepresentative, so this is not the flaw.
- (D) The argument does not suggest there is any cause or effect.
- (E) The argument decides that correlation did not imply causation, so this cannot be the answer.

### 12. Question Type: Assumption
The conclusion is that the edifice qualifies as art.
- (A) Even if some things qualified as art without causing debate among experts, the edifice could still be art, so this fails the negation test.
- (B) This would not allow the conclusion to be drawn, as it would suggest that no expert could be certain that the edifice was art.
- (C) The argument does not suggest that it should not be opposed, so this cannot be the assumption.
- (D) Correct. If objects that fulfilled the purpose of art did not qualify as art, then the conclusion could not follow.
- (E) The argument makes no claim about whether the commission should purchase it or not, so this cannot be the assumption.

### 13. Question Type: Conclusion
The conclusion is the second sentence. The first and third are both premises supporting this sentence.
- (A) This is a premise, as is suggested by the phrase "it is a given that."
- (B) Correct. This paraphrases the second sentence, so it is the answer.
- (C) This is used to support the second sentence, as evidenced by the word "for" at the beginning of the sentence.
- (D) This is a reversal of the second sentence, so this is not the conclusion.
- (E) The passage is about instilling curiosity in others, so this is not the conclusion.

### 14. Question Type: Assumption
The conclusion is the final half of the last sentence. This is only true if theater managers think films attractive to younger audiences are more likely to be profitable.
- (A) While this would support the argument, it does not make it logically sound because we do not know if it is less enough that movies will not be profitable.
- (B) The conclusion could still follow if they often did appeal to older audiences as well, so this fails the negation test.
- (C) Since the managers only care about overall profit, where it came from does not affect the argument and cannot be the assumption.
- (D) Correct. This paraphrases our predicted answer. If theater managers did not believe this, the conclusion would not follow.
- (E) Almost never is too extreme here; the adult films only need to be less likely to generate a profit than the younger films.

### 15. Question Type: Most Supported/Must be True
- (A) We only know that most research is, not most advances.
- (B) This is not supported, as we only know that most research is funded by the government, not how often government research produces breakthroughs.
- (C) This is not supported, as we do not know how many of the advances are made by research funded from each group.
- (D) Correct. If there is no funding except from these groups, and there are no ethical dilemmas without funding, then there can only be an ethical dilemma if one of these groups funded it. This means that if there was no funding from these groups, there could not be an ethical dilemma.
- (E) It will only give rise to dilemmas if advances are made, and we do not know if advances will continue to be made.

## PrepTest 58, Section 1 (LR) Continued...

**16. Question Type: Assumption**
The conclusion is the final sentence. This only follows if changing a core corporate philosophy requires becoming a different corporation.
(A) This is too extreme; the argument only suggests that some businesses will have to adapt by changing their core philosophies. This does not suggest that all must in order to survive.
(B) Becoming less efficient is not the same as not being efficient anymore, so this would not make the conclusion properly drawn.
(C) Even if some corporations have the same corporate philosophy, when one changes its core philosophy, it could be becoming a new corporation.
(D) It is suggested that some businesses must change their core philosophies to continue to exist, so this cannot be the answer.
(E) Correct. This paraphrases our predicted answer. If this were not the case, the conclusion could not follow.

**17. Question Type: Resolve the Paradox**
A survey ten years ago showed that people were happy with their living conditions, even though they were below the national average. A survey this year found that people were unhappy with their living conditions, even though they are now at the national average.
(A) How those in adjacent areas value living conditions does not have an effect on those in L, so this does not explain the change in L residents' feelings.
(B) Correct. This would mean that even though L's living conditions were now the national average, the conditions would be below where they were 10 years ago, which would explain their change in feelings. There is a distinction between relative improvement and actual improvement. (This is a common distinction on the LSAT).
(C) Optimal living conditions does not explain anything about this situation.
(D) What needs to be explained is why the residents are unhappy, despite going from below national average to at the national average. This does not explain that in any way.
(E) This does not explain why they would be unhappy now, so this is not the answer.

**18. Question Type: Flaw**
The conclusion here is the last sentence. The argument assumes that having reliable statistics means the airline will be safe; it is possible that an airline that does not have enough data yet is safer than one that has enough data. The correct answer will likely mention this.
(A) The total number is not what matters but the proportion, so this is not the flaw.
(B) Some airlines do have enough data, so this is not the answer.
(C) Correct. This paraphrases our predicted answer. It points out the reason the conclusion does not follow from its premises, thus exposing the argument's vulnerability.
(D) This is a reversal of the assumption, so it is not the correct answer.
(E) The argument is about how safe an airline is; it does not suggest that a safe airline will have no accidents whatsoever, so this is not the correct answer.

**19. Question Type: Assumption**
The conclusion is the last sentence. This only follows if lowering taxes will cause people to spend more. The correct answer will likely paraphrase this.
(A) Even if this did not cause prices to decrease, the conclusion could still follow, so this fails the negation test.
(B) Even if increasing spending did not cause an increase in income, the conclusion could still follow, so this fails the negation test.
(C) Even if consumer wages did not decline when income taxes were not lowered, the conclusion could still be true, so this fails the negation test.
(D) Correct. This paraphrases our predicted answer. If consumers were not less reluctant, the conclusion could not follow.
(E) Government spending has nothing to do with the argument, so this cannot be the assumption.

**20. Question Type: Most Supported/Must be True**
(A) This is not true, as those in group A had increased risk of heart disease.
(B) The argument does not compare the cholesterol levels of the two groups, so this is not supported by the

prompt.
(C) The prompt does not include any information about whether people changed anything else in their habits or not, so this is not supported.
(D) The only group that switched lipid profiles, the A group, had no reduction in cholesterol. Therefore, a reduction in cholesterol could not have been responsible for switching.
(E) Correct. This is true of the type A group that switched to type B, which indicates higher risk of heart disease.

### 21. Question Type: Principle

The principle is that something (exploiting depraved tastes for financial gain) can be allowed but not be morally acceptable.
(A) The principle here would be that freedom should not be limited except when people think someone is being depraved. This is quite different from the principle in the prompt.
(B) The prompt says nothing about having the freedom to refrain from anything, and this answer fails to include anything about whether something is right or wrong. Therefore, this does not follow the same principle.
(C) Correct. The principle here is that something (publishing books that pander to depraved tastes) is allowed but not necessarily morally right. This is just like the principle in the prompt, so this is the answer.
(D) The principle in the prompt does not suggest that anything should be limited by the government, so this is not the answer.
(E) The argument does not suggest anything about when someone should or should not criticize others, so this does not follow the same principle.

### 22. Question Type: Assumption

The conclusion is the final sentence. Note that the conclusion is the first mention of the idea of "deference." Is deference the same as "valuing advice?" Not necessarily. We need to link the two.
(A) This is implied by the prompt, meaning that it is essentially repeating a stated premise.
(B) It does not matter how much the experience is practical but how much the youth believes it is practical.
(C) Correct. This matches our prediction.
(D) It does not matter how relevant the experience is but how much the youth believes it is relevant.
(E) It does not matter how much the experience is practical but how much the youth believes it is practical.

### 23. Question Type: Principle

The principle is that we should act to keep a unique way of life from vanishing by imposing tariffs.
(A) The argument is not about economic interest but attempting to keep a way of life.
(B) The argument suggests that producers in other countries should be hindered, so this cannot be the answer.
(C) Correct. This would explain the desire to lower economic efficiency (raising a tariff so less efficient farmers can stay around) for a social reason (keeping a way of life around).
(D) It is not clear that this is in the interest of the citizens, so this is not the answer.
(E) In this case, the government would be creating less economic efficiency, so this cannot be the answer.

### 24. Question Type: Weaken

The conclusion is that the bear population in the valley will increase if the road is kept closed. This only follows if the population in the valley itself has actually increased over the past eight years; it is possible that the bears have simply migrated to the Preserve. The correct answer will likely suggest that this assumption is incorrect.
(A) Since we do not know where the migration is from, it is possible that the population in the valley has increased as well, which would mean the conclusion was still likely. Therefore, this does not weaken the argument effectively.
(B) This would strengthen the argument, as it would suggest that some of the population increase must have come from other things. This would mean the conclusion was still likely.
(C) If they migrated from outside of the valley, then they increased the population in the valley. Therefore, this would strengthen the argument.
(D) Since we don't know how much it has decreased, this does not imply that the valley's population as a whole has not been increasing.
(E) Correct. This paraphrases our predicted answer. It suggests that the increase in the preserve has not meant

## PrepTest 58, Section 1 (LR) Continued...

an increase throughout the valley, meaning there is no reason to believe the conclusion. Therefore, this weakens the argument effectively.

**25. Question Type: Assumption**

The conclusion is the final sentence. This only follows if all medium to expensive wigs have hand-made foundations, as this would imply human hair and then dry-cleaning.

(A) Correct. This paraphrases our predicted answer. If this were not true, the conclusion would not follow, so this passes the negation test.
(B) This is a reversal of the correct answer, and the usage of more expensive rather than listing a price range is also a problem.
(C) The use of "any" makes this answer too extreme. Meanwhile, even if this were not true, the conclusion could still be true, so this fails the negation test.
(D) This is a reversal of the correct answer.
(E) Even if some that were dry-cleaned did not have handmade foundations, made-to-measure wigs could need to be dry-cleaned. Therefore, this fails the negation test.

**26. Question Type: Method of Reasoning**

The conclusion is the final sentence. The argument suggests that an argument is incorrect (that animals don't have rights) because it is based on a premise (only human beings are capable of obeying moral rules) that has been proven incorrect by an example (wolves, foxes and dogs).

(A) Correct. This paraphrases our predicted answer.
(B) The argument does not say anything about all animals, so this is incorrect.
(C) The argument does not cast doubt on this principle; rather, it suggests that the premise used in conjunction with that principle is false.
(D) No logical contradiction is mentioned, so this is not the correct answer.
(E) The argument is attempting to broaden morality, so this cannot be the answer.

# PrepTest 58, Section 2 (RC)

**Passage 1**

The first sentence begins with "traditional sources of evidence." The word "traditional" will usually signal that we're going to read about something non-traditional in contrast. Next sentence: "Those investigating the crafts practiced by women in ancient times, however, often derive little information from these sources." This is particularly true of textile production. Further down: "Yet despite these obstacles," we can learn about ancient textiles. So we've got a complex picture: there are obstacles to analysis of ancient textiles, but we can still learn a lot.

Paragraph 2. Technological analysis has helped. Several examples of this are given in lines 23 through 26. Also, the philosophical shift to preserving everything has helped.

Paragraph 3. Another thing that's helped is recreating the process of making cloth.

The point here is that there are obstacles to learning about textiles, but we can still learn a lot, due to various advances in archaeology.

1. Looking at that prediction, the best answer is **(B)**—the only one that preserves both the focus on textiles and the changes in archaeology that have made the advances possible. (A) is too broad—it discusses archaeology in general. (C) is too narrow: it discusses production techniques only. (B) is the Goldilocks choice – just right.

2. Questions about the author's attitude can often be narrowed by eliminating the choices that are negative if the piece was positive, or vice versa. So cross (A) through (C) off the list right away. As between (D) and (E): is the author optimistic, or satisfied? You might say "optimistic," but you'd better read the rest of the choice: he's not interested in recruiting archaeologists but in learning about ancient textiles. So choice **(E)** is correct.

3. The example given in the paragraph about recreating ancient techniques (paragraph 3) is the bit about the two statues of Athena (lines 50-51 ff.). That's choice **(E)**.

4. We're referred to line 1—read that line, and the rest of the sentence. "Traditional sources" are archaeological remains and ancient texts. Which of the choices is neither of those? Choice **(D)** is.

5. The passage isn't argumentative—it's merely descriptive. So go through the choices and see which matches. Is the passage a defense? No. A recommendation? Nope. A rejection? No again. A summary, or an account? Maybe. Read those two more closely. It's not a summary of hypotheses, so choice E is wrong. That leaves choice **(C)**.

6. You're asked which item was an element "in the transformation of archaeology." Well, how did archaeology change, according to the passage? It started using technology, and it stopped throwing things away. Choice **(E)** mentions one of those two changes, so is correct.

7. Choice **(A)** is correct. The issue of textiles is particularly difficult—the first paragraph describes that.

**Passage 2**

The first paragraph describes Emeagwali's approach to computer design, based on natural principles. He achieved breakthroughs in parallel systems, which are described.

Paragraph 2 describes the complexity of the problem of describing the movement of oil; it also discusses Emeagwali's solution, and its origin in Emeagwali's observation of trees.

The third paragraph describes a similar breakthrough, in which the design was like a honeycomb.

What's the point? Emeagwali uses natural inspiration to develop breakthroughs in computer architecture.

## PrepTest 58, Section 2 (RC) Continued...

8. The main idea is best expressed in choice **(D)**. The other choices miss the mark, largely by being far more abstract than the passage is.

9. Emeagwali's "breakthrough" was in parallel computer systems, which he used to model oil fields. "Breakthrough" makes you the first person to do something. So that's choice **(C)**.

10. Emeagwali, according to the passage, believes that natural forms can inspire computer design. That might make choice (C) tempting. But choice (C) says "most computer designs" will be that way, which overstates the case. The right answer is choice **(A)**, which essentially says the same thing, but uses "some" rather than "most."

11. Look at the sentences referred to. They're describing the complexities inherent in modeling oil fields. The only close choice is **(B)**. (It says, immediately earlier in the passage, that supercomputers were unable to handle this type of complexity.)

12. The prediction referred to states that natural models will become more common in computer architecture. Choice **(A)**—a recent awareness of natural principles by computer scientists—would make that likely.

13. Choice **(E)** is suggested by lines 32-35. People had thought of it (eliminating choice (B)), but hadn't been able to find a way to get the computers not to interfere with each other.

**Passage 3**

The first sentence starts "Proponents of the tangible object theory...." We can expect the opponents to weigh in sooner or later. Watch for that—in this case, the opposing viewpoint doesn't come in until the very end.

The first paragraph describes the tangible-object theory of copyright.

The second paragraph highlights an advantage of that point of view: like with any other object, "if the owner transfers ownership of an object, the full component of rights is not necessarily transferred."

The third paragraph gives two objections to tangible-object understandings of copyright law—first, there isn't always a tangible object, and second, "more importantly," the creator of the object is not always the creator of the work.

So the structure is, we've introduced a concept, we've explained its advantages, and we've shown how it's inadequate. Your main idea should encompass that structure—especially that little flip at the end.

14. As noted, choice **(B)** is what you're looking for—the main idea is that tangible object theory is inadequate.

15. Choice **(A)** is correct. Look at lines 3-6.

16. "Directly answers" means the passage will contain the answer fairly literally—no inferences necessary. The one choice in that category is **(B)**. See the sentence that begins at line 24.

17. One of the two big flaws with tangible-object theory is that the creator of the object is not always the creator of the work. Tangible-object theory vests IP rights in the creator of the object (lines 7-11). In this case, that's the engineer. Choice **(A)**.

18. Choice **(E)** is correct; see lines 36-39. Notice that choice (D) is mentioned in the passage, but it's ascribed to the opponents of tangible object theory.

19. Choice **(C)** is correct; See lines 11-13, which appear in the description of tangible-object theory. The other choices are an inference too far—they rely on assumptions the passage doesn't make.

20. The author finds tangible-object theory inadequate, so we're looking for a choice that expresses that. That's

## PrepTest 58, Section 2 (RC) Continued...

choice **(D)** (which fixes the "the creator of the idea may not be the creator of the object" problem).

**Passage 4, Comparative reading**

Passage A: In music, we like at least a certain amount of complexity to arouse our curiosity, but not too much. That's true of how we see language, too—we need structure, but not chaos. If music is like this, that might explain why soothing music tends to be more continuous and rhythmical: sudden sounds = danger.

Passage B: Certain patterns in music create expectations that others will follow. When they don't immediately follow, that creates tension, whose resolution allows us to relax. This factor can be used to create "musical emotions"—withhold the release, and create negative emotions. Resolve all the patterns, and create positive emotions. In general, we need a certain level of this unpleasant emotion (but not too much) in our music to keep it interesting.

21. Both passages discuss complexity (choice **(E)**) as creating a good musical experience. (Line 1; line 61).

22. What question is addressed by both passages? Basically, both passages ask what it is about music that makes us like it. That's best expressed by choice **(C)**.

23. The first paragraph expresses our preference for coherence. So does choice **(B)**.

24. Passage B is about how music creates "musical emotion." Choice **(A)** is correct. Note that choice (C) is contained within the passage, but is not the main idea. While the passage does contain a statement about experienced listeners, it's a statement nothing like choice (B), so that choice is also incorrect.

25. Remember what Passage A said about how music relaxes? By being continuous and rhythmical (see the first sentence of paragraph 3). What would undermine this? Either an irregular sound that's also relaxing, or a continuous sound that's also non-relaxing. The latter of these is reflected in choice **(C)**.

26. Both passages are about how music affects us emotionally. So that leaves it as between choice (A) and (B). But only the first passage was remotely biological; both passages discussed psychology. Choice **(B)** is correct.

27. **(D)** is correct—both passages state that unpredicted elements in music are not relaxing (see 21-22; 35-37). Why isn't (A) correct? In #21 we said that both passages talked about complexity. But the relationship between complexity and enjoyability is...complex. Too much complexity is also bad (lines 5-6; line 54-56).

# PrepTest 58, Section 3, Game 1

This is an advanced linear game. We're putting 6 monuments in 5 spaces, so we know there will be multiples. It seems like there is actually quite a bit of variability until we get to Rule 4, which significantly limits the options.

F G H L M S* = 6

```
                    H/   H/
___  ___  ___  ___  ___
 1    2    3    4    5
                ~M   ~M
```

## Rules

#1: G < L < F
#2: H no earlier than 4 (insert into diagram)
#3: M earlier than 4 (insert into diagram)
#4: 2 in Year 1, no other year with >1 (insert into diagram)

Discussion: There's no need to limit your diagram "601" – 1 is fine. Make sure to read Rule 4 carefully. There are 6 monuments, each of which go once. There are 5 spaces; in only 1 of those spaces are there 2 monuments. That means that Year 1 has 2 spaces in our diagram, and the rest have 1. It's worth your time to put in the exclusion rules based on Rule 1. Note that S is a floater, unbound by any rule. Make sure to consider what can go first and last. First is especially valuable here since there are 2 spaces. We know L, F, and H can't go first, which leaves us just G, M, and S to fill Year 1.

```
G/M/S
G/M/S              H/   H/
___   ___  ___  ___  ___
 1     2    3    4    5
~L    ~F        ~M   ~M
~F              ~G   ~L
~H                   ~G
```

We can go one space further with L as well. L can't go first or last. We can also deduce that it can't go 4th; if it did, F and H would both have to go behind it which won't work. So L can only go 2 or 3.

```
G/M/S
G/M/S  L/   L/   H/   H/
___   ___  ___  ___  ___
 1     2    3    4    5
~L    ~F        ~M   ~M
~F              ~G   ~L
                     ~G
```

---

1. List question..
   a) Violates Rule 4
   b) Violates Rule 2
   c) Violates Rule 1
   d) Violates Rule 3
   e) **Correct**

2. On questions that ask about the latest a certain variable can go, start with the latest and work backwards to eliminate. We know L can't go last because F must go after. Can it go 5th? No; not only must F go after L, but H must also go 4 or 5. So L can't go 5 because H and L would both have to go after. Can L go 4? Work it out on a quick diagram:

```
        S
G   M   L   F   H
1   2   3   4   5
```

**c) Correct.**

3. The most restricted part of the game is that first space; only 3 variables can go in the two spaces of Year 1. Start, then, by working on answer choices with G, M, or S. Put each option into the diagram, and as soon as you run into uncertainty or variability, you can eliminate that answer.

a) F in 3 forces L into 2 and G into 1, as per Rule 1. M would also have to go first, because it must go before 4 and there aren't other spaces left. However, H/S can go 4/5 interchangeably.
b) G in 2 forces M and S into 1. L would then have to go 3rd, but we're not sure how H and F are organized.
c) We run into trouble with S, which can go in any space here (except 5).
d) M in 2 forces G and S into 1, but we'll still run into trouble with H/S in 4/5.
e) **Correct.** S in 4 forces H into 5. G and M would be 1, with L in 2 and F in 3. We know the arrangement exactly.

4. Since S can go anywhere, we can quickly eliminate b) and d). We've also know that M and S can be in 1, so we can eliminate E. We have a) and c) to consider.

a) **Correct.** M must go 1, 2, or 3 (Rule 3). F must have at least 2 years before it (Rule 1), so the very earliest it could go is year 3, in which case F would have to go earlier than 3.
c) F could go last, with H in 4.

5. This is an unusual question as it presents a conclusion (that L must be in 2) and asks you to find the evidence that leads to it. You'll need to eliminate here. The WRONG answers here allow the possibility that L could be elsewhere than 2.

Think this through. Your goal is total certainly about L's position. What's the most uncertain part of the game? S! It might help to start with S as you scan the choices.
a) If F is in 5, H must be in 6. However, it's not clear where to go from here as S, L, or M could all be in 2 in various configurations.
b) If G was in 1, M could be with it and either L or S could be in 2.
c) If H were 4, F could be 5. Either L, S, or M could be 2.
d) With M in first, G could also be first; S/L could both be 2.
e) **Correct.** With S in 3, G and M must be in 1. F/H must go 4/5, so L would indeed have to be in 2.

6. Make sure to combine this new local rule (L < M) with your old sequencing rule (actually do this on your paper).

```
        ┌─→M
G < L < F
```

M going late in the order forces G and S to go first.
a) With G and S first, we'd put L 2nd so F can go in 3. But that forces M in to 4 or 5, violating Rule 3.
b) G must be first.
c) **Correct.** G S, L, M, F, H
d) This leaves 2 empty as F, M, and H all have to go after L if it were in 3.
e) S must be first.

# PrepTest 58, Section 3, Game 2

This is an in-out grouping game with a ton of conditionals. This game type has become less popular, but if you examine older LSATs you will see many of this type of game. It tests your ability to quickly evaluate many conditional rules methodically as you work through the problems.

F L M R S T V = 7

|  In  |  Out  |
|------|-------|
| (volunteers) | (Doesn't volunteer) |

Rules
#1: R → M
#2: M → T
#3: ~S → V
#4: ~R → L
#4: T → ~F and ~V

Contrapositives
~M → ~R
~T → ~M
~V → S
~L → R
F or V → ~T

Discussion: If you do not list out your contrapositives here, you will be totally lost. Make sure to write them out clearly.

Some students like combining conditional rules (e.g. R → M → T), but we have found that doing so can take more time than it's worth; every time you see R, you'll make that connection very quickly anyway. It you prefer to explicitly combine rules, you certainly can do so, and it looks like this:

$$R \to M \to T \to \begin{matrix}\sim F \\ \text{and} \\ \sim V\end{matrix} \to S$$

You want to be especially aware of rules where a negative leads to a positive. For instance, Rule 3 tells us that if we don't have S, we have V, and if we don't have V we have S. So we must either have S, V, or both. Rule 4 is similar. It can be helpful to list these as placeholders in your diagram:

**In　Out**

S/V / both
R/L / both

7. List question..
a) Violates Rule 4 (R is out, so L must be in)
b) Violates Rule 2
c) **Correct**
d) Violates Rule 1
e) Violates Rule 5

8. On this and similar questions, you must put the new information in, go through each rule and find the inferences based on that info, then repeat to find the inferences from your inferences.

Here are the steps in detail; these are the same steps for nearly all questions in in-out conditional grouping games.

Step 1: We are given V.
Rule 2)

| In | Out |
|---|---|
| V | |

Step 2: from V we know ~T (contrapositive of Rule 5).

| In | Out |
|---|---|
| V | ~T |

Step 3: From ~T we get ~M (contrapositive of Rule 1)

| In | Out |
|---|---|
| V | ~T |
| | ~M |

Step 4: from ~M we get ~R (contrapositive of Rule 1)

| In | Out |
|---|---|
| V | ~T |
| | ~M |
| | ~R |

Step 5: from ~R we get L (Rule 4)

| In | Out |
|---|---|
| V | ~T |
| L | ~M |
| | ~R |

From here, we have no more moves; knowing L doesn't help us link up to any more rules. We now have a complete list of everything that must be true given V.

a) We know R is out.
b) **Correct.**
c) M is out.
d) T is out.
e) T is out.

9. Given ~T we know ~M. ~M gives us ~R. ~R gives us L. Also, remember our 2 placeholders; we are given L, but we should also remember and mark that either S or V or both must be in (Rule 3).

| In | Out |
|---|---|
| L | ~T |
| S/V/both | ~M |
| | ~R |

a) Could be true.
b) L in fact MUST be in.
c) **Correct.** We know R must be out.
d) Could be true.
e) Could be true.

10. Given M, we know T. T gives us ~F and ~V. ~V gives us S.

| In | Out |
|---|---|
| M | ~F |
| T | ~V |
| S | |
| R/L/both | |

a) F is out.
b) **Correct.** L could be in.
c) V is out.
d) S must be in.
e) T must be in.

11. Given F, we know ~T. ~T gives us ~M. ~M gives us ~R. ~R gives us L.

| In | Out |
|---|---|
| F | ~T |
| L | ~M |
| S/V/both | ~R |

a) **Correct.** L must be in.

b) through e) could be true (but do not have to be).

12. The correct answer here is a pair of variables one of which must be in; that means that the 4 wrong answers could have both variables out. That means to eliminate, try putting each pair "out" and see if you run into trouble.

a) **Correct.** If L is out, we know R. However, if M is out, we know ~R, a contradiction.

The other choices feature two variables both of which could be out.

# PrepTest 58, Section 3, Game 3

This is a complicated advanced linear game with matching aspects. There are 4 sets of variables, making the game complex: flight order, flight letter, airlines, and domestic/international. In fact, it's not immediately clear what the diagram might look like until you read the first two rules, which help structure the game. Games that seem complicated often have big inferences, and this is no exception.

Pf Qf Rg Sg Tg = 5

## Rules
#1: one plane at a time*
#2: D or I (not both)

#3:

#4: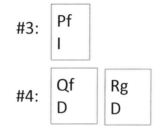

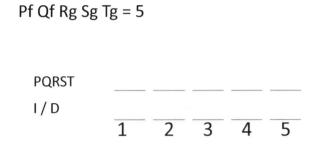

#5. All I before any D

#6: Gateway D < Flyhigh D

*This is how we know there's a linear aspect to the game, which isn't immediately obvious.

Discussion: First we can do some basic diagram maintenance. We don't know whether S and T are domestic or international, but we do know there are at least 1 international and 2 domestic flights (from Rules 3 and 4).

```
PQRST   ___  ___  ___  ___  ___
I / D    I         D    D
         1    2    3    4    5
```

Is there a variable that reoccurs in multiple rules? Not explicitly, but if you look at the constraints Qf actually appears in Rules 4, 5, and 6. We know that P must be before Q because international goes before domestic. We also know that R goes before Q because any Gateway domestic goes before any Flyhigh domestic. What about S and T? We don't know whether they are international or domestic. But let's look at both options.
- If S and T are domestic, they would go ahead of Q because all Gateway domestics go before any Flyhigh domestics (Rule 6).
- If S and T are international, they still go before Q because all internationals go before any domestics
So we have found a major inference – Q must be last.

```
PQRST   ___  ___  ___  ___   Q
I / D    I         D    D
         1    2    3    4    5
```

13. List question. This one isn't as susceptible to our standard eliminate-by-rule strategy since you need to combine the variables with their airline and I/D status to make sense of it. The easiest way is that if you found the inference you can quickly eliminate a), b), and c).

e) Is out because it has P, an international, after D, a domestic.

**d) Correct.**

14. We know Q is out; that's our key inference (so eliminate d) ). Can the other variables all go second? Yes; any international flight could go second. If P is the only international flight, R could also go second (making S and T also domestics).

**d) Correct.** All the variables but Q could go second.

15. S coming before P means that S will be International. We can't make further inferences, so proceed to eliminate.
a) S could go first, e.g. S P R T Q
b) **Correct,** S cannot go third. If S goes third, P must go 4$^{th}$ since Q is always last. That forces R, a domestic flight, in front of both S and P, international flights, violating Rule 4.
c) T could go second, e.g. S T P R Q
d) T could also go third, e.g. S P T R Q
e) T can go fourth; see diagram for a).

16. Oftentimes on games with one big inference, there will be a question later that simply tests that inference. If you didn't find the inference you can still get this question by process of elimination, but it will take some time. Importantly, if you are going that route and find that Q MUST depart last, make sure to integrate that inference into your diagram at that point.

**b) Correct.** Q must depart last.

17. S going third doesn't lead to big inferences since we don't know if S is international or domestic. We'll have to eliminate.
a) Could be true; R would have to be second with P the lone international flight in first.
b) Could be true; T could go 1$^{st}$ or 2$^{nd}$.
c) **Correct.** If S is third, there are only 2 spaces after it to accommodate R, T, and Q. (Note that this would be much more challenging if we did not know Q must be last).
d) Like B, T could go 1$^{st}$ or 2$^{nd}$.
e) T could go first.

# PrepTest 58, Section 3, Game 4

This is an in/out grouping game with lots of conditional rules. We have some additional structure from the fact that the student must take at least 3 classes. However, the questions on this game can be quite time-consuming as there is a good amount of trial and error, making this a challenging game.

H L* M P S T W = 7

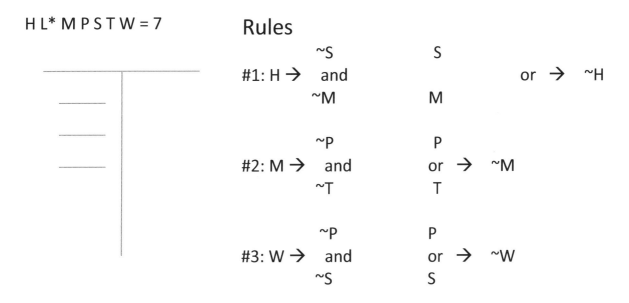

Discussion: Each of these rules suggests a conflict between the variables; each rule necessitates that at least one other variable will be out. This helps us a bit as we know that not all 7 variables will be in. Rather than spending a lot of time trying to examine the rules, on a in/out grouping game it's usually best to get to the questions.

If you try many different configurations of this game, it is possible to deduce that there are a maximum of 4 variables in, however this is one of those deductions that you are probably not *expected* to make. See question 19 for a complete walkthrough.

18. List question.
a) Violates rule 1
b) Violates rule 2
c) **Correct**
d) Violates rule 3
e) Violates rule 2

19. This question points us to an important inference that we can add to our main diagram, but one which is very difficult to find without working through the options.

We know seven is not the answer because each rule eliminates others. How about 6? That won't work either; if we have any one of either H, M, or W, that would eliminate 2 others. How about 5? We can start by selecting variables other than H, M, and W: L (which is unrestricted), S, T, and P.

| In | Out |
|---|---|
| S | |
| T | |
| L | |
| P | |

From here, we can't add H, M, or W – each would eliminate the variables we already have. Any way you work it, you'll find that 4 is the maximum. **b) is correct.**

20. We are given ~P and ~W and asked to choose 2 other variables that could be out. On each answer choices, we are really being asked whether or not the remaining 3 variables can be in. (There is nothing to deduce directly from ~P and ~W).
a) This implies M S T are in. Will that work? No; we know from Rule 2 that M → ~T.
b) **Correct.** L, S, T would be in; T triggers ~M, which is true, and S triggers ~H and ~W (by the contrapositives of rules 1 and 3), which are both true. This works.
c) Implies L, M, T. Rule 2 tells us M → ~T, so this is a contradiction.
d) H S and T would be in. Rule 1 tells us H → ~S, so this won't work.
e) H L and M are in. Rule 1 tells us H → ~M.

21. Given M, we know ~P and ~T from Rule 2 and ~H from the contrapositive of Rule 1.

| In | Out |
|---|---|
| M | ~P |
| ___ | ~T |
| ___ | ~H |
| ___ | |

Of L, S, and W, which must be in? We'll have to eliminate; we do this by seeing if it's possible to have each of the variables out. If we put S out and it works, for example, we know that S is not a class the student must take.

Could S be out? Yes, if S were out L and W would be in. L doesn't give us anything; W gives us ~P and ~S, which would be true. Could W be out? Yes; we'd have L and S; S triggers ~H which is already true. Could L be out? No, it can't be out; if L is out, S and W are in. W gives us ~S, a contradiction.

**b) Is correct – L must be in.**

22. Make sure to make use of past diagrams here for elimination; most of these options can be eliminated. You're looking for past diagrams where both of the choices are out.

**b) Is correct.** If L and T are both out, there's not a valid combination that will work.

23. We're looking for a restriction that has the same effect as Rule 2.
a) This forces us to take S or W if we also take M. This is tempting but doesn't work. If M is in, P, T, S, and W could be out (H and L would be in).
b) **Correct.** This is exactly the same rule as #2, written the other way. Rule 2 says that if we have M we can't have P or T; b) says that if we have M we could ONLY have L, S, or W (the other variables left). We know that H and M can't coexist because Rule 1 is still in effect.
c) and d) don't really address M.
e) Is tricky because it looks like the contrapositive to rule 2, which would be a great answer to this question. However, the contrapositive says T OR P then ~M; e) says T AND P then ~M.

# PrepTest 58, Section 4 (LR)

**1. Question Type: Resolve the Paradox**
The paradox is that automatic flight technology can fly an aircraft reliably, but human error can still occur.
(A) This would not explain how human error could play a factor while it was functioning correctly, so this does not explain the prompt.
(B) This would not explain the human error part, so this is not the answer.
(C) This would not explain how human error could play a factor while it was functioning correctly, so this does not explain the prompt
(D) This does not explain anything from the prompt, so it is not the answer.
(E) Correct. If humans have to give the automated flight technology commands, then even when the technology is functioning properly, human error can cause problems. Therefore, this explains the paradox.

**2. Question Type: Weaken**
The conclusion is the first sentence.
(A) This does not suggest that the conclusion or reasoning is incorrect, so it does not weaken the argument.
(B) Warmer is relative term that was not in the prompt; the prompt only discussed keeping things warm, not getting them warmer.
(C) Correct. Since such temperatures can occur in winter, this would suggest the conclusion was incorrect. Therefore, this weakens the argument.
(D) The argument does not say it is the most effective way, so this does not affect the argument.
(E) Since the prompt did not suggest the physical effort would do this, this does not suggest the argument is incorrect.

**3. Question Type: Conclusion**
The conclusion is the first sentence. The last sentence is a sub-conclusion used to support the first sentence. The second and third sentences are premises that support the sub-conclusion and, indirectly, the main conclusion.
(A) Correct. This paraphrases the first sentence, so it is the main conclusion.
(B) and (C) These are premises supporting the sub-conclusion.
(D) This is part of the sub-conclusion.
(E) This is never stated, but it is very close to one of the premises that supports the sub-conclusion.

**4. Question Type: Principle**
The principle here is that people can tell when something deserves a certain label (grammatical) without being able to explain why it deserves that label.
(A) The principle here is that people can be good at one type of writing but not another kind; this is nothing like the first principle.
(B) The principle here is that those who use a set of rules for practical applications know those rules better than the people who discovered those rules; this is nothing like the first principle.
(C) Correct. The principle here is that people can tell when something deserves a certain label (waltz) without being able to explain why; this is just like the principle in the prompt.
(D) The principle is that those who enjoy something are not always the best at describing it; this is very different from the prompt.
(E) The principle here is that many people can know how to do something while most of them do not know how to do it well. This is different from the principle in the prompt.

**5. Question Type: Flaw**
The argument assumes that everyone who has worked at the top consulting firms is one of the best managing consultants available. The correct answer will likely point this out.
(A) Correct. This paraphrases our predicted answer.
(B) The argument generalizes from the fact that the firms are in the top 1% to the fact that employees of those firms are the best available. There is no reason to believe that the sample was too small. The generalization is flawed, but not because of the sample size.
(C) This is the reverse of the assumption.
(D) It does not presume that whoever they select will accept, just that someone from the top firms will accept.
(E) It does not suggest anything about other tasks, so this cannot be the answer.

*PrepTest 58, Section 4 (LR) Continued...*

**6. Question Type: Most Supported/Must be True**
(A) The argument does not suggest one is better at this, just that one does this and the other does not.
(B) The argument does not provide any support for this statement, as it never makes any suggestions about what players should do.
(C) The prompt does not suggest how one can improve, so this is not supported.
**(D) Correct.** Expert players recognize patterns from past games, so they must be able to remember those games well.
(E) The prompt does not suggest how players can improve, so there is no support for this answer.

**7. Question Type: Resolve the Paradox**
The paradox is that the farmer knows the best way to achieve popcorn corn is to do one thing, but the farmer does something different.
**(A) Correct.** This would explain why the farmer did something different; s/he was unable to use the technique that produced the best results.
(B) This would not explain using a different method, so this is not the answer.
(C), (D) and (E) do not explain why the farmer would not use the best way, so these are not the answer.

**8. Question Type: Flaw**
The argument states one way the prices could be lowered and then claims that that way must be done. Therefore, the argument assumes that it is the only way to lower prices.
(A) The argument does not need to take this into account, as it is only worrying about how its prices compare to competitors, not how the price changes over time.
**(B) Correct.** This paraphrases our predicted answer.
(C) There is no evidence to suggest that the manufacturing equipment is outdated because the prices are high, so this is not the answer.
(D) The argument does consider causes, so this is not the answer.
(E) It does make a definite recommendation, so this is not the answer.

**9. Question Type: Most Supported/Must be true**
**(A) Correct.** This is implied by the recent shipment of African pythons, which have a high likelihood of having the liver disease.
(B) The argument does not say anything about which are more susceptible, so this is not supported.
(C) It is possible that a python contracted the disease a month after hatching, in which case it could die of the disease when it was 7 months old.
(D) The prompt suggests that this is because of the number of new arrivals, not the liver disease.
(E) The argument does not say anything about pythons elsewhere, so this is not supported.

**10. Question Type: Weaken**
The conclusion is the last sentence
(A) This would strengthen the conclusion, so this is not the answer.
(B) This does not affect the argument, as it might suggest some who had less than 5 servings did not need to take them, but some who had five or more servings of the wrong kinds of vegetables could need the pills. Therefore, it neither strengthens nor weakens the conclusion.
(C) This does not affect the fact that they agree people need 5 servings, so this does not affect the argument.
**(D) Correct.** This would suggest that people did not need vitamin pills to meet daily requirements, despite having less than 5 servings of fruits and vegetables. Therefore, it would weaken the argument.
(E) This would not weaken the argument, which is only about getting enough vitamins. Whether people need fiber or not does not affect this argument.

**11. Question Type: Assumption**
The conclusion is that armadillos do not move rapidly into new territories. The argument assumes that the armadillos did not move further away while the researcher was gone and then return before the researcher got back. The correct answer will likely paraphrase this.
(A) The argument bases its claim on the fact that a majority of the tagged armadillos had moved very little, so it does not matter how many were tagged, as long as he had a large enough population for the data to

*PrepTest 58, Section 4 (LR) Continued...*

be reliable.
(B) This would weaken the argument, so it cannot be the assumption.
(C) Even if predators had killed some, the conclusion could still follow, so this fails the negation test.
(D) Even if some armadillos were able to remove their tags, the conclusion could still follow, so this fails the negation test.
(E) Correct. This paraphrases our predicted answer. If they had moved to a new territory in the intervening summer and then moved back, the conclusion could not follow.

**12. Question Type: Method of Reasoning**
R suggests that S's conclusion is incorrect because one of his/her premises relied on an assumption that was not necessarily true.
(A) Correct. This identifies R's rebuttal of S's assumption, so it is the answer.
(B) It does not provide support, so this cannot be the answer.
(C) R does not accept S's conclusion, so this is not the answer.
(D) R does not accept S's premise, so this is not the answer.
(E) R does not suggest there is a contradiction, so this is not the answer.

**13. Question Type: Most Supported/Must be True**
(A) The argument only states that a frog cannot live somewhere if it will get too dehydrated and that small ones cannot live in arid climates. Therefore, there is no support for this statement.
(B) The prompt suggests that frogs will be larger in arid climates, which would suggest the opposite of this.
(C) Correct. Since large frogs could live in the arid north and the wet south, and small frogs could only live in the wet south, this answer is supported.
(D) The argument does not suggest this, as they can both live there, and no information is given about how many might be there of each.
(E) The argument does not suggest that any frogs have less permeable skin, so this is not the answer.

**14. Question Type: Flaw**
The argument assumes that because people think crime is increasing that it actually is. The correct answer will likely point out this assumption.
(A) The survey results are not actually inconsistent, so this cannot be the answer.
(B) The argument does not draw such a connection, so this cannot be the answer.
(C) The argument only suggests what the government needs to do now about a current issue; what surveys in the past indicated has no bearing on this argument.
(D) Correct. This paraphrases our predicted answer.
(E) The argument does not presume this, so this cannot be the answer.

**15. Question Type: Most Supported/Must be true**
(A) The argument only suggests that proofs that depend crucially on computers, to the extent that the computation could not be done by a human, are questionable. Therefore, this answer is too general.
(B) Correct. This is supported by the argument, which states that computations a human cannot double-check are questionable.
(C) This is only the case if the computer was doing something a human could not double-check.
(D) The argument does not suggest that one can be completely certain when humans can double-check, just that there is less certainty when a human cannot do this.
(E) This is not impossible, as people supplement human cognition with computers for proofs; just because these are less certain does not mean that human cognition was not supplemented.

**16. Question Type: Principle**
(A) This is not suggested by the prompt, as it makes no claim about what is most important.
(B) Correct. The issue discussed is the over-simplification of farming; therefore, the prompt is suggesting that farming should be looked at in a more complicated way.
(C) We only know that the farmer is better at farming than industrialists, so this is not suggested by the prompt.
(D) The argument does not suggest that this is never true; it simply suggests that industrialists tend to

*PrepTest 58, Section 4 (LR) Continued...*

oversimplify and gives an example.
(E) The argument does not say it is fundamentally flawed but that it does not work for farming.

### 17. Question Type: Assumption
There is a missing link between possessing nobility and believing in fate, so the correct answer will likely make this link.
(A) If this did depend on the audience, the conclusion could still be true, so this fails the negation test.
(B) The argument only suggests that people no longer believe this; it does not require that fate does not govern human endeavors.
(C) Even if most were not misclassified, the conclusion could still follow, so this fails the negation test.
**(D) Correct.** This correctly creates the link between fate and nobility. If this link were false, then the conclusion could not follow, so this passes the negation test.
(E) Even if ignoble characters could be in tragedies, the conclusion could still be true, so this fails the negation test.

### 18. Question Type: Flaw
If most of them do not know about the attempt, it cannot be that most of them are against it. Meanwhile, just because many who do know about it do not support it does not mean that they are against it. (There is indeed a distinction between not approving and disapproving of a union or anything else.) The correct answer will likely point out one of these flaws.
(A) No long-standing practice is mentioned, so this is not the answer.
(B) Since it was not established that a majority disapproved, this cannot be the answer.
(C) It does not presume that it is not a good idea but rather that most are against it, so this is not the answer.
(D) Since it was not established that it would not pursue graduate student interests, this cannot be the answer.
**(E) Correct.** This paraphrases the second flaw mentioned in our predicted answer.

### 19. Question Type: Assumption
The conclusion is that Griley does not believe in democracy. This only follows if believing popular artwork is bad means that one does not have a high regard for the wisdom of the masses.
(A) Even if this were not true, the conclusion could still follow, so this is not the correct answer.
**(B) Correct.** This paraphrases our predicted answer. If it was not true, the conclusion would not follow, so it passes the negation test.
(C) Even if this were not true, the conclusion could still follow, so this fails the negation test.
(D) Even if some such people did not believe this about popular artwork, the conclusion could still follow, so this fails the negation test.
(E) Even if Griley could have a high regard for the wisdom of the masses without believing in democracy, the conclusion could still follow, so this fails the negation test.

### 20. Question Type: Resolve the Paradox
The paradox is that those who had high blood pressure and reduced salt intake lowered their blood pressure, but those who consumed a lot of salt and had low blood pressure maintained low blood pressure despite continuing to consume a lot of salt. (This is more of a process-of-elimination question as (E) isn't that great of an answer.)
(A) This would not explain the second half of the prompt, so this is not the answer.
(B) This does not explain the second half of the prompt, so this is not the answer.
(C) This fails to explain the second half of the prompt, so this is not the answer.
(D) This would only add a new piece of information that needs explaining, so this is not the answer.
**(E) Correct.** This explains how some people can have a high salt intake yet not have high blood pressure (because they started off with very low blood pressure).

### 21. Question Type: Assumption
The conclusion is the second half of the last sentence. This only follows if when people become aware of something, they think it is likely to happen to them. The correct answer will likely paraphrase this.
(A) Even if most people did not do this because the odds against were downplayed, the conclusion could still follow, so this fails the negation test.

## PrepTest 58, Section 4 (LR) Continued...

(B) Even if others did receive great attention, the conclusion could still follow, so this fails the negation test.
(C) Even if people might overestimate their odds for some other reason, the conclusion is still possible, so this fails the negation test.
**(D)** Correct. This paraphrases our predicted answer. If this did not occur, the conclusion could not follow, so this passes the negation test.
(E) Even if there were no people like this, the conclusion could still follow, so this fails the negation test.

### 22. Question Type: Parallel Reasoning
The argument involves a compound conditional, in which two conditions together are sufficient to bring about something else. It is then assumed that because one of these conditions and the outcome were true, the second condition must have been true.
(A) This is incorrect because the compound part of the conditional is on the "then" side instead of the "if" side.
(B) This argument generalizes from a conditional that is true this year to what must have been true last year. This is different from the logic in the prompt.
**(C)** Correct. This has the compound conditional with the two conditions on the "if" side. One of the conditions and the outcome is true, so it is assumed that the second condition must have been true. This is exactly like the reasoning in the prompt.
(D) There is no flaw in the reasoning here, so this cannot be the answer.
(E) There is no flaw in the reasoning here, so this cannot be the answer.

### 23. Question Type: Strengthen
The conclusion is the second half of the last sentence. This only follows if it is assumed that meteorites cannot hit in a linear pattern if they are of different ages. The correct answer will likely suggest that this assumption is correct.
(A) This would not suggest anything about the case in the prompt, as the fact that they were of different ages was important.
**(B)** Correct. This supports the assumption mentioned in our predicted answer.
(C) This would not strengthen the argument, as it would merely suggest that nothing else either supported or denied the conclusion.
(D) This would weaken the conclusion, as it would suggest that one of the premises was incorrect and that meteors would have had to create the craters with high-pressure shocks.
(E) This does not strengthen the argument, as there is no reason to believe the craters would have to have been created by a single meteor shower if they were created by meteors. In fact, because they were different ages, they could not have come from a single meteor shower.

### 24. Question Type: Assumption
The conclusion is that creative geniuses tend to anger the majority. This only follows if demonstrating the falsehood of popular opinions tends to anger the majority.
(A) This would suggest that the creative geniuses were angry, not that people were angry at them, so this cannot be the answer.
**(B)** Correct. This paraphrases our predicted answer. If it were not true, the conclusion could not follow, so this passes the negation test.
(C) Even if this were not true, the conclusion could still follow, so this fails the negation test.
(D) Even if they did not enjoy this, the conclusion could still follow, so this fails the negation test.
(E) Even if they were not dissatisfied, the conclusion could still follow, so this fails the negation test.

### 25. Question Type: Principle
Both of L's analogies are cases in which she acts preemptively but reasonably. She therefore suggests that people can salt their food before tasting it if they know that food at restaurants is not as salty as they want it to be.
**(A)** Correct. This explains the exact situation described in the predicted answer and applies it to C's argument effectively.
(B) L does not suggest this in any way; she merely suggests that one of C's supposed indicators of a job-related behavior is not well-reasoned.
(C) L suggests that salting food before tasting does not mean what C thinks it does; this has nothing to do with

## PrepTest 58, Section 4 (LR) Continued...

whether one can generalize or not.
(D) Social expectations have no role in the argument, so this is not the correct answer.
(E) L suggests the evidence in a particular is faulty, not that evidence cannot be used for a negative assessment.

# PrepTest 59

## PrepTest 59, Section 1, Game 1

This is a grouping game. While the diagram has many spaces, it's a fairly straightforward diagram and game. Just make sure to create a diagram that represents the setup graphically.

F* H I L P S* T = 7

Top     ___  ___  ___
Middle  ___  ___  ___
Bottom  ___  ___  ___

**Rules**

#1: (P T)

#2: [H / I]

#3: [L _ _ _ _ _]

Discussion: Rules 2 and 3 combine to make a powerful inference: L must occupy the entire top or middle floor. (It can't be in the middle because H and I must be on adjacent floors, and no other department can go on the same floor as L.) So there are two options:

Top     L
Middle  H  ___  ___
Bottom  I  ___  ___

Top     H  ___  ___
Middle  I  ___  ___
Bottom  L

1. List question.
a) Violates rule 2
b) Violates rule 1
c) **Correct**
d) Violates rule 3
e) Violates rule 2

2. Given that I must be in the middle, we can place all of the variables contained in Rules 1-3.

Top     H  ___
Middle  I   P   T
Bottom  L

a) **Correct.** Family law could take the last spot in the middle floor.

b) through e) are eliminated by the inferences in the diagram.

3.
a) This arrangement works with F, H, P, and T on the top floor
b) F, I, P, and T could all be on the middle or bottom floor
c) **Correct.** If F P S and T fill one of the floors, we would have to split H and I on two different floors which won't work since we need an entire floor for L.
d) This group could go on the top or middle floors.
e) I, P, S, and T could go on the top or bottom floors.


4. If F and S are together, think of the implications. That means that our two unconstrained variables must go together. With L on it's own floor, the other 2 floors will have one of either H or I and either PT or FS. We'll have two floors with 3 departments and one floor with just L.

a) Only L can be by itself in this configuration, and L can't go on the middle floor.
b) No floor can have 4 departments here.
c) Again, we can't have 2 departments on a floor with this configuration.
d) **Correct.** The bottom floor would have I and either PT or FS.
e) We can't have 4 departments with this configuration.

5. P (and with it, T) are assigned to the middle floor. There are two ways this can work out. Remember that the question specifies that there are exactly 2 other departments with P.

| | | | | | | | | |
|---|---|---|---|---|---|---|---|---|
| Top | L | | | | Top | H | | |
| Middle | P | T | H | | Middle | P | T | I |
| Bottom | I | | | | Bottom | L | | |

As we can see, F and S only have one place to go in each configuration, so we can solve the entire game:

| | | | | | | | | |
|---|---|---|---|---|---|---|---|---|
| Top | L | | | | Top | H | F | S |
| Middle | P | T | H | | Middle | P | T | I |
| Bottom | I | F | S | | Bottom | L | | |

c) **Correct.** F must go with S in both configurations.

All the other choices could be, but do not have to be, true.

# PrepTest 59, Section 1, Game 2

This is a relatively straightforward linear game.

F G H I K L M = 7

```
 F/                           F/
 ___  ___  ___  ___  ___  ___  ___
  1    2    3    4    5    6    7
 ~H              ~M   ~M   ~M   ~M
```

## Rules

#1:

#2: H < K;  H not first (into diagram)

#3: (I L)

#4: M is 1, 2, or 3 (into diagram)

#5: F is 1st or 7th

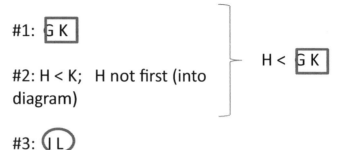

Discussion: Rules 1 and 2 can be combined. We can then do exclusion rules with the combined rule. Note that since H can't be first, G can't go second because it must go after H.

```
 F/                           F/
 ___  ___  ___  ___  ___  ___  ___
  1    2    3    4    5    6    7
 ~H   ~G   ~K   ~M   ~M   ~M   ~M
 ~G   ~G                       ~H
 ~K   ~K
```

6. List question.
   a) Violates rule 1
   b) Violates rule 2
   c) **Correct**
   d) Violates rule 3
   e) Violates rule 5

7. Given I right before G, we can combine with rules 1, 2, and 3 to get:

H < [L I G K]

We still have to place M and F, but since those variables are also both constrained we have a pretty good idea of how this will go. Do make sure to actually write out this new rule.

a) G in 4th gives us:

| F/ | L | I | G | K |   | F/ |
|----|---|---|---|---|---|----|
| 1  | 2 | 3 | 4 | 5 | 6 | 7  |

That won't work because H would have to go first (before L) and M would also have to go first because it must go in the first 3 (Rule 4)
b) H 4th won't work because we have 4 variables that must go after H here and only 3 spaces.
c) If I is 3rd, H and L have to go before it. But M always has to go in the first three, so we'll run out of spaces.
d) Similarly to c), if L goes second we'd need H and M both in first. M can't go third because G must follow L immediately given the new rule.
e) **Correct.** If M is third, we could have: F H M L I G K

8. Process of elimination; since we are looking for a fully-determined configuration, as soon as we see variability or ambiguity in an answer choice, we can eliminate. Do give some thought to what the hardest variables will be to place; of all the variables, I and L will be the trickiest. While they must be next to each other, we don't have any idea in what order.
a) With G in 4 we'd have K in 5. Then there are a variety of options such as F H M G K I/L I/L (but there are many other ways as well).
b) With H in second we know that the two blocks of GK and IL will have to go after it, but we don't know the order of IL, and either M or F could still go first.
c) With I first, L could go either first or third (with M taking the spot L did not).
d) **Correct.**

| L | I | M | H | G | K | F |
|---|---|---|---|---|---|---|
| 1 | 2 | 3 | 4 | 5 | 6 | 7 |

With L first, I must be second. M must always be in the first 3, so M would be third. We also know F must be last since it can't be first in this configuration. Then we just have H, G, and K, and we know in what order they must go.
e) Looking at the configuration above, if M is third, I and L can go first and second but in either order.

9. With M in second, we know that both blocks (GK and IL) will be going after it, but there are a couple different arrangements for H and F. Time to eliminate.
a) Works, e.g. F M H G K I L
b) **Correct.** If H goes 4th, there isn't room for 2 2-variable blocks.
c) Works, e.g. F M I L H G K
d) Works, e.g. F M H G K I L
e) Works, e.g. F M I L H G K

10. This is particularly tricky because the new rule we substitute must both put H in front of K and rule out H from first. Importantly, the question makes clear that this new rule must have the same effect on the entire game, not just those 2 variables – so if the new rule puts some random constraint on I, for example, it would be wrong. This is a complicated question which takes a lot of hard work. This question would be good to skip if you are regularly time-pressured on the exam.

a) If F is 7, H is 2, which puts it before K. But consider if F isn't second. If F is first, H can't be first which is good, but then we don't have a constraint that K must go after H.
b) This replaces the rule adequately, but it also places other major constraints on the rest of the game that weren't there before, so it's not a good answer.
c) While this rules out H being first, it doesn't do anything to place H before K.
d) **Correct.** Let's examine both options. If H is second, we're in good shape because it's not first and it's before K without setting other constraints on the game. If H is not second we're told it is between M and G. This immediately gives us a check for placing H before K because GK is still a block. It also rules H out for first place, because it must come after M.
e) We get H < K out of this, but there's no reason H couldn't be first.

## PrepTest 59, Section 1, Game 3

This is an in/out grouping game. We get a good deal of structure since we know Alicia takes exactly 4 classes. The only little trick is that Statistics is offered twice; you should simply treat it as two variables, so while the game says there are 7 classes, there are in effect 8.

G J M P R S9 S3* W = 8

| In | Out |
|---|---|
|  |  |
|  |  |
|  |  |
|  |  |

Rules
#1: ~R → J
#2: M → ~J
#3: S9 → ~W
#4: P → S9
#5: G or W (not both)

Contrapositives
~J → R
J → ~M
W → ~S9
~S9 → ~P

Discussion: Keep in mind that Statistics can't be taken twice, so there's a rule implied: S9 ←|→ S3. It pays to include Rule 5 in your diagram with placeholders G/W in each column. Again, it's possible to do some rule combinations like M → ~J → R, but doing so won't save much time if you are moving through the questions properly.

Many students benefit from re-writing Rules 2 and 3 with the double-sided not arrow, which is implied by combining those rules with their own contrapositives.

| In | Out |
|---|---|
| G/W | G/W |
|  |  |
|  |  |
|  |  |

Inferences
S9 ←|→ S3
M ←|→ J
S9 ←|→ W

11. List question.
a) Violates rule 4 (she takes psychology but not statistics)
b) Violates rule 1
c) Violates Rule 2
d) **Correct**
e) Violates rule 5 (she takes neither G or W)

12. Use past diagrams to eliminate if possible.
a) G and W cannot both be included.
b) J and M can't coexist according to Rule 2.
c) Given W, we know ~S9 (contrapositive of Rule 3). However, we also know ~S9 → ~P (contrapositive of Rule 4), which is a contradiction.
d) Given P, you know ~S9 (Rule 4). However, ~S9 → ~P (contrapositive of Rule 3), which is a contradiction).
e) **Correct.** This is a little tricky. Given W, we know ~S9 – you have to realize that ~S9 does not rule out S3, which would have to be in.

| In | Out |
|---|---|
| R | S9 |
| S3 | P |
| W | G |
| J/M | J/M |

13. Carefully follow along with the rules for each answer choice and you can quickly find whether there are multiple options for each configuration. Remember to do this in a diagram (not in your head).

**c) Is correct.** Given R and P, we know S9. Given S9 we know ~W. ~W gives us G (we always have either W or G). That fills up our in column, so the rest of the variables would have to be out and the diagram is completely determined.

14. This question asks two things: can the given configuration work with S3, and can it also work with S9? S3 is not restricted, but if a given configuration rules out working with S9 that won't be a correct answer.

a) **Correct.** Starting with S9, G, and J, see if we can make this work. Since we have G we know ~W; we can also get ~W from S9. J gives us ~M. Either R or P can be the final variable which goes in.
b) P forces us to take S9. Since Alicia can't take statistics twice, that means she can't take S3.
c) S9 gives us ~W, so they can't coexist.
d) Similar to b, P forces S9, which rules out S3
e) W rules out S9

15. If we know S3 we can deduce ~S9; from ~S9 we can deduce ~P. From G we can deduce ~G. We still have to consider M, J, and R.

| In | Out |
|---|---|
| S3 | S9 |
| G | P |
|  | W |

M and J are essentially interchangeable, but they can't go in together. That means that R must be included along with either M or J.

**d) Correct.** R must be in.

16. This question changes Rule 4 to read:

$$P \rightarrow \begin{matrix} S3 \\ \text{or} \\ S9 \end{matrix}$$

(The contrapositive of this rule doesn't come in to play since we can never have S3 and S9.)

a) **Correct.** P, R, S, and W works. Previously to this question, P would lead to S9, which would rule out W. But since P could lead to S3 in this new local rule, W can still be included.
b) Doesn't work; ~R → J, which isn't in.
c) Doesn't work; P still infers S, which is missing from this list.
d) Similar to c), P infers S, which is missing.
e) G and W can't coexist.

# PrepTest 59, Section 1, Game 4

This is a basic linear game that has a couple split-block rules.

L M N* T V W = 6

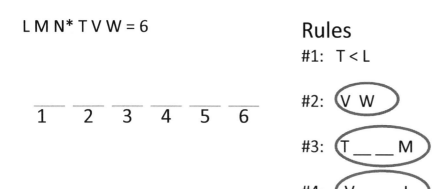

```
___  ___  ___  ___  ___  ___
 1    2    3    4    5    6
```

Discussion: Note that N is unconstrained. There aren't very simple rule combinations, because either of the split blocks can go either way. For example, Rules 2 and 4 could be "WV__ __ L" or "VW __ L". If you like, you can list out all the possibilities, but there are many of them and working through each takes time. You can probably make better use of your time by going through the questions directly instead. You can add the inferences from Rule 1.

```
     ___  ___  ___  ___  ___  ___
      1    2    3    4    5    6
      ~L                   ~T
```

17. List question.
a) **Correct**
b) Violates rule 1
c) Violates Rule 4
d) Violates Rule 2
e) Violates rule 3

18. Work through the options quickly; you can eliminate most options based on past diagrams.
a) through d) can be eliminated with past diagrams or with a quick sketch.

e) **Correct.** Though you'll likely get here by eliminating other diagrams, there's no way to arrange N and W except with 2 spaces between them. This is also an inference you can use in future questions.

19. Work through process of elimination.
a), b), c), and e) leave multiple configurations.

d) Is correct: the only way V can go first is: V W T L N M. V in first forces L in 4th and W next to V in 2nd. T must go before L so it will have to go third, placing M last. N can only go 5th.

20. You can eliminate liberally here as you've used W in several different spaces in past diagrams. If you have a few options left over where you have not seen W go, just try them quickly. W is not constrained and can go in any space, thus **e) is correct.**

21. If M is first, T must be 4th. Is there an answer choice that revolves around that small inference?
a) Works, e.g. M V W T L N
b) Works, e.g. M T V T N L
c) Works, same diagram as a)
d) Works, same diagram as b)
e) **Correct.** L in 3 puts L before T.

22. Eliminate quickly, putting options in diagrams if there isn't a clear initial solution.
a) L must go after T and thus can't go first.
b) **Correct, e.g. T N L M N V**
c) M in 3 forces T in 6, which doesn't work because L must come after T.
d) Similarly to c), V in 4 puts L in first, but L must go after T.
e) Again, T cannot go last.

23. You can use past diagrams to eliminate many options.

b) **Correct.** If L and W go together, it forces a space between V and W, breaking a rule:

LW _ V
V _ WL

# PrepTest 59, Section 2 (LR)

**1. Question Type: Strengthen**

The question includes data, and the prompt concludes from a correlation of two things that one causes the other, which is a flaw. To strengthen the argument, some logical reason to believe this causal link exists must be established. The correct answer will likely do so.

(A) Correct. If the fruits caused the atypical symptoms, then stopping eating the fruits would mean the symptoms should go away. This answer suggests that is the case, which supports the claim that the fruits caused the symptoms.

(B) This does not strengthen the argument because the argument only makes a claim about those who did eat the fruit (that their symptoms were caused by eating it). What others did has no bearing on this claim and thus does not strengthen it.

(C) This does not strengthen the argument because the argument makes a claim about one thing causing certain symptoms, while this answer suggests that something else can cause those symptoms.

(D) This would actually weaken the argument, as the ten who ate more of the fruit would show that the fruit did not cause the symptoms.

(E) Whether or not the fruit contains certain vitamins does not affect whether or not it causes certain symptoms, so this does not support the argument.

**2. Question Type: Point at Issue**

The correct answer will be a statement that one speaker will definitely agree with and the other speaker will definitely disagree with.

(A) While we know P agrees with this statement, we don't know that A disagrees; A only suggests that this is not the primary responsibility, not that it isn't one at all.

(B) While we know A agrees with this statement, we don't know that P disagrees.

(C) Nothing implies that either would agree or disagree with this statement.

(D) Correct. P clearly believes this, and A clearly disagrees.

(E) Nothing implies that either would agree or disagree with this statement.

**3. Question Type: Strengthen**

(A) Correct. This would suggest that the bank's internal audit system would catch the accidental credit with the program that double-checked large transactions.

(B) This would not suggest anything about when a mistake was made, so it is not the answer.

(C) Sending this statement would not ensure that the bank notices accidental credits, so this would not strengthen the claim.

(D) and (E) These do not suggest anything about when an accidental credit is made, so neither is the answer.

**4. Question Type: Flaw**

The argument concludes from data that shows two events to be correlated that one caused the other. However, correlation does not logically imply causation, so this is a flaw in reasoning.

(A) The argument makes no claim regarding how harmful something is, so this is not a flaw.

(B) The argument does not draw a general conclusion, as evidenced by the words "in this case" in the conclusion.

(C) The argument does not generalize, as mentioned in the explanation for answer (B).

(D) While the argument does this, it is not a logical flaw. An argument can be logically correct even if one of the premises is incorrect.

(E) Correct. This paraphrases our predicted answer.

**5. Question Type: Strengthen**

To strengthen S's argument, we need a reason to use her criterion for "natural" over G's.

(A) Even if they dropped the ingredient, the label in question was from before they dropped it. Therefore, this does not strengthen her argument.

(B) This has no effect on her argument, as the chemical in question is an ingredient and is not used as part of the manufacturing process.

(C) In S's argument, it doesn't matter whether they were synthesized or not, so this does not support her argument.

(D) All of those labels could be mistaken, so this does not support S's argument.

*PrepTest 59, Section 2 (LR) Continued...*

(E) Correct. This supplies a reason to use her criterion for natural, under which the label would not be mistaken. Thus, it strengthens her conclusion that it is not mistaken.

### 6. Question Type: Flaw

The conclusion is that her negative review relies on a mistake. However, just because the other works were popular does not mean that the research methods were acceptable. The correct answer will likely point this out.

(A) No scholar's view is used to contest that of J, so this is not the answer.
(B) The argument does not attack J, so this is not the answer.
(C) Correct. This paraphrases our predicted answer. The argument suggested that because Y's older books were popular and used the same research methods, Y's new book must have been accurate.
(D) There is no general conclusion, so this is not the answer.
(E) The argument does not presume this, so it cannot be the answer.

### 7. Question Type: Method of Reasoning

The argument suggests that one explanation for the observation that concerts are better than recordings is incorrect.

(A) The argument attempts to show that the explanation for the observation is incorrect, so it is not what it meant to show.
(B) It is not the reason given but a phenomenon described.
(C) The argument does not offer an explanation, so this cannot be the answer.
(D) The argument does not suggest this is incorrect, just that the given explanation for it is incorrect.
(E) Correct. This describes its position as an observation that is explained by another statement but that this argument suggests is not the true explanation.

### 8. Question Type: Flaw

The argument assumes that because two things are correlated, one caused the other.

(A) The dairy farmers have the data, and the relevant pieces of the data are presented (the sharp decline in one and the doubling in the other).
(B) Correct. This points out that one of the correlated things (decline in ice cream sales) could be caused by something else.
(C) There is no reason to believe that the dairy farmers would be biased, as they would be involved in the production of both ice cream and cheddar cheese.
(D) This is not presumed, so it cannot be the flaw.
(E) This is not presumed, so it cannot be the flaw.

### 9. Question Type: Parallel Reasoning

The flaw in reasoning is that there could be some other position that members have at the group.

(A) There is no flaw in this answer, so it cannot be correct.
(B) There is no flaw in this answer, so it cannot be correct.
(C) Correct. This uses the same logic that if you can't be two things at the same time, then if you are not one, you are the other. It is flawed in the same way as the prompt, so this is the answer.
(D) There is no flaw in this answer, so it cannot be correct.
(E) There is no flaw in this answer, so it cannot be correct.

### 10. Question Type: Conclusion

The conclusion is the second sentence, which is supported by the other sentences and does not support any other claim.

(A), (B) and (C) None of these lists the sentence we found in our predicted answer.
(D) Correct. This correctly paraphrases the sentence from our predicted answer. All of the information about worms and chemical fertilizers given supports the idea that chemicals should not be used.
(E) This sentence is used to support the claim that chemicals should not be used, so it cannot be the main conclusion.

## PrepTest 59, Section 2 (LR) Continued...

**11. Question Type: Resolve the Paradox**
The paradox is that a diet is more healthy, but those who are on it for decades have more health problems.
(A) This fails to explain why they have more health problems and thus fails to resolve the paradox.
**(B)** Correct. This would explain why those who are on the diet tend to have more health problems, despite the fact that it is more healthy. Therefore, it resolves the paradox.
(C), (D), and (E) These fail to explain why those on the diet have more health problems and thus fails to resolve the paradox.

**12. Question Type: Complete the Argument**
The rest of the argument will probably be something like "not all of history's main trends can be captured by historical analysis."
(A) This answer is way too extreme; some benefits are mentioned in the prompt.
(B) No evidence for this statement is given, so it does not fit in the blank.
**(C)** Correct. This is a paraphrase of our predicted answer. This statement is supported by the rest of the prompt, and it fits as a conclusion to the earlier statements.
(D) This answer is a jumble of words from the prompt that are rearranged to mean something completely different. As such, it is not supported and cannot be the logical completion of the prompt.
(E) This answer is too extreme; differences are mentioned in the prompt.

**13. Question Type: Principle**
The last sentence is the conclusion.
(A) Because the conclusion does not suggest psychologists try to understand why, this principle does not support the conclusion.
(B) This principle has no suggestion as to what should be done, so it does not support the conclusion.
**(C)** Correct. This would suggest that the conclusion should be done, as it would lower the number of nightmare-prone adults. Therefore, it supports the conclusion.
(D) This principle does not suggest what should be done, so it does not support the conclusion.
(E) This does not suggest anything about what psychologists should do with children who are likely to have nightmares as adults, so it does not support the conclusion.

**14. Question Type: Assumption**
(A) The argument does not make any mention of health impact, so this cannot be the answer.
(B) Awareness does not make a difference to the argument.
(C) The argument made no mention of health benefits, so this cannot be the answer.
**(D)** Correct. If this were not true, and doughnut-eaters did add substances, the conclusion could not follow. This answer thus passes the negation test.
(E) This does not affect the argument, so it cannot be the answer.

**15. Question Type: Flaw**
**(A)** Correct. The word anarchy is first defined as absence of government and later defined as chaos. The shift in definition allows the thinker to reason that a position is incorrect, but only by distorting that position.
(B) The argument does not need to show this, as its claim only depends on showing that anarchy does not promote peace and order.
(C) The argument does not suggest that anything is true or false based on the number of people who believe it, so this is not the answer.
(D) The argument makes no mention of flourishing, so this is not the correct answer.
(E) It does not reject the view for being extreme, so this cannot be the answer.

**16. Question Type: Parallel Reasoning**
The reasoning is correct and can be diagrammed as follows:
$$P + \sim E \rightarrow W$$
$$L \rightarrow P$$
$$\sim E + L$$
$$\text{Therefore, } W$$
(A) This answer has a mistaken reversal of the second premise and thus is false. Therefore, it cannot be the

correct answer.
(B) The reasoning can be diagrammed as follows:

P + ~D + ~C → L
P → W
P + ~D + ~C
Therefore, W

The reason this is not the correct answer is that the entire first line is unnecessary for the argument. Meanwhile, it was required for the reasoning in the prompt.
(C) This reasoning is flawed, so it cannot be the correct answer.
(D) This reasoning is flawed, so it cannot be the correct answer.
(E) Correct. This reasoning is just like that in the prompt. It can be diagrammed as follows:

RB + ~LY → FC
TH → RB
~LY + TH
Therefore, FC

### 17. Question Type: Assumption

There is a missing link between losing respect and hiding ignorance. The correct answer will likely establish that link.
(A), (B), (C), and (D) None of these establishes the missing link, so none of them makes the conclusion properly drawn.
(E) Correct. This correctly establishes the link between losing respect and hiding ignorance. If students didn't lose respect when this happened, the conclusion would not follow, so this passes the negation test.

### 18. Question Type: Method of Reasoning

The conclusion is the first half of the last sentence. The statement in question is a premise that the author suggests will no longer be true in the future.
(A) It is not a hypothesis, as it is presented as a fact.
(B) It is not used as evidence for anything, so this cannot be the answer.
(C) The argument does not suggest that it supports M's argument, so this cannot be the answer.
(D) Correct. This paraphrases our predicted answer.
(E) The argument mentions nothing of inadequate evidence, and the statement is treated as fact rather than as a hypothesis.

### 19. Question Type: Must be True

These statements and their contrapositives can be diagrammed as follows:

B → A     ~A → ~B
L → ~B    B → ~L

(A) This is a mistaken reversal of the first statement and is not supported.
(B) This would require a mistaken negation of the first statement, so it is not supported.
(C) Correct. This must be true, as those Bs that are As are not Ls, so some As are not Ls.
(D) This is exactly the opposite of the contrapositive of the second statement.
(E) This would require a mistaken negation of the first statement, so it is not supported.

### 20. Question Type: Flaw

The prompt states that twenty percent of those sent by the field testers were defective; this does not logically imply that more than five percent of all manufactured products were defective. It is possible that the field testers sent ones that were more likely to be defective.
(A) We do not know how large the sample is, so we have no reason to believe this is a flaw.
(B) This would mean they assumed that the products were 50% defective, which was not presumed.
(C) The argument does not overlook this; even if most of them were from one or two plants, the percentage could still fall below the contracted amount.
(D) Correct. This paraphrases our predicted answer. If the field testers did do that, then the inference that the manufacturers had broken the contract would be incorrect.
(E) The number of visits has no effect on the reasoning in the argument.

# PrepTest 59, Section 2 (LR) Continued...

### 21. Question Type: Weaken
The conclusion is the final part of the last sentence.
(A) This would strengthen the argument that the cause of extinction was microorganisms.
(B) This would not affect the argument, as it would not affect whether the microorganisms caused extinction in other animals.
**(C) Correct.** This would weaken the argument. If the extinctions were caused by microorganisms and not hunting, then whether or not an animal was hunted would not have affected if it went extinct or not.
(D) This would not affect the argument, as it would not affect whether the microorganisms caused the extinction in specific animals.
(E) The argument seeks to explain the extinction less than 2,000 years after, so what happened after that does not affect the argument.

### 22. Question Type: Strengthen
The argument assumes that because those at B were not given a free nutritious breakfast, they did not have nutritious breakfasts that month. The correct answer will likely support this assumption.
**(A) Correct.** This would suggest that the assumption is correct, meaning that the argument is more likely to be true.
(B) This would not strengthen the argument, as there is no logical reason to believe that starting at a different time would alter productivity. The argument would require another statement about starting at different times in addition to this answer for it to be logically related.
(C) This does not strengthen the argument, as we have no knowledge of which plant had a more nutritious diet before.
(D) Vacation has no effect on the causal link in the argument, so this is not the answer.
(E) This does not affect the argument, which merely concludes that having a nutritious breakfast will increase one's productivity, not that the plant with the most nutritious breakfast will be the most productive.

### 23. Question Type: Principle
(A) This does not fit the prompt, as the residents of H did not know anyone at either town.
(B) This does not fit the prompt because it brings up the irrelevant fact of how much people like government relief programs.
(C) No information is given about how publicized any of the disasters was, so there is no support for this.
**(D) Correct.** This is supported by the prompt, as the residents of H gave more after they were hit by a tornado.
(E) We don't know that H ever had a similar disaster; all we know is that it is also a river town. Therefore, this is no support for this answer.

### 24. Question Type: Complete the Argument
The first sentence suggests that consumers don't care much about the interest rates on their card because they plan to pay them off before interest accrues. The second sentence says that credit card companies focus on what consumers care about in their marketing. This suggests that the blank will say that credit card companies tend not to focus on interest rates when marketing cards.
(A) This would completely ignore the second sentence, so it is not the correct answer.
**(B) Correct.** This is a paraphrase of our predicted answer.
(C) This would completely ignore the second sentence, so it is not the correct answer.
(D) The first sentence suggests this is incorrect, so this cannot be the correct answer.
(E) The number of places is not mentioned in the first or second sentences, so this does not fit with the rest of the prompt.

### 25. Question Type: Weaken
The conclusion is the last sentence. The "only if" in the preceding sentence means that the level of greenhouse gases must have been higher. However, there is no reason to believe that carbon dioxide was higher; other gases could have been higher. The correct answer will likely point this out.
(A) This would strengthen the argument, as it supports the second to last sentence.
**(B) Correct.** This paraphrases our predicted answer. If methane levels were much higher, then there is no reason to believe that carbon dioxide levels were higher. Therefore, this information would weaken the argument.

## PrepTest 59, Section 2 (LR) Continued...

(C) This would strengthen the argument, as it supports the premises of the argument.
(D) This is completely unrelated, so it does not weaken the argument.
(E) This is completely unrelated, so it does not weaken the argument.

**26. Question Type: Assumption**

The conclusion is the last part of the last sentence. The advertised prices and written estimates constitute an ability to contact many sellers to see their prices. This means that the argument must be assuming that consumers are unable to compare these prices to what the items are truly worth.

(A) The argument only says that people have to have the ability to contact sellers and compare, not that they have to exercise this ability. Therefore, this does not affect the argument.
**(B)** Correct. This would mean that the consumers were unable to compare the prices to the items' true values. Meanwhile, if people did know the true worth, the conclusion would not follow, so this passes the negation test.
(C) If all gave estimates, the argument could still follow, so this fails the negation test.
(D) Even if very few charged more, the conclusion could still follow, so this fails the negation test.
(E) This does not affect that argument, so it cannot be the answer.

# PrepTest 59, Section 3 (LR)

**1. Question Type: Resolve the Paradox**
The paradox is that investment is very risky, but some are willing to invest.
**(A)** Correct. This would explain why some investors were willing to invest in such risky ventures.
(B) What has happened in the last decade does not affect whether any more breakthroughs will occur in the future.
(C) and (D) These do not explain why people were investing in risky stocks, so neither can be the answer.
(E) This is unrelated, so it does not resolve the paradox.

**2. Question Type: Weaken**
The chair's argument is that the book was chosen for academic and not monetary reasons. Her evidence is that the committee gave it the highest rating. This only proves the conclusion if it is assumed that the committee was not affected by the money. The correct answer will likely suggest this assumption is incorrect.
**(A)** Correct. This paraphrases our predicted answer.
(B) This does not affect the reasoning, so it cannot be the answer.
(C) This has no bearing on whether the money affected their decision or not.
(D) This implies that one member of the committee knew about the donation; it does not suggest that the conclusion was incorrect, though.
(E) This has no bearing on the argument, so it cannot be the answer.

**3. Question Type: Must be True**
(A) This is not supported; all we know is that the molecule will be more effective at capturing oxygen, not that it will definitely be successful.
(B) This is not supported; the argument never stated that nothing else came into play, so we have no reason to believe that to be true.
**(C)** Correct. We do know that the molecule becomes more effective the more oxygen molecules it has captured, so this must be true.
(D) There is no support for this statement.
(E) The argument leaves open the possibility that hemoglobin molecules can fail to pick up oxygen at the lungs, so this answer is not supported.

**4. Question Type: Resolve the Paradox**
The paradox is the way in which passengers affect the likelihood of getting in an accident is different between short and long drives.
(A) This does not explain the difference, so it does not resolve the paradox.
(B) This fails to explain the effect of the passenger, so it does not resolve the paradox.
**(C)** Correct. This would explain why driving with no passenger on a long trip increases the likelihood of getting in an accident, so it resolves the paradox.
(D) This merely adds another fact to explain and fails to resolve the paradox.
(E) This does not explain the difference. The likelihood of an accident is the probability of having an accident, not the total number of accidents. So even if people take more short drives and thus get in more short accidents, this does not affect the difference in likelihoods.

**5. Question Type: Flaw**
The point of C's statement was that the increase in jobs did not give jobs to people living in the city; rather, people from outside the city came with the jobs. M ignores this when replying.
(A) The mayor does not take this for granted, so this cannot be the answer.
(B) This does not need to be considered, as it does not affect the argument.
**(C)** Correct. This paraphrases our predicted answer.
(D) This was not C's claim, so this cannot be the answer.
(E) M does not do this, so this cannot be the answer.

**6. Question Type: Principle**
The principle is something like "it is unfair to criticize a group for not attempting to do something that it is unable to do."
(A) This is different in that is is possible to use the same number of layers as used to be used.

# PrepTest 59, Section 3 (LR) Continued...

(B) Correct. This follows the paraphrased principle in our predicted answer.
(C) This claims it is unfair to criticize a group for something, but it is very different from that in the predicted answer.
(D) Sacrificing another subject is possible, even if it is not desirable. Therefore, this does not conform to the same principle.
(E) It is possible to use economic theory where it is irrelevant, so this follows a different principle.

### 7. Question Type: Must be True

(A) Correct. Those who could imagine remote benefits would see those benefits more clearly, allowing them to outweigh more immediate gains.
(B) This would suggest that they would be less likely to stop their habitual behavior, as they could perceive it continuing for longer than it actually would.
(C) This is not supported, as the argument makes no mention of how success in the past affects ability to get rid of bad habits.
(D) This is not supported, as the argument makes no mention of how awareness of behavioral characteristics affects ability to get rid of bad habits.
(E) This is not supported, as we don't know how to compare the pains of the past and the pains of the present, so we cannot determine how perceiving past pains affects ability to get rid of bad habits.

### 8. Question Type: Flaw

The argument assumes that because the scribes had mathematical competence, the people in general had a strong grasp of sophisticated math. This generalization seems questionable, as the scribes were probably better educated than most people.

(A) No definition is necessary, as the colloquial and dictionary definitions suffice.
(B) Correct. This correctly paraphrases our predicted answer.
(C) The argument is only about one civilization, so overlooking other civilizations is not an error in reasoning.
(D) Scientific is only used in one sense, so this is not a flaw in the argument.
(E) No correlation is mentioned, and no causation is assumed.

### 9. Question Type: Conclusion

The conclusion is the first sentence. The following sentences are used to support it, and it does not support either of the following sentences.

(A) and (C) These are both premises and thus not the conclusion.
(B) This is never stated, so it cannot be the conclusion.
(D) Correct. This paraphrases the first sentence.
(E) This is never stated, so it cannot be the conclusion.

### 10. Question Type: Assumption

The conclusion is the very first part of the last sentence. The conclusion only follows if any action that leads to restrictions of what can be viewed is censorship.

(A) Even if there could could be some restriction under these conditions, the conclusion could still follow, so this fails the negation test.
(B) Even if this was impossible, the conclusion could still follow, so this fails the negation test.
(C) Even if some such shows did not have an audience, the conclusion could still follow, so this fails the negation test.
(D) Even if there was not widespread agreement, the conclusion could still follow, so this fails the negation test.
(E) Correct. This paraphrases our predicted answer. If this were not the case, the conclusion would not follow, so this passes the negation test.

### 11. Question Type: Strengthen

The conclusion is that the predictions are incorrect.

(A) This does not add anything to the argument, so it does not strengthen it. It only suggests that electronic books are better for scholars and research, which is already stated.
(B) Correct. This suggests that the predictions are incorrect because publishers will create books in a

*PrepTest 59, Section 3 (LR) Continued...*

non-electronic format, which will be stocked in book stores and hence keep the electronic book from replacing printed books.
(C) Where they conduct their research does not affect whether print books will be replaced by electronic books or not.
(D) and (E) These would weaken the argument, as they both suggest the predictions are coming true.

**12. Question Type: Assumption**
A causal link between humidity and illness is assumed from a correlation. Meanwhile, it is assumed that the visits to the nurse were due to illness. The correct answer could mention either of these.
**(A)** Correct. This mentions the second assumption in our predicted answer. If they had gone to the nurse for some other reason, the conclusion could not follow, so this passes the negation test.
(B) Even if some did not suffer, it is possible that a number were made ill, so this fails the negation test.
(C) The argument makes no mention of viruses, so this cannot be the answer.
(D) Even if the numbers are not that exact, the conclusion is still possible, so this fails the negation test.
(E) How it affected costs has no bearing on the conclusion, so this is not the answer.

**13. Question Type: Weaken**
The conclusion is the final sentence. This assumes that large and small cars get in the same number of accidents; if large cars got into more accidents, they could have more injuries despite a lower percentage of accidents with injuries.
(A) The speed limit does not affect the argument.
(B) It does not matter if they can sometimes drive larger cars; the argument is only about what happened when they were in each size car.
(C) The argument is only about those who drove large and small cars, so the medium cars were simply left out. Therefore, this does not weaken the argument.
**(D)** Correct. This paraphrases our predicted answer, suggesting that the assumption is incorrect.
(E) This does not affect the argument, as the size of the percentages is not given.

**14. Question Type: Method of Reasoning**
The argument makes use of an analogy to try to show that something is not a good idea.
(A) No assumption is mentioned, so this cannot be the answer.
(B) The argument does not suggest that an analogy is faulty but rather uses an analogy to show that a particular action will not work.
**(C)** Correct. This paraphrases our predicted answer.
(D) No mention of the authority of a source is made, so this cannot be the answer.
(E) No disastrous consequences are mentioned, so this cannot be the answer.

**15. Question Type: Parallel Reasoning**
The logic is that if one thing is okay under certain circumstances, and another thing is okay under certain circumstances, there must be some circumstance when it is okay to do both.
(A) This reasoning here is that if one thing is okay in two different circumstances, it must not be okay in any other circumstances. While this is also flawed, it is not very similar reasoning.
(B) While this reasoning is flawed, it is nothing like that in the prompt.
**(C)** Correct. Two things are okay under certain circumstances, so it is assumed that it is okay to do both of them.
(D) This reasoning is very different from that in the prompt.
(E) The reasoning here is that if one thing causes two events, then when those two events happen simultaneously, the first thing happened. This is pretty different from that in the prompt.

**16. Question Type: Assumption**
The conclusion is the last sentence. The conclusion only follows if restoring the enzyme to normal levels means that people will definitely not have periodontitis at all. This is a leap because the prompt only says that those with low levels of cathepsin have a lower risk of gum disease, not that they don't have gum disease at all. The assumption must make this link.
(A) Even if there were other ways, it is possible that this way would eliminate it, so this fails the negation test.

## PrepTest 59, Section 3 (LR) Continued...

(B) Even if there are other causes, it is possible that restoring levels to normal will eliminate the condition, so this fails the negation test.
(C) The argument does not suggest anything about how long it will take; it can be true if it takes 1 year or 100 years. Therefore, this is not the correct answer.
(D) Even if people who did not have the genetic mutation still got gum disease, the conclusion can still follow, so this fails the negation test.
(E) Correct. This is our prediction.

### 17. Question Type: Resolve the Paradox EXCEPT
The paradox is that most movies use a plot that has been seen many times before, but people still enjoy seeing new movies. Four of the answers will resolve the paradox, and the correct answer will not.
(A) Correct. This would not explain why people enjoy new movies, so it fails to resolve the paradox.
(B), (C), (D), and (E) These would all explain how people could enjoy new movies despite the recycled plots.

### 18. Question Type: Principle
The conclusion is the first sentence. The argument is that governments should continue funding projects that have had unintended benefits in the past.
(A) This uses very little of the reasoning in the prompt and thus does not justify it.
(B) The argument mentions nothing about underestimating, so this does not justify the reasoning.
(C) The important thing is that the unintended consequences were beneficial, which is not mentioned in this answer. Therefore, this does not justify the reasoning.
(D) Correct. This paraphrases our predicted answer.
(E) The argument does not mention the welfare of society, and this fails to mention the unintended consequences, so this does not justify the reasoning.

### 19. Question Type: Must be True
The first sentence is not taken as a premise to be believed, and the author seems to disagree with it.
(A) While under the first sentence this would be true, there is no reason to believe the first sentence is true, so it is not the case that this answer follows logically.
(B) The author seems to believe this, but it has not been mentioned in the argument, so we have no logical reason to believe that this follows.
(C) There is no reason to think that the second part of this answer follows, since we have no reason to believe that uttering words means one understands them.
(D) There is no reason to believe the second half of this sentence.
(E) Correct. If babies sometimes utter words that they don't know the dictionary definition for and they understand the words they utter, then understanding a word must not require knowing the dictionary definition.

### 20. Question Type: Flaw
The argument assumes that because the lightest moths contrasted most, the darkest moths contrasted least. However, it is possible that some intermediate shade contrasted least. The correct answer will likely point out this assumption.
(A) This is not a flaw, as it would strengthen the argument if it were true.
(B) This is not taken for granted, so it is not the flaw.
(C) The argument justifies this by suggesting that the coloring is related to how well it can hide.
(D) Correct. This paraphrases our predicted answer.
(E) The argument does not presume this is its only defense mechanism but rather that it is the most important one.

### 21. Question Type: Must be True
(A) This is not implied by the argument; the argument only says that people can type as much as twice as fast, not that anyone will immediately type faster using a different configuration.
(B) The argument does not compare older typewriters to newer typewriters, so this is not supported.
(C) There is no reason to believe this; they still had to keep people from jamming the keys on the typewriters of the time.

*PrepTest 59, Section 3 (LR) Continued...*

(D) The argument makes no mention of the benefit to society, so it does not support this statement.
(E) Correct. The reason the layout was designed to limit typing speed was that typewriters had a particular limit. Since computers did not have this limit, the layout would not have been designed to limit typing speed.

### 22. Question Type: Flaw
The actions assume that because one thing (making an agreement) is sufficient for another thing (being obligated to fulfill that agreement), it is also necessary for that thing.
(A) Whether the consequences are good or not has nothing to do with the argument, so this is not the flaw.
(B) The argument takes the opposite of this for granted.
(C) The argument does not have logically equivalent premises and conclusions, and it states nothing about what actions one should agree to perform.
(D) Correct. This correctly identifies the flaw in our predicted answer. It also notes an additional flaw.
(E) The term "action" is not ambiguous and causes no problems in the argument. Also, people can be unwilling to do things they are obligated to do, so this is not a problem with the argument.

### 23. Question Type: Method of Reasoning
The argument suggests that the definition of inventing something is exactly the same as what one does when attempting to predict an invention. This means that one finishes predicting something when it has just finished coming to pass, meaning it wasn't actually predicted at all.
(A) No counterexample is given, and no hypothesis about the future is given, so this cannot be the method of reasoning.
(B) Correct. The argument appeals to the definition of inventing something to show that predicting an invention is impossible.
(C) No hypothesis is mentioned, so this cannot be the answer.
(D) No problem is mentioned as being widely thought of as scientific.
(E) This is too broad; only predicting inventions is said to be impossible, not predicting anything.

### 24. Question Type: Flaw
The conclusion is the final part of the final sentence. However, this is assuming that no new aesthetic theory can be developed that encompasses the newer art forms. The correct answer will likely point this out.
(A) The argument does not take this for granted, so this cannot be the flaw.
(B) It does justify this idea by saying that they were rebelling against earlier aesthetic theory.
(C) The argument makes no mention of geography as making a difference, so it does not presume this.
(D) The argument never suggests this is true, so this cannot be the flaw.
(E) Correct. This paraphrases our predicted answer.

### 25. Question Type: Assumption
The conclusion is the final sentence. It is assumed that the reviewing scientists do not share any biases with the researchers.
(A) Even if they have their own biases, they can still remove biased interpretations of researchers.
(B) Correct. This paraphrases our predicted answer. If this were not the case, the conclusion could not follow, so this passes the negation test.
(C) If this were not true, the conclusion could still follow, so this fails the negation test.
(D) The argument only makes statements about biases in interpretation of data, so this does not affect it.
(E) Even if there were some other way, it is possible that this way would still get rid of all of the biases. Therefore, this fails the negation test.

# PrepTest 59, Section 4 (RC)

**Passage 1, Comparative reading**

Summarize both passages first.

Passage A: Sophisticated computer models of weather or the oceans are possible to make. But actually performing the calculations is beyond the capacity of current computing power—the number of calculations is simply far too large. This may be solved if multiple, networked computers shared the calculation load—this type of project has been successful in the past.

Passage B. Many problems are naturally parallel. For example, one ant is pretty simple, but a mass of ants can behave in a more complex way. When solving a massively parallel problem, it may be best to use massively parallel computing—thousands of computers working at once.

1. **(C)** is correct; The real point about Passage B is that computer science is changing towards parallel computing, in response to the need to solve massively parallel problems. Choice (A) doesn't encompass that paradigm shift. The other choices are further off.

2. The key word in the prompt is "large scale." The large-scale example in Passage B is the behavior of a mass of ants. That's choice **(C)**.

3. Both authors would agree with **(E)**. That's a statement made pretty directly by the first passage. But why would the second author also agree? Because it's clear that the climate is a massively parallel problem as Passage B is using the term.

4. The point of mentioning the public is to emphasize that if you want large numbers of computers to help with your project, you must capture the public's interest. Public engagement is something you need to succeed. So choice **(B)** is correct.

5. The second passage gives the theory behind parallel computing. The first passage talks about how climate modeling can best be solved by parallel computing. B is the theory behind A—that is, A is an example of B. (If you flipped the order, the two would almost work together as a single coherent essay.) So choice **(C)** expresses it best.

6. The passages advocate parallel computing to solve parallel problems. (Passage B does so more generally than Passage (A). The best choice for their common purpose is **(B)**. Note that Passage A focuses on just one computing task—climate modeling. So choices saying this method works for many or most problems—(A) and (D)—are wrong.

7. Why the reference to computers in describing the ants? Basically, just to emphasize that the mass of ants is greater than the sum of its parts. Choice **(A)**.

8. Here's another case where the most conservatively worded answer is right. **(E)** – one of the main themes of each passage was the power of parallel computing.

**Passage 2**

Paragraph 1: Statutory interpretation is a vital part of practice of law, but it's not emphasized enough in law school.

Paragraph 2 elaborates that statutes are an important part of practicing law, so it should be taught in law school.

Paragraph 3 states that another benefit is that statute interpretation would teach synthesis—the ability to understand how parts of the law interact with each other.

## PrepTest 59, Section 4 (RC) Continued...

Paragraph 4 answers the objection that because statutes vary from state to state, teaching them can't have nationwide applicability. The answer is that the method of statutory interpretation is being taught, and is applicable anywhere.

So the point here is that law schools should focus more on statutory interpretation. Let's see if that main point prediction is presented as a choice in the first question.

9. It's choice **(C)**. Why not (A) or (B)? They both overstate the case. The author argues for neither a standard curriculum nor a full-scale reversal of law schools' curriculum priorities.

10. The reason given for not studying statutes is in that last paragraph ("One possible argument against..."). And it's **(E)**.

11. The author's argument is that law schools need to place more emphasis on statutes. This is undermined by choice **(B)**, which states that lawyers can learn statutory interpretation on their own (i.e., that law schools don't need to teach it).

12. The third paragraph gives synthesis as a positive result of what the author advocates. See lines 26-28. So choice **(A)** is correct.

13. Choice **(E)** is answered in the passage (lines 5-11). So it's correct. Note that (D) sounds promising until you notice that it mentions "regionally oriented law schools." The objection in the fourth paragraph talks about nationally oriented law schools.

14. Essentially, when you're asked what the author would agree with, you're asked to draw an inference from the passage. Here, choice **(B)** is easily inferred from lines 22-25.

15. Note the word "except"—flip the question on its head. We're looking for a choice that the author would disagree with—that is, something that would not result from more study of statutes. Choice **(A)** is about judicial decisions, so that fits the bill.

**Passage 3**

This passage traces the development of Noguchi. The first paragraph describes him as inquisitive and original. The second paragraph, describing his experiences as another sculptor's stonecutter, shows how Noguchi became interested in positive-light sculptures. Paragraph 3 describes this coming to fruition. The fourth paragraph analyzes these positive-light sculptures. The last paragraph states that Noguchi then moved on again.

16. The point about gold is that it's non-oxidizing—it doesn't lose its luster. So choice (C) is correct.

17. Choice (D) is in the passage (see the last five lines). The others are not.

18. This is one of those questions where none of the answers seems all that great. The least-wrong one is (D); it can be supported by the information in the first paragraph, and the hints in the last paragraph. Noguchi "veered off at wide angles" from the way artists normally progress.

19. So what's the relationship between Ford and Noguchi? Ford developed and made available the metal that Noguchi sculpted with. The best analogy is choice (C).

20. If a positive-light sculpture depends on reflections from the environment, a negative-light sculpture clearly does not. Choice (E) is correct.

21. You may have forgotten what the passage said about Noguchi's sculptures before 1927. Look at lines 11-14. Human forms are mentioned. So (B) is your choice.

22. The idea here is that Noguchi developed the innovative positive-light sculptures in reaction to what he saw at Brancusi's studio. This argument would be weakened if Noguchi had actually seen positive-light sculptures from Brancusi: the development would have not been Noguchi's, nor would it have been a reaction to Brancusi. So choice **(A)** is correct.

**Passage 4**

Paragraph 1 describes the "rules" of the Ultimate Game.

Paragraph 2 describes the results of the game and question why a responder would ever reject an offer.

Paragraph 3 offers one explanation – prehistoric desires for community. "But" (line 35) there are problems with that theory.

Paragraph 4 offers the author's preferred explanation, which is that humans aren't wired to act in strictly one-off social interactions. Responders reject low offers to maintain self-esteem useful in future encounters (even though in this situation there won't be any).

The main idea should reflect that the Ultimate Game raises an interesting question regarding rejections of low offers. While some have hypothesized that it's about community standards, in fact, it's about maintaining self-esteem in future interactions.

23. **(B)** – this reflects the problem around rejection of low offers and discusses the evolutionary explanation.

(C) is interesting because it more specifically addresses the author's explanation, but it doesn't discuss the ultimate game at all and is thus too general.

24. **(D)** – we know this is one-shot; that's addressed in the final paragraph.

25. From our main idea we know the passage is trying to explain a curious result from the Ultimate Game. **(D)** reflects this. (A) is wrong because we aren't simply surveying interpretations, the author is advocating for one over another.

26. The last paragraph is concluding that self-esteem in future interactions explains the results of the Ultimate Game. **(C)** continues this thought by explaining another result of the Ultiate Game through the author's lens of long-term social esteem.

27. **(D)** is correct. The problem the author gives with the first explanation is that it fails to explain why responders reject low offers. (D) explains this -- responders in social groups don't want to be out-competed.

# PrepTest 60
## PrepTest 60, Section 1 (LR)

**1. Question Type: Find the flaw**
Jim knows that anything which contains iron will be attracted to a magnet, but he doesn't know that everything which is attracted to a magnet must be iron. Other substances could also be attracted to magnets, and the one he's testing may be one of those. So the answer is D.
(A) This answer choice contradicts one of Jim's premises: according to the prompt, "magnets attract iron." Remember, on flaw questions you're looking for flaws in the prompt's reasoning, not in its premises.
(B) It doesn't matter what else iron is attracted to: Jim is trying to check whether his substance is iron by using a magnet.
(C) This would matter if Jim had discovered that the substance was not attracted to a magnet: maybe he just pointed the magnet the wrong way. But since it was, this shouldn't matter.
**(D)** Correct.
(E) The difference in degree doesn't matter here: Jim is just looking for attraction or lack thereof.

**2. Question Type: Method of Argument**
First, let's identify the conclusion: "the book must have been either misplaced or stolen." How does the prompt go about convincing us that this is true? Well, it spends a lot of time eliminating other possibilities: the book isn't in use, it's not being reshelved, etc. The right answer should have something to do with that. Thus (E) is the correct answer: "The conclusion [that the book has been misplaced or stolen] is supported by ruling out other explanations [in use, reshelving, etc.] of an observed fact [that the book isn't in place.]"
(A) There's no "general conclusion about similar objects": the whole argument is about one book.
(B) The argument isn't demonstrating a deficiency in the system, even though we might infer one.
(C) There's no "generalization" going on here.
(D) No generalization is rejected: the conclusion is about a particular book.
**(E)** Correct.

**3. Question Type: Inference**
In an inference question, you're looking for something that must be true given the prompt. So you should avoid answer choices that merely seem likely given the prompt. In this question, answer choices A, C, and E all predict consequences of future actions, but the prompt is all about the past ten years, so we can't be sure of any of them. The correct answer is (B), since it draws a conclusion about the past which must be true if everything in the prompt is true.
(A) We can't know what will happen in the next few years—scientists may perfect cold fusion, or the world may end! So there's no way to prove that sulfur dioxide will continue to increase.
**(B)** Correct.
(C) Again, this is a prediction and the prompt only discusses the past.
(D) The prompt doesn't tell us anything about whether power plants are major or minor contributors to air pollution.
(E) We can't know this from the prompt, since again it's a claim about the future.

**4. Question Type: Method of Argument**
The ecologist's conclusion is that a certain "prediction… is therefore unsound." Which prediction? The claim that "there will inevitably be a crisis in landfill availability." So the ecologist is refuting this claim, and the right answer is (D). This prompt is trying to trick you into thinking the ecologist believes the claim about landfill crisis just because he quotes it—to avoid this trap, look out for phrases like "some people say" or "it is often claimed," which generally mark the speaker's disagreement with what he's about to say next.
(A) "Some people" think that the claim about landfill crisis follows from the ecologist's first sentence, but the ecologist himself explicitly disagrees with this, so it can't be right.
(B) The main conclusion is what comes after "therefore" in this case, so B is clearly wrong.
(C) The argument's conclusion is the opposite of this claim, so again that can't be right.
**(D)** Correct.
(E) An intermediate conclusion would lead to the main conclusion; in this case, the main conclusion is to reject the statement about landfill crisis, so clearly E is wrong.

## PrepTest 60, Section 1 (LR) Continued...

### 5. Question Type: Resolve the paradox

What's the "discrepancy" or paradox here? Well, it seems on the one hand as though Country X is pretty good at dealing with disease P, since so few people contract it there, but on the other hand as though Country X isn't so great at dealing with it, since those who do get it are likely to die of it. What's going on? The only answer choice which explains why this might be is C: it's not that fewer people are getting the disease, it's just that few people who get the disease get diagnosed with it, and only those with very severe cases are diagnosed. So it turns out that Country X may have more of disease P than we expected, and it also makes sense why so many of those who get P die of it.

(A) The prompt is about Country X, but this answer has nothing to do with Country X.
(B) This is irrelevant.
**(C)** Correct.
(D) This isn't specific to Country X.
(E) This only deepens the paradox, since from the prompt it seems that fewer cases of illness occur in Country X than in most places.

### 6. Question Type: Find the flaw

The wording of the question is important here: "Which one of the following... most seriously calls into question evidence offered in support of the conclusion above?" In other words, we're looking to challenge the evidence we see—the statistics on otter rehab—rather than the conclusion that the rehab was not worthwhile. Only B does this, so it's the right answer.

(A) Other species don't matter, and areas not affected by the spill don't matter, so this is totally irrelevant.
**(B)** This question directly challenges the argument's claim that "only a fifth of the otters that died immediately were found." If we didn't find those otters, how do we know how many there were? This undermines the prompt's claim that a very small percentage of all otters affected were helped by the rehabilitation.
(C) This is irrelevant because we're worried only about otters affected by the spill.
(D) Again, we care only about otters in this prompt.
(E) This is a very strong answer choice, since it challenges the conclusion of the argument: that "the effort was not worthwhile." To know whether it was worthwhile, wouldn't we have to know how much effort was put into it? Yes. But this answer choice demands new evidence instead of undermining the given evidence, so it's not quite an answer to the question asked here.

### 7. Question Type: Assumption

The psychologist's conclusion is that support groups may have value. It's pretty clear what's missing from his argument: he draws no connection between stress and a weak immune system. So (C) is the correct answer.

(A) This may be true, but it's not relevant to the psychologist's claim.
(B) This is an extreme claim, and not one that the psychologist needs to make for his argument.
**(C)** Correct.
(D) This is an extreme claim—surely talking doesn't eliminate the stress of cancer—and it doesn't make the connection to a weak immune system that we're looking for.
(E) The psychologist must think that support groups -> lower stress -> stronger immune system. If stress were merely a symptom of a weak immune system (weak immune system -> high stress), then we couldn't improve someone's immune system by treating this symptom.

### 8. Question Type: Main Point

When you're faced with a main point question, try summing up the argument in your head. In this case you'll probably get something like: "Adobe is good to build with in deserts because it doesn't let the house get too hot or too cold, unlike other materials." If we use this as our prediction, it's easy to see that the correct answer is E.

(A) This conclusion is more general than the argument—the argument is just about deserts in particular.
(B) This isn't the main point of the argument, since it doesn't contrast adobe with other materials.
(C) The argument is about deserts, which aren't mentioned here.
(D) The argument is about adobe, which isn't mentioned here.
**(E)** Correct.

# PrepTest 60, Section 1 (LR) Continued...

**9. Question Type: Resolve the paradox**
The paradox here is pretty clear: two studies of the same population found very different numbers. What's the deal? Remember, we're looking for an answer which clearly explains why the first study got such a high number, not just information which casts doubt on the accuracy of the studies.
(A) The first study didn't find more patterned plants, it found a higher percentage of patterned plants. So the total population shouldn't matter.
(B) This is irrelevant: We only care about this species.
(C) Again, the total number of plants studied shouldn't make a difference, since we're explaining a discrepancy in the percent of plants.
**(D)** Correct: A broader definition of "patterned" would cause the first study to count more plants as patterned than the second study, thus explaining the different results.
(E) The reason why the studies were conducted doesn't explain their different results.

**10. Question Type: Find the flaw**
The argument's conclusion is: "The approach you propose would damage commercial fishing operations." But the only evidence provided is that a bunch of people signed a petition disagreeing with the proposed plan. We have no reason to believe that these people know what they're talking about. Thus the answer is (D).
(A) We don't know the editor's view, so we can't tell whether it's been distorted.
(B) The argument's main conclusion is against the editor's proposal, not for the alternative. Thus it's not essential that the argument prove whether the alternative is viable.
(C) We don't know what the letter-writer's self-interest is, nor would it matter if we did: an argument can be valid even if the person who's making it is motivated by self-interest.
**(D)** Correct.
(E) The argument is against the editor's proposal, not for the alternative, so it doesn't matter whether some third option might work.

**11. Question Type: Strengthen**
The conclusion here is that "most universities offer a more in-depth and cosmopolitan education than ever before." The prompt provides only one example to demonstrate this, and the example isn't rock-solid: are more extensive textbooks good evidence of an "in-depth and cosmopolitan education"? This is a major hole in the argument, so we expect an answer choice which fills it, and only (C) does so.
(A) The argument isn't about what interests students, so this is irrelevant.
(B) This does strengthen the conclusion a bit, since study-abroad programs seem cosmopolitan (though they may not be in-depth), but it has the same problem as the prompt's example: we're not sure if this is evidence of a "cosmopolitan and in-depth" education.
**(C)** Correct. If this statement is true, then the example of textbook coverage given in the prompt is a "strong indication" that its conclusion is true. Since we're trying to strengthen this conclusion, C is the right answer.
(D) This would weaken the argument.
(E) This shows that bad textbooks aren't enough to guarantee a cosmopolitan and in-depth education, but it doesn't prove that good textbooks are enough to guarantee it, which is what the prompt is arguing.

**12. Question Type: Find the flaw**
The conclusion here is: "such disclosure actually undermines the government's goal of making the public more informed," since airlines will avoid making safety information public. But clearly the public will get some information out of the safety reports, even if it's not complete information, so even if the speaker is correct in thinking that airlines will hide information, it's not clear that this will lead to less information than there is now. The prompt fails to consider that a solution which isn't perfect may still be partly effective. Thus the answer is (A).
**(A)** Correct.
(B) The prompt argues against informing the public, so it certainly doesn't assume the public has a right to know.
(C) The prompt focuses on government disclosures and makes no claims about other ways to find this information, so this is irrelevant.
(D) The prompt doesn't discuss who "should be held responsible" for disclosure, only what the airlines are likely to do in practice.

(E) Revenues aren't directly relevant here.

### 13. Question Type: Weaken

This is a tough question—getting the right answer depends on recognizing a subtle shift in vocabulary. The prompt argues that economists are wrong about financial rewards, but it quotes surveys on the issue of high salaries. The first time you read through this you're likely to think financial rewards are the same as high salaries, but if this were false, the argument would be very weak. Thus (C) is the answer. But most test-takers will only realize this once they've eliminated the other answers, so be sure you know why each other answer is incorrect.

(A) The argument is about what motivates people to take jobs; whether people can get all the goods they desire is scarcely relevant.
(B) The prompt argues against the idea that money is "the strongest incentive" to take a given job. B merely shows that money is an incentive, not the strongest, so it's not sufficient to weaken the argument.
**(C)** Correct: Economists may be right that "financial incentives" like pensions and healthcare are very important, even if salary isn't.
(D) This suggests another reason a person might take a job besides money, but doesn't show that this is a stronger incentive than money, so it's not relevant.
(E) This is irrelevant, since it doesn't tell us whether time or money is a stronger incentive.

### 14. Question Type: Assumption

The prompt argues that reducing class size won't make students "more engaged in the learning process," but the study it cites only shows that students' grades won't improve after a reduction in class size. So the argument works only if no increase in grades indicates no increase in engagement. (After all, teachers at better schools may give out the same number of As for better work, in which case the study provides no evidence concerning whether schools with smaller class sizes are better.) Thus the answer is (D).

(A) The prompt doesn't mention large schools in particular.
(B) This isn't important, since the question isn't about whether some students will get more attention than others but whether students who get more attention on average will do better.
(C) This is irrelevant, since the overall number of teachers isn't at issue.
**(D)** Correct.
(E) The prompt doesn't need to assume that parents want smaller classes solely for one reason or another; it merely needs to show that this particular reason (increased engagement) is incorrect.

### 15. Question Type: Find the flaw

Rebecca says that she has saved some money on her water bill, but she doesn't say how much. She's trying to prove that "it is not true that the manufacturers' claims are exaggerated." To know whether the manufacturers' claims are exaggerated, we have to know whether she saved as much as they claimed she would. The answer is B; Rebecca assumes that she is saving not just some money but as much money as she was told she would.

(A) This answer is almost right, but it misses the main point: to know whether the manufacturers' claims are exaggerated, we need to know not just whether she's saving money, but whether she's saving as much money as the manufacturers claim.
**(B)** Correct.
(C) The consistency of different manufacturers isn't at issue here.
(D) The argument isn't about satisfaction with water volume but about monetary savings.
(E) Rebecca isn't taking this for granted, since her argument doesn't depend on how many water-saving faucets she owns.

### 16. Question Type: Weaken

The company spokesperson proves that old cars are a bigger problem than the company's plants overall, but that doesn't mean that the company's proposed solution to this problem will be more effective than redesigning its plants. After all, unless the company buys up all the old cars in the area, it won't reduce pollution by a full 30%; how much pollution is reduced will depend on how much money the company spends and how many cars it buys. The answer is C: If most of the cars the company buys aren't running anyway, its car-buying plan won't affect pollution much at all, and the claim that this plan will reduce pollution more than plant redesign falls apart.

## PrepTest 60, Section 1 (LR) Continued...

(A) This doesn't affect the argument, since even if only a small proportion of cars predate 1980 they are still responsible for 30% of pollution.
(B) This shows that the company has a self-interested motive for its car-buying plan, but does not prove that the plan will not have the desired effect.
**(C) Correct.**
(D) Even if this is true, the company's plan to focus on old cars may still reduce pollution.
(E) We have no way of knowing whether the lower number of complaints corresponds to a lower level of pollution.

### 17. Question Type: Parallel reasoning

This argument reasons from an evident effect (human survival) back to its necessary cause (sacrifice for close relatives), then points out that this cause (sacrifice) must in turn have a further cause (at least partial altruism.) We could diagram it as follows:
No self-sacrifice -> no survival
Survival (observed) -> self-sacrifice
Self-sacrifice -> altruism
Answer choice (A) is a close parallel here:
No increased study time -> no improved grades
Improved grades -> Increased study time
Increased study time -> Time management
Thus (A) is the answer.

**(A) Correct.**
(B) This argument is clearly not parallel: Among other things, it argues for what a given group doesn't have (photosynthesis), unlike the prompt, which shows what a group does have.
(C) This argument is about the future (effects of government action) instead of the causal implications of a present state of affairs (as in the prompt, where species survival is taken as a given and we reason back from it.)
(D) Again, this argument aims at the effects of future actions rather than the necessary precursors of present facts.
(E) The conclusion of this argument is an either/or, which is not parallel to the prompt.

### 18. Question Type: Principle

The bus driver concludes that he should not be held responsible for the accident, even if he could have prevented it by reacting more quickly, simply because he wasn't violating traffic regulations. Note that the argument here is negative: the bus driver doesn't say who should be held responsible or when, only who shouldn't be. Thus the answer is (E): If we assume (E), the driver's conclusion follows clearly from his evidence. He wasn't violating traffic law, so he shouldn't be punished.

(A) This looks like a good answer—but it's much broader than the bus driver's claim. He doesn't deny all responsibility for the collision, or claim that all responsibility should go to the other driver—he merely denies that he should be reprimanded.
(B) We don't know whether the police report confirms that "the collision was completely the fault of the driver of another vehicle," only that it says the bus driver was not violating any laws.
(C) The bus driver says nothing about when the company should reprimand a driver, only about when it shouldn't. Thus this principle is irrelevant.
(D) We know from the prompt that the bus driver might well have been able to avoid this accident if he had reacted more quickly, so (D) actually works against his argument.
**(E) Correct.**

### 19. *Removed from Scoring*

### 20. Question Type: Assumption

The historian's evidence is narrow, and his conclusion is quite broad: he shows that people used to exercise their imagination when they listened to the radio, and that people use less imagination when they watch TV, but concludes quite generally that people today use their imagination less frequently overall. This will be true only if people today have no other ways of exercising their imagination than watching TV. This is exactly what

# PrepTest 60, Section 1 (LR) Continued...

answer choice (D) says: the historian must be assuming that people today don't exercise their imagination in any other way that has replaced radio. So the answer is (D).

(A) The precise amount of time devoted to each medium is irrelevant.
(B) The historian's argument isn't about change within a medium (as people become more familiar with it) but about change between media (from radio to TV).
(C) We may suspect that the historian believes this value judgment, but it certainly isn't required by his argument; his argument could be true even if he thought TV was superior to radio.
**(D)** Correct.
(E) The historian discusses imagination, not thought.

### 21. Question Type: Parallel flaw
The pattern of reasoning here is:
All A (candidates) are B (small business owners).
Most B (small business owners) are C (competent managers).
      All C (competent managers) are D (have skills to be a good mayor.)
Therefore Most A (candidates) are D (have skills).
The flaw here is that just because most small business owners are competent managers doesn't mean most of those who are running for mayor are competent managers. If most of a set has a given property, that doesn't mean most of any subset of that set has a property. (Think about it: It can be true that most days in May 2011 were sunny but still false that most Sundays in May 2011 were sunny.) B has precisely the same structure as the prompt:
All A (items on the menu) are B (fat-free).
Most B (fat-free) are C (sugar-free)
All C (sugar-free) are D (low calories).
Therefore Most A (items on the menu) are D (low calories).
Thus B is the right answer.

(A) This argument isn't actually flawed: if most of the company's management has worked in sales, and everyone who has worked in sales understands marketing, it must be true that most of the company's management understands marketing.
**(B)** Correct.
(C) This can be eliminated immediately, since the conclusion doesn't contain the word or concept "most," so it can't have the same flaw as the prompt.
(D) This argument changes terms (from avant-garde films to films at the film festival), which is a flaw, but not the one in the prompt.
(E) This argument confuses "most" of one set (helmets with rubber) with most of another set (helmets in the store), which is a different flaw from that of the prompt.

### 22. Question Type: Sufficient Assumption
In an assumption question, always look for a word or concept that is in the conclusion but not in the premises. In this case, independent invention of money is the new concept. We know that money was invented from the premises (since it's not innate), but not that it was invented independently in more than one society. We need evidence for this—evidence that money was invented more than once. Only A provides such evidence, so it's the right answer.

**(A)** Correct.
(B) The conclusion of the argument is about money, so this isn't relevant.
(C) This isn't required by the prompt—there may be universals which aren't invented, but the prompt specifically says that money was invented.
(D) This is irrelevant, since the prompt doesn't need to explain why money is widespread—only that it is.
(E) This contradicts the premise of the argument that money is "universal," so it can't be an assumption required by the argument.

### 23. Question Type: Principle
The conclusion here is that "strong laws against libel can make it impossible for anyone in the public eye to have a good reputation." Yet the evidence provided is just that with strong libel laws, "no one will say anything bad about public figures." We need a principle which explains why only when people say bad things about

## PrepTest 60, Section 1 (LR) Continued...

public figures can any public figure have a good reputation. E provides such an explanation: if some public figures need to have bad reputations in order for others to have good reputations, it makes sense that laws which prevent people from having bad reputations will also prevent people from having good reputations. Thus E is correct.

(A) This clearly contradicts the prompt's conclusion.
(B) This doesn't explain why with strong libel laws no one will have a good reputation.
(C) This is irrelevant to the argument's conclusion, which is about reputation, not what should be considered libel.
(D) This contradicts the prompt's statement that in countries with strong libel laws "no one will say anything bad," so it can't help justify the prompt's argument.
(E) Correct.

### 24. Question Type: Most strongly supported

This prompt contains many long words, so it can be tough to parse. But it's clear from the prompt that (a) beta-glucans prevent cancer by stimulating immune cells, and (b) beta-glucans are better at preventing cancer as the "degree of branching" increases. This implies that more-branched beta-glucans are better at stimulating immune cells, so (C) is the answer.

(A) The prompt says mammals can't digest cellulose, but cellulose may have some positive health effect without being digested, so this isn't supported.
(B) We know that beta-glucans in mushrooms prevent cancer, but there may be some other way in which mushrooms can prevent cancer even without beta-glucans; (beta-glucans -> prevent cancer) doesn't imply (prevents cancer -> beta-glucans).
(C) Correct.
(D) Beta-glucans don't function by killing cancer cells, but we get no information from the prompt on how immune cells function.
(E) The prompt says that mushrooms can make beta-glucans from cellulose, but not that everything that can digest cellulose produces beta-glucans.

### 25. Question Type: Method of argument

It's clear that the only comparison made in the argument is between laws and manners: "Just as manners… so societal laws…" But this isn't that helpful, because every answer choice involves manners. Why are manners brought up exactly? The prompt's point is that manners are obeyed not because we'll be punished if we don't follow them but because we've gotten used to following them, and that laws work the same way: we comply with them because we're used to doing so. The answer is (C).

(A) The speaker may agree with this, but that's not the point of the comparison: the main point of the argument is that compliance with laws is customary, not that it varies from society to society.
(B) The prompt doesn't raise the issue of why laws are adopted, only why they're complied with.
(C) Correct.
(D) The prompt doesn't say whether compliance with laws or manners is ethically required; it only states that people don't comply because it's ethically required, but because it's customary.
(E) The prompt doesn't say whether those who fail to comply with laws or manners are punished, only that people don't comply because of punishment; rather, they comply because of custom.

# PrepTest 60, Section 2, Game 1

This is a straightforward grouping game; we have 6 spots for 6 workshops.

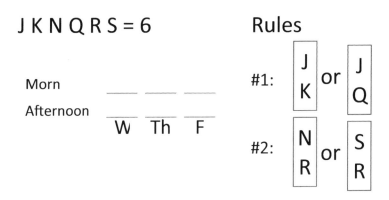

#3:  Q (day before) < K / N

Discussion: There aren't major inferences to be had here, but it is helpful to add the sequencing inferences from Rule 3. You also know that J can't be in the afternoon and R can't be in the morning. On Rule 3, it's important to note that Q must be on a day before both K and N; it wouldn't be sufficient for Q to go in the morning on a day in which K or N go.

```
Morn        ___  ___  ~R
Afternoon   ___  ___  ~J
             W   Th    F
            ~K       ~Q
            ~N
```

1. List question.
a)  Violates Rule 3
b)  **Correct.**
c)  Violates Rule 3
d)  Violates Rule 2
e)  Violates Rule 1

2. You'll be able to eliminate with past diagrams; anything left you can quickly insert into a diagram and make work.
**c) Correct,** Q can't be on Thursday morning. This would force both K and N to Friday. J would have to go in the only morning spot remaining, Wednesday, but neither K or Q are available to go with it, violating Rule 1.

3. This will be process of elimination.
a) Correct. K can't go on Wednesday because there will be no room for Q.
b) Works, e.g. JQ, NR, KS
c) Works, e.g. QS, JK, NR
d) Works, e.g. SQ, NR, JK
e) Works, e.g. SR, JQ, KN

4. If K is Friday morning, we know we'll need to have JK together (since JQ is ruled out). There are therefore two options:

| | | | | | | | | |
|---|---|---|---|---|---|---|---|---|
| Morn | | J | | K | Morn | | J | K |
| Afternoon | Q | | | | Afternoon | Q | | |
| | W | Th | F | | | W | Th | F |

Then we need to fit in Rule 2. In the first option, either NR or SR will work. For the second option, it will have to be SR because the block goes on Wednesday, and we can't put N before Q.

| | | | | | | | | |
|---|---|---|---|---|---|---|---|---|
| Morn | J | N/S | K | | Morn | S | J | K |
| Afternoon | Q | R | N/S | | Afternoon | R | Q | N |
| | W | Th | F | | | W | Th | F |

As an aside, drawing these diagrams out not only helps you solve this question but gives you ample valid diagrams with which to use on questions 2, 3, and 6.

a) **Correct.** J could be on Thursday morning. All other options are ruled out.

5. If Q is in the morning, we know that JK will have to go together. That helps us enormously; N will still have to go after Q, and it clearly can't go with JK, so it will have to go on a third day. That means Q will have to go on Wednesday. We know we have to put R in the afternoon, and it can go with either N or S. But if R goes with S, N would have to go with Q, which we know is not permitted. So we know that QS go on the first day, followed by either JK or NR (but we don't know in what order).

| | | | | | | | | | |
|---|---|---|---|---|---|---|---|---|---|
| Morn | Q | J | S | | Morn | Q | N | J |
| Afternoon | S | K | R | OR | Afternoon | S | R | K |
| | W | Th | F | | | W | Th | F |

e) Correct. S must be given on Wednesday.

6. At this point we have a ton of past diagrams to look at. In Wednesday morning so far we've seen J (#1), S (#4), and Q (#5). Which variables do we know for sure can't go on Wednesday? K and N, because they must go after Q. That just leaves R, but we know R can never go in the morning (Rule 2).

c) **Correct.** Only J, S, and Q can go on Wednesday morning.

# PrepTest 60, Section 2, Game 2

This is a basic linear game..

G H J L M P = 6

**Rules**

```
___ ___ ___ ___ ___ ___
 1   2   3   4   5   6
                     ~G
```

#1:  ...L... < H
     M

#2:  ...L... < J
     P

#3:  M < P → H < G      G < H → P < M

#4: G not 6 (insert into diagram)

Discussion: There are several exclusion rules that can be inserted from Rules 1 and 2.

```
                          H/J
___ ___ ___ ___ ___ ___
 1   2   3   4   5   6
~H                      ~G
~J                      ~L
                        ~P
                        ~M
```

The contrapositive of rule 3 would technically be ~(H < G) →  ~(M < P), but since none of the variables can go simultaneously we can simplify by reversing the order of each side and just write G < H →  P < M.

It's worth thinking about the world in which M < P to look for inferences (because it triggers Rule 3), but it doesn't really get you anywhere; we'll know that G has to go after L, M, and H, but that's not enormously useful. Although we'd like to combine rules to make a big inference, it's not possible here.

7. List question.
a) Violates Rule 2
b) Violates Rule 3
c) Violates Rule 1
d) Violates Rule 4
e) **Correct**

8. You can do some elimination with past diagrams.
a) H can go before G, e.g. L M P H G J
b) Could work, e.g. L P M J G H
c) **Correct.** L must have both H and J behind it, so L can't go 5$^{th}$.
d) Could work, same diagram as b)
e) Could work, same diagram as b)

9. According to our master diagram, only H and J can go last. **D is correct.**

10. We're given the new rule J < M. Make sure to combine this with your other rules. This gives us:

$$\begin{matrix} L \\ \cdots \\ P \end{matrix} < J < M < H$$

G is not assigned, but we know it can't be last.

a) **Correct.** This fits our new rule.
b) Can't work, has H before L
c) Can't work, has H before P
d) Can't work, has G last; we know only H or J can go last, and J has to go much earlier here.
e) Can't work, has G last. This is the same logic as d).

11. We're given the new block of LG . We'll still need to have H and J after this block.
a) G can be 4$^{th}$, e.g. P M L G H J
b) H could be last, but J could be last as well.
c) **Correct.** L needs to have G, H, and J behind it, so it can't go later than third.
d) Could be false, e.g. L G P M H J
e) Could be false, see d)

12. If M is first, we know that Rule 3 is triggered, thus H < G. If H < G, H can't be last, so J has to be last.

**c) Correct.** J must be 6$^{th}$.

# PrepTest 60, Section 2, Game 3

While this is essentially a linear game, there are only 2 variables and they repeat several times; it's not like any other recent game.

3 M, 4 S = 7

**Rules**
(Cleaned between types)
#1: Max 3 cleanings
#2: 5=M

```
                    M
___ ___ ___ ___ ___ ___ ___
 1   2   3   4   5   6   7
```

Discussion: There aren't big inferences to be made here. It's possible to list out dozens of possibilities, but doing so tends to take more time than it could possibly be worth, especially given that you'll just work through those possibilities when you get to the questions. You can determine that 2 M's must be together. (If not, there would have to be more than 3 cleanings).

13. On this and most questions for this game, quick elimination on a diagram works wonders.
a) This gives us M's every other space, requiring 5 cleanings
b) Requires 4 cleanings
c) Requires 4 cleanings
d) Requires 4 cleanings
e) **Correct.** Requires 2 cleanings (between 3/4 and 6/7)

14. Again, quick process of elimination works well.
a) Could be false: M M S S M S S
b) Could be false: M S S S M M S
c) Could be false, see a)
d) **Correct.** 2 mulches must be together else 4+ cleanings are required.
e) Could be false, see a)

15. If 3 and 5 are both M, we know that we'll need the third M to be next to either of those, putting S in 1 and 7.
a) Could be false: S S M M M S S
b) Could be false: see a)
c) Could be false, see a)
d) Could be false: S S M M M S S
e) **Correct.** Were M first, we wouldn't have consecutive M's, which forces us into 4+ cleanings

16.
a) **Correct.** If M is in 2, we'd need at least 3 cleanings: M M S S M S S, S M M S M S S, etc – no configuration will work.
b) Could be false; S S S M M M S
c) Could be false: S S M M M S S
d) Could be false; see c)
e) Could be false; see c)

17. If no more than 2 loads go consecutively, we'll need a grouping of consecutive M's, and one M separating the rest of the S's.
a) Must be false; if S is first, we'll get either a group of 3 consecutive S's or 4+ cleanings
b) **Correct, e.g. M M S S M S S**
c) Must be false; 4 can't be mulch because we'd have a block of 3 M's, but if it's not we'd have too many cleanings.
d) Must be false; forces 7 and to be mulch, which will end in too many cleanings.
e) Must be false; forces S into 6, which will generate too many cleanings.

This is a grouping game with some matching aspects. We are managing 3 sets of variables: stories, interns, and the profession of the intern. If the diagram is structured correctly, the setup is straightforward.

F G H J K L = 6

| | | | |
|---|---|---|---|
| Rom | p | w | |
| Spain | p | w | ~S |
| Tusc | p | w | J |

### Rules
#1: G and L same field (implies G and L can't be on the same story)
#2: F and K different fields
#3: Hp
#4: J to Tuscany (insert into diagram)
#5: K not to Spain (insert)

Discussion: it's important to integrate the professions directly into the diagram so you know when you've filled a certain profession.

Think about each of the professions. For photography, we know that H is definitely included. We also know that F/K are in different fields, so photography must have both H and one of either F/K. This leads to a big insight: with 2 interns locked in photography (because we would have 4 photographers), G and L (which must be in the same field) can't also both be photographers, so they must be writers! We know we also have to have F/K in the writers' column, which fills it up. J would therefore have to be a photographer.

```
        H      G
       F/K     L
        J     F/K
```

| | | | |
|---|---|---|---|
| R | p | w | |
| S | p | w | ~K |
| T | p | w | J |

Since we know J has to go to Tuscany by Rule 4, and we know he must be a photographer (because of the above inference, we know exactly where J goes.

```
        H      G
       F/K     L
        J     F/K
```

| | | | |
|---|---|---|---|
| R | p | w | |
| S | p | w | ~K |
| T | Jp | w | |

By using the placeholder F/K, we unlocked a key inference that will make this game quite manageable.

18. List question. If you found the inference you can quickly eliminate B, C, and E, but the rule-by-rule elimination method works as well as ever.
a) **Correct.**
b) Violates Rule 1
c) Violates Rule 2
d) Violates Rule 3
e) Violates Rule 5

19. If F is assigned to Romania, F can be either a photographer or writer:

| | | | | | | | | |
|---|---|---|---|---|---|---|---|---|
| R | Fp | w | | | R | p | Fw | |
| S | p | w | ~K | | S | p | w | ~K |
| T | Jp | w | | | T | Jp | w | |

If F is a photographer, H must go to Spain because it's the only photographer we have left. We're not sure about the writers (other than that K doesn't go to Spain).

If F is a writer, K must be a photographer. But K can't go to Spain, so it must go to Romania. That means H is the photographer in Spain because that's the only photography space left.

**b) Correct.** Hall must be assigned to Spain.

20. If F and H go on the same story, they must cover Spain. If H covered Romania, K would be the only photographer left to cover Spain, which is not allowed.

| | | |
|---|---|---|
| R | Kp | G/Lw |
| S | Hp | Fw ~K |
| T | Jp | G/Lw |

**b) Correct.** G could cover Romania.

21. Similarly to #20, if F is a writer then K must be a photographer and also must be assigned to Romania (because Jp covers Tuscany as always, and R cannot cover Spain by rule). That means H will cover Spain as a writer and G, L, and F float in the writers' column.

**d) Correct.** K and L could cover Romania.

22. We have the same logical pattern again as we did in 20 and 21. G is always a writer, so K will have to be a photographer. If K is a photographer, it will have to go to Romania (because Tuscany has J and K cannot cover Spain). That means that G will also cover Romania, H will be the writer for Spain, and F/L will be writers in Spain and Tuscany.

**e) Correct.** L could be the writer for Spain.

23. This is simple if you made the right inferences. **c) is correct;** H can't cover Tuscany because H must be a photographer, and J is always the photographer that covers Tuscany.

# PrepTest 60, Section 3 (LR)

**1. Question Type: Resolve the paradox**

In "resolve the paradox" questions, it's important to be clear about what the "paradox" is exactly. Here, it's pretty clear: when measures are undertaken to fight congestion, congestion actually increases. We're looking for an answer choice that explains why more traffic happens on the new roads. Answer choice WWW DOT DIORREFERRAL DOT COM does just that: If wider roads attract more cars, it makes sense that there will be more traffic on them.

**(A)** Correct.
(B) This answer would only deepen the paradox by ruling out one possible explanation: If population isn't increasing, why does traffic continue to increase?
(C) This is irrelevant, since the question has nothing to do with accidents.
(D) This is irrelevant, since the prompt refers only to "urban areas," not to rural ones.
(E) This is irrelevant, since the contrast in the prompt isn't between rural and urban areas but between urban areas before and after road improvement.

**2. Question Type: Strengthen**

The prompt claims that the advertisements caused people to buy the product. But we can't know whether the ads were the reason people bought the product—maybe it was a coincidence. So the argument would be stronger if we had evidence that the ads changed people's behavior—and only (B) provides this. So **(B)** is correct.

(A) The prompt isn't about how many people went through the checkout line in total, but about how likely those who did check out were to buy a particular product. Since (A) is about the total number, it's irrelevant.
**(B)** This is very good evidence that people's behavior is changed by the ads—if they weren't going to purchase the product before they heard the ads, the ads likely had something to do with it.
(C) This is definitely the second-best answer, but it doesn't show that the ads caused people to buy products: after all, the store may advertise products which many people buy anyway.
(D) This would weaken the argument—be careful not to let opposite answers trick you!
(E) This might slightly strengthen the argument—if people don't buy the product often, but did now, the ad may be the cause. But it doesn't demonstrate the causal link as clearly as B does.

**3. Question Type: Assumption**

This prompt has a pretty glaring gap: It says the library won't be finished on time unless either the permit is obtained on time or building process can be sped up. We know the permit can't be obtained on time, but we don't know whether the building process can be sped up. Only if we knew this was impossible would the conclusion that the library won't be finished on time follow logically. So we're looking for an answer choice which says the building process can't be sped up, and (A) is the answer.

**(A)** Correct.
(B) This makes the conclusion probable, but we're looking for an assumption which will make the conclusion follow logically without a hint of chance, so this won't work.
(C) This tells us something we already know (that the permit won't be obtained by February 1), not something we need to assume.
(D) Again, we know that the permit won't be on time, so we don't need to assume anything further about it.
(E) The premise of the prompt is that either the building permit must be obtained or construction must be sped up if the library is to be completed on time. Thus the prompt rules out the possibility of starting construction early. Remember, don't choose an answer that directly contradicts the argument's premises!

**4. Question Type: Weaken**

The results of the study will be weakened if there is "sample bias"—if the groups who inhaled peppermint and bitter orange weren't the same in all other respects. If this is true, the scent may not be the cause of the difference in getting to sleep found by the study, because some other factor may come into play. (B) is the correct answer because if the people who inhaled peppermint were already more insomniac than the people who inhaled bitter orange, they may have had more trouble getting to sleep for this reason, and the study may not tell us about the effects of the scent.

(A) The argument is about peppermint's effects on insomnia, so people who don't have insomnia are irrelevant.
**(B)** Correct.

## PrepTest 60, Section 3 (LR) Continued...

(C) While this may bias the results of the study, the effect should apply to bitter orange and peppermint equally—so it doesn't explain away the difference found by the study.
(D) This is irrelevant, since it doesn't tell us anything about the difference between peppermint and bitter orange.
(E) This is very vague—we don't know whether "dramatically affect" means increase or decrease insomnia, and we don't know what scents they're talking about, so there's no way this information can be applied to this particular study.

### 5. Question Type: Method of argument

What is the prompt trying to prove? Clearly, it offers a study as evidence for the first sentence, its conclusion. Thus (D) is the answer. Note that this argument has flaws—we don't know, for example, whether dogs trained only with hand signals would be better than those with both voice and hand signals—but that's not relevant here: we can still tell that the speaker believes that his study supports his first sentence.

(A) The argument doesn't prove other things given the first sentence, so it's not a premise.
(B) Nothing stated explicitly in the argument could be an "implicit premise."
(C) This isn't background information, it's the main point.
(D) Correct.
(E) What would count as the "main conclusion" here? There's no conclusion besides the first sentence.

### 6. Question Type: Parallel reasoning

The structure of this argument is pretty simple:
> None of Group A (test pilots) had experience X (difficulty) in the past.
> Therefore, the next member of group A (tomorrow's pilot) also won't have experience X.

Only (D) follows this structure exactly:
> None of Group A (book reviewers) had experience X (enjoyment) in the past.
> Therefore, the next member of Group A (the local reviewer) will have experience X (enjoyment).

(A) This argument shifts from "book reviewers" to "average readers," but the prompt contains no such shift—it stays within the group of test pilots.
(B) This argument is about many book reviewers who read the book, but the prompt is about all test pilots who flew the plane.
(C) This argument is almost parallel, but not quite: It cites just two reviewers, whereas the prompt has many pilots.
(D) Correct.
(E) This answer switches groups (reviewers -> general public), whereas the prompt stays within the group of test pilots.

### 7. Question Type: Method of argument

The scientist starts off with a necessary condition for a theory to be taken seriously: it must affect our perception. But he wants to show it's not sufficient: not everything which affects our perception should be taken seriously. He gives astrology as an example to make sure we understand that the condition (affecting our perception) isn't sufficient: astrology does affect our perception, but clearly he thinks it shouldn't be taken seriously. The answer is (C).

(A) The scientist does think that astrology shouldn't be taken seriously, but he brings it up specifically because it does affect our perception of the world, to show that this condition isn't sufficient to take a theory seriously.
(B) The scientist doesn't say anything about what should be considered a theory.
(C) Correct.
(D) The scientist does thing that astrology affects our perception, but he clearly doesn't think it should be taken seriously. (He's a scientist, after all!)
(E) The scientist says clearly that a theory should be taken seriously only if it affects our perception, so this can't be right.

### 8. Question type: Flaw

Clark's mistake is to think that just because critical acclaim is "one of the main factors" determining which plays get performed, every play performed must have critical acclaim. In fact, there may be other factors

## PrepTest 60, Section 3 (LR) Continued...

which will cause a play to get performed even if it doesn't have critical acclaim—so his conclusion that Michaela's play has critical acclaim may be false. He "treats one factor considered in the selection of plays [critical acclaim] as though it were a condition that must be met [as though every play performed has it]"—so (C) is correct.

(A) This seems relevant, but he doesn't give any conditions necessary for a play to be critically acclaimed, so it can't be right.
(B) This is almost right: If the wording was "several causes may produce the same effect," then this would be equivalent to (C) and correct. (He thinks that since being critically acclaimed can cause performance, anything performed must have critical acclaim.) But the actual answer is reversed, so this is irrelevant.
(C) Correct.
(D) His source is the production director, and we have no reason to believe she's unreliable.
(E) He believes that being performed is a result of being acclaimed, and he does provide evidence: the production director says so.

### 9. Question Type: Principle

The legal theorist's conclusion is that the government should not be allowed to use personal diaries to prosecute. His evidence is that a person's diary is intended only for himself. There's a missing link between the evidence and the conclusion: we don't know why evidence that a diary is intended for oneself is evidence that it shouldn't be used in prosecution. To draw this conclusion, the theorist must believe that words intended for oneself shouldn't be used in prosecution. Thus the answer is (C).

(A) Interoffice memos are not intended for oneself, so they're outside the scope of the argument.
(B) This is the opposite of what the theorist is saying: he thinks evidence should be restricted.
(C) Correct.
(D) "Personal correspondence" means letters to other people, whereas the theorist is discussing writing only for oneself.
(E) This is the opposite of what the theorist is saying, since he's proposing a limit on government power.

### 10. Question Type: Most strongly supported

This is a relatively easy question: we're told to assume that the theories described are correct, so we know that
(1) the ring of gas has a radius of 49 kilometers and (2) this can be true only if the black hole is spinning. Thus the black hole must be spinning, and (C) is the answer.

(A) We know that black holes with rings less than 49 kilometers are spinning, but we can't infer from this that black holes with rings greater than 49 kilometers are stationary.
(B) This goes well beyond the information we're given. There may be other types of gas rings not described in the prompt.
(C) Correct.
(D) We can't infer any causal relationship because the prompt says nothing about causes.
(E) We can't infer this—there may be stationary black holes with no gas rings at all.

### 11. Question Type: Assumption

Note that the prompt's conclusion is simply that black water of this intensity didn't enter the bay at any time in the past two centuries. The prompt doesn't take a position on whether the black water was natural or caused by human activity. The prompt supports its conclusion by noting that 200-year-old corals were destroyed by the black water; if black water had entered the bay in the past 200 years, presumably it would have destroyed this coral and there wouldn't be any 200-year-old coral. But it's possible that black water destroyed the coral this time only because it was already damaged; if this were true, it would be possible that black water had entered the bay in the past 200 years and simply hadn't destroyed all the coral. We need an assumption that excludes this possibility, so the answer is (D).

(A) This would contradict the argument, so it's certainly not an assumption required by the argument.
(B) It's not necessary that every species be harmed; only the five referred to in the prompt are relevant, and we know they were destroyed.
(C) This is irrelevant, since the argument is based on coral.
(D) Correct.
(E) If this were true, it would weaken the argument, since it would imply that the old corals were wiped out only because they were old, and that they may have withstood earlier black water events. Thus it's certainly

## PrepTest 60, Section 3 (LR) Continued...

not an assumption required by the argument.

### 12. Question Type: Inference
We're given two types of information here: Information about how nurseries label miniature tress (they label them differently, and some label Stark Sweet Melody as miniature) and a sufficient condition for correctly labeling something miniature (it must be suitable to grow in a pot). We don't know whether Stark Sweet Melody is suitable for growing in a pot, but we do know that if it were not suitable, the nurseries which labeled it as miniature would be labeling it incorrectly. So the answer is (E).
(A) We aren't told anything about what "most" nurseries do.
(B) Even if SSM were suitable for growing in a pot, some nurseries might be labeling it correctly—the ones which label it as miniature. So it's not true that some nurseries mislabel it only if it's not suitable for growing in a pot.
(C) We can't know this, since we don't know whether SSM is suitable for growth in a pot.
(D) We know that if a nectarine tree (1) is not suitable for growing in a pot and (2) is labeled miniature, then it's labeled incorrectly. We don't know what conditions would have to hold for a tree which is not labeled miniature to be labeled incorrectly, so we can't know whether these trees are mislabeled.
(E) Correct.

### 13. Question Type: Weaken
The psychologist concludes that, since identical twins who grow up separately share many tastes, many tastes must be genetic. If we discover that identical twins in other situations don't share many tastes, that will weaken his argument, since it will show that many tastes aren't genetic. Only answer choice (D) provides such evidence—identical twins who grow up together behave differently—so (D) is the answer. Note that (D) doesn't entirely refute the psychologist's argument, since even if (D) is true many of our tastes may be genetic, but it does weaken his argument by showing evidence of another source of our tastes.
(A) Radical changes in lifestyle may be caused by genetics, just as puberty is, so they don't provide any evidence against genetic causes.
(B) The psychologist argues only that many of our inclinations are genetic, not all or even most, so "a few differences" won't weaken his argument.
(C) Even if scientists can't discover the exact mechanism by which genes determine inclinations, evidence that those with the same genes have the same inclinations still indicates that genetics determine inclinations. So this doesn't weaken the psychologist's argument.
(D) Correct.
(E) This strengthens the psychologist's argument, since twins with different genes are not similar but twins with the same genes are similar.

### 14. Question Type: Conclusion
The prompt shows (a) that humans are happy only when they're motivated by love and friendship (love motivation is a necessary condition for happiness), but (b) that economic needs can be satisfied even when love and friendship don't motivate actions (love motivation is not a necessary condition for satisfying economic needs). Clearly, these two statements imply that economic needs can be met even when the necessary condition for happiness is not met. Thus (D) is the answer.
(A) The prompt says that love motivation must be the primary motive in a happy society, not that no other motivations can be at work. So it doesn't imply that economic motives can't be "a motivator"—just that they can't be the main one.
(B) The prompt says nothing about economic needs being a condition for happiness. We might believe this, but there's no evidence for it in the prompt.
(C) The prompt provides one example of a society in which economic needs are satisfied without friendship, but doesn't say that economic needs couldn't be satisfied this way.
(D) Correct.
(E) The prompt clearly contradicts this: economic needs may be satisfied in a society (e.g. a merchant society) where happiness has not been achieved.

### 15. Question Type: Main point
Clearly, the gist of this argument is that even though hydrogen infrastructure doesn't exist yet, it will come

*PrepTest 60, Section 3 (LR) Continued...*

about quickly. Gasoline is brought up as a historical comparison to prove this point. (D) summarizes the argument well, so it's the right answer.
(A) If this were the main point, there would be no reason to discuss infrastructure, yet most of the argument is concerned with infrastructure.
(B) The argument says this, but it's not the main point, since the prompt brings up gasoline to show that the infrastructure will soon exist.
(C) This answer is much broader than the prompt, which addresses only hydrogen infrastructure, not infrastructure in general.
(D) Correct.
(E) The prompt may assume this, but it's not the main point of the argument, since consumer demand is introduced only to explain why infrastructure will grow.

**16. Question Type: Find the flaw**
Remember, when we look for a flaw in an argument we're looking for a problem with the way it gets from its premises to its conclusion. We're not looking for false premises; we have to assume that all the premises of the argument are true. So we might think that it's not true that interfering with the environment always makes it harder for non-endangered species to survive, but we have to take that truth as given and figure out why the argument is flawed even if that's true. So what's the flaw? The argument says we shouldn't interfere to save endangered species because it may harm non-endangered species—but it may well be more important to save endangered species than to worry about the welfare of species that aren't endangered, so it's not clear that we shouldn't interfere. The answer is (E).
(A) The prompt doesn't argue that wildlife managers couldn't save endangered species, only that they shouldn't.
(B) This isn't a flaw in the argument—if this were true it would support the argument by suggesting that we should avoid harming non-endangered species lest they become endangered.
(C) The argument doesn't discuss diversity, so this is irrelevant.
(D) The argument isn't making a comparison between various endangered species, but between endangered and non-endangered species, so this is irrelevant.
(E) Correct.

**17. Question Type: Must be true**
Like many "must be true" questions, this prompt throws a lot of information at us. But from the first sentence we can see that all food that is not both sterilized and sealed can contain disease-causing bacteria. So it is true that any food which hasn't been sterilized can contain disease-causing bacteria. It's also clear that some acceptable preservation techniques don't involve sterilization, since some merely "slow the growth of disease-causing bacteria." Thus any non-sterilized food, even if it's preserved, can contain disease-causing bacteria, and the answer is (D).
(A) This isn't true, since the prompt tells us that some preservation techniques merely "slow the growth" of bacteria.
(B) We don't know what the relationship is between destroying enzymes and sterilization.
(C) We know that many preservation techniques prevent enzymes that cause spoiling, but we don't know whether sterilization does this more than other techniques.
(D) Correct.
(E) We know that any food which hasn't been sterilized can contain bacteria, but we don't know whether it does. Some food may just happen not to have bacteria, even without preservation. So even if we see that a food item has no bacteria, we can't know whether it has been preserved.

**18. Question Type: Principle**
We are given two conditions either one of which is necessary and sufficient (if and only if) to make a life-risking activity acceptable: either (a) the person who takes the risk must gain something that he couldn't get otherwise, or (b) he must accept it voluntarily. If either one of these conditions holds, the risk is acceptable. In answer choice (C), the motorcyclist bears the risk voluntarily, so condition (b) holds and the risk is acceptable.
(A) This answer choice is almost correct, but it's not clear whether in declining to buy a new car the salesperson is risking only his own life (antilock brakes might save other motorists as well, for example), so it doesn't quite conform to condition (b).
(B) In this case, the risk to life is "minimal," so the principle in the prompt doesn't apply.

# PrepTest 60, Section 3 (LR) Continued...

(C) Correct.
(D) This judgment appears to conform to condition (a), since people are bearing a risk to get a reward, but it's not clear whether the reward (inexpensive travel) can be gained only by undergoing the risk (since there may be other ways to get cheap travel), so it doesn't quite conform to the principle.
(E) Since there's no risk to life, the principle in the prompt doesn't apply.

### 19. Question Type: Flaw

The ecologist has tested each compound separately, but the butterfly uses all the compounds together. So it may be that they have an effect together that wasn't tested by separating them. Thus the answer is (D): the ecologist infers incorrectly that just because no member of a set (no single compound) has an effect (repulsing predators), the whole set together doesn't have that effect.

(A) It's not essential to the ecologist's argument that the theories be incompatible: the butterflies may avoid predators both by appearance and by chemicals. He merely sets out to refute one of the theories.
(B) The ecologist has isolated the chemicals in different pellets, so he can validly infer causation.
(C) The ecologist doesn't dispute the butterfly's ability to avoid predators; his argument is about how this happened.
(D) Correct.
(E) The conclusion that chemicals don't explain the butterfly's capacity to avoid predators clearly is not present in any of the premises.

### 20. Question Type: Principle

The principle provides two conditions which are both necessary for criticizing the words or actions of another: it must (a) not seriously harm the person and (b) one must hope that it benefits the other. In the application in the prompt, it seems as though Jarrett lacks condition (b): he didn't benefit anyone. If this is so, it doesn't matter whether he lacks condition (a), since each is separately necessary. But is it totally clear that he lacks condition (b)? The principle says not that one is unjustified if the criticism doesn't benefit anyone, but that one is unjustified if one does not hope or expect it to benefit someone. To be sure that the application is correct, we must know what Jarrett was expecting. Only (A) tells us that Jarrett knew his actions would benefit no one, so (A) is correct.

(A) Correct.
(B) We know the criticism didn't benefit anyone, so it doesn't matter why this was the case.
(C) The principle says nothing about "antagonizing" anyone, and antagonizing isn't equivalent to serious harm.
(D) Whether Jarrett planned to benefit himself is irrelevant to the principle, which speaks only about whether one benefits others.
(E) This answer is almost right, and seems very similar to (A). But even if Jarrett knew his criticism wouldn't benefit Ostertag, he might have thought it would benefit someone else in the class, so E doesn't give us what we're looking for.

### 21. Question Type: Strengthen

The safety consultant reasons that since minivans are associated with fewer injuries per licensed vehicle, yet do not seem better at preventing injuries in the event of a crash, it must be the drivers of minivans who are safer, not the cars themselves. He neglects an important possibility: maybe, even though minivans are no better at protecting passengers when a crash happens, they are more likely to avoid a crash than similar vehicles—maybe their brakes are better, for example. This is a major hole in his argument; by filling the hole and guaranteeing that minivans are no better at avoiding crashes than similar vehicles, (E) strengthens the argument.

(A) Minivans don't perform better on crash tests than comparable vehicles, so this doesn't strengthen the idea that low-risk drivers drive minivans.
(B) This would weaken the argument: we would expect low-risk drivers to get into fewer crashes, but this implies that's not the case.
(C) This makes it all the more surprising that minivans have fewer injuries, but doesn't strengthen or weaken the safety consultant's argument about the cause of this phenomenon.
(D) The prompt compares minivans to other vehicles of the same size, so whether they're better or worse than smaller vehicles is irrelevant.
(E) Correct.

*PrepTest 60, Section 3 (LR) Continued...*

**22. Question Type: Assumption**
This argument looks pretty solid: it concludes that the government is responsible for increased gas prices and shows that the government's policies led to just this. In an assumption question, always look for the word or concept that's in the conclusion but not in the premises. In this case that concept is responsibility: just because the government's policies ultimately led to increased gas prices, that doesn't mean that it's responsible. We need an assumption which guarantees that the government is responsible for things its policies may cause; thus the answer is (A).
**(A)** Correct.
(B) We don't know whether the consequence was unforeseen, so this doesn't necessarily apply.
(C) We don't need to know whether an increase in demand must cause an increase in price; we need only to know that in this case it did cause an increase, and the prompt tells us that.
(D) The prompt doesn't argue that the government shouldn't have instituted these policies, only that it is responsible for them. So it doesn't matter what the government's obligation was.
(E) We don't need to know whether the government is the only factor which can cause gas prices to rise, since we know from the prompt that in this case it did cause gas prices to rise.

**23. Question Type: Parallel flaw**
The flaw here is relatively simple: the prompt states that a condition (frequent mutations) is necessary for something to occur (surviving dramatic changes), but its conclusion assumes that this condition is also sufficient. Answer (C) makes the same mistake: it establishes that being honest is a necessary condition for being morally upright, then assumes that it's sufficient to make one morally upright. Thus (C) is the answer.
(A) This argument has no flaw: its premises establish necessary conditions, and its conclusion is about a necessary condition. It doesn't switch to a sufficient condition the way the prompt does.
(B) This argument is in no way parallel to the prompt; its flaw is to show that a play performed before the same audience will get different reactions, then infer that a play performed before different audiences will get different reactions.
**(C)** Correct.
(D) Again, this argument has no flaw: it stays with necessary conditions and does not mistake a necessary condition for a sufficient one.
(E) This argument is flawed in that it switches from "healthful diet" to "healthy person," but it does not switch from necessary to sufficient conditions, so it's not parallel.

**24. Question Type: Principle**
The music critic argues that sales are no mark of an underground band's success: that is, we can't infer from bad sales either that the band is successful or that it's not successful. This is because bad sales may reflect either authentic undergroundness or mere incompetence. The argument is about success, however, and the music critic doesn't explain what success means. Answer choice (B) explains that incompetence and trendiness are both signs of being unsuccessful, so both good and bad sales may reflect being unsuccessful. This justifies his argument, so (B) is the correct answer.
(A) The critic says that sales don't reflect anything about a group's success, so this principle wouldn't justify his argument.
**(B)** Correct.
(C) The critic says nothing about meeting the criteria of other underground musicians, so this doesn't help his argument.
(D) The critic doesn't say that good sales definitely make an underground unsuccessful, only that they may indicate trendiness and therefore being unsuccessful. So it's possible that a band may be successful even if its recordings sell well.
(E) The critic clearly thinks that both these things are marks of success, so this wouldn't justify his argument.

**25. Question Type: Point at issue**
The point at issue here is not whether computers are "smarter" than people—both Graham and Adelaide agree that a computer beat a chess master at chess. Rather, they disagree on whether that success indicates computer intelligence; Graham thinks it does, but Adelaide points out that it may merely reflect the intelligence of computer programmers. Thus the answer is (C): they disagree on who's responsible for the computer's victory.
(A) Neither Graham nor Adelaide tells us whether chess is "the best" example of anything.

## PrepTest 60, Section 3 (LR) Continued...

(B) Neither Graham nor Adelaide tells us whether chess is typical. Graham seems to imply this, but we can't tell whether Adelaide disagrees.
(C) Correct.
(D) Graham clearly agrees with this, but we can't tell whether Adelaide agrees, so it's not the point at issue.
(E) Neither Graham nor Adelaide addresses tools.

# PrepTest 60, Section 4 (RC)

## Passage 1

Paragraph 1 describes the formation of urban sprawl, and introduces the New Urbanism critique of that sprawl—it "contributes to the decline of civic life and civility." The first paragraph continues with the first half of that—suburbs eliminate civic spaces.

The second paragraph introduces the idea of a "de facto economic segregation" caused by suburbs, and the fact that suburbanites are forced to spend time in automobiles. Thus, people don't learn to interact with each other. The New Urbanists advocate a return to small urban neighborhoods and a "gratifying public realm."

The third paragraph addresses the critique that moving to suburbs is an individual choice. The response is that the point of the movement is to question the values that are reflected in, e.g., zoning policies.

The main idea is that New Urbanism criticizes suburbs—as what, exactly? As destroying a sense of community. They want to undo that.

1. The main idea (described above) is given by **(D)**.

2. The problem with cars, according to the passage, is that they shut people off from each other. Not specifically parents and children, so choice (E) is wrong. It does so more generally—leading to antisocial behavior. So that's choice **(C)**.

3. Again, the author's problem with sprawl is that it destroys peoples' sense of community. The design of the suburbs thus influences people's values. The design is also influenced by the residents—see the last paragraph's first sentence. The answer is thus **(D)**.

4. Look at the parts of the passage that are identified. The first "communities" is in the phrase "low-density communities"—so community in a housing sense. The second one, "the concept of community" is using the word more abstractly. To put that in different words, **(B)**.

5. We're looking to weaken the position of the critics of New Urbanism. Their position was that people move to the suburbs as a matter of free choice. If it's not altogether a matter of free choice, then that position is weakened. So look at choice **(D)**.

6. The correct choice is **(E)**. The authors suggest that rigid separation between housing and commercial zones could and should be eliminated. This would bring stores and schools back into the neighborhoods. Note that (A) is wrong: the author isn't keen on zoning, but doesn't advocate its complete elimination.

7. The paragraph discusses economic segregation. That'll happen if people of like incomes live together. That will only occur if people don't deliberately live in a poorer area than they could afford. So choice **(A)** is a necessary assumption in the paragraph.

## Passage 2, Comparative reading

Passage A deals with how bees "dance" to communicate. There was disagreement on how the mechanism actually works. Finally, a honeybee robot (!) demonstrated that sounds are in fact the explanation.

Passage B covers much of the same ground. In this case, an experiment demonstrating that vervets communicate via sound is described. The honeybee situation from Passage A is summarized, but another experiment is described in which the bees ignore information that is likely to be false.

8. Both passages are about animals using sound to communicate; both describe experiments that were designed to verify that fact. Choice **(C)** is correct. Choice (A) ("human-like intelligence") far overstates the case; choice (D) is wrong because the second passage isn't focused on the bee issue as a main aim.

## PrepTest 60, Section 4 (RC) Continued...

9. Don't overthink these things. Passage A focuses on honeybees; Passage B does too, but also talks about vervets. So choice **(A)** is accurate (if simplistic).

10. There are two Gould experiments described. In one, the foragers dispatched bees to a place they had not been; in the other, the bees had been to the middle of the lake, but their dispatch suggestions were ignored. Those two experiments are described by choice **(D)**.

11. Von Frisch discovered the dance of the bees, and is mentioned in both passages. Clearly, both writers believe that he was important. So choice **(D)** is correct.

12. Once again Passage A is all about the honeybees, while Passage B uses the honeybees as one example. Put more abstractly, that relationship is given by choice **(C)**.

**Passage 3**

Luis Valdez is credited with developing Chicano theater, according to paragraph 1. His discussions with Cesar Chavez are described. The second paragraph describes Valdez's use of workers' improvisational, satirical skits to develop the actos—skits that were to be performed as political theater. The third paragraph criticizes this point of view towards Valdez's work: actos weren't invented by Valdez. The workers' contributions can't be ignored, nor can an earlier form called carpas. But Valdez was still important.

The main idea should reflect that Valdez contributed to the creation of actos; however, the contribution of workers to the creation of both actos and earlier forms of theater should not be ignored.

13. The best summary of the main point is **(C)**. The other choices all misstate one or more aspects of the passage. (E) is closest but misses the mark because it understates Valdez's involvement; he didn't simply use connections to popularize the form, he contributed to its development.

14. As ever, when asked about a specific word in context, go read the context. "Because actos were based on participants' personal experiences, they had palpable immediacy," according to lines 37-39. The immediacy involved is thus the lack of an intermediary between the audience and the experience. That point is expressed in choice **(E)**.

15. What's Cesar Chavez doing here? Context, basically. It tells you why the actos were being created. So choice **(A)** is best.

16. All of the things listed apply only to actos, not to carpas, except for **(D)**. Both forms involve satire. We're told that in line 36 (for actos) and line 47 (for carpas).

17. You're asked what Valdez would believe, not what the author would. So your only source here is what the author says about Valdez. We know that he developed his theatrical form based on the improvisations of workers. We can therefore infer that he didn't require trained actors. So choice **(D)** is correct.

18. The author quotes Broyles-Gonzalez with some approval (note the word "rightly" in line 41). Broyles-Gonzalez believed that actos developed in part from carpas, with which the workers were acquainted. Choice **(C)** expresses this. (No one said Valdez was acquainted with carpas, so choice (D) is wrong.)

19. The first paragraph suggests that the Teatro was started after the United Farm Workers had already gained recognition. See lines 5-12. So choice **(C)** is correct.

20. Both the carpas and the actos are described as satirical. So we know that comedy was a prominent feature of Chicano theater. Choice **(B)** is correct. Choice (A) is wrong: We know that at least one critic noticed carpas, but that doesn't mean that they were widely discussed. The other choices make statements about Valdez's later career that simply aren't supported by the text.

## PrepTest 60, Section 4 (RC) Continued...

**Passage 4**

Paragraph 1. A proposal is given for contingent fees in Western Australia.
Paragraph 2. The proposal in question would be an "uplift fee" (an additional percentage of the lawyer's fee is added to his regular fee). Only clients unable to pay the fee would qualify.
Paragraph 3. There are problems with this arrangement. One is that investigating whether to charge such a fee would be onerous for the lawyer.
Paragraph 4. Another problem is that it's unfair to clients who are not indigent; the reasons for entering into a contingent fee apply to all clients.

21. It's necessary for you to understand the fee arrangement. The lawyer gets more than his usual fee (by a certain percent) if he wins, but nothing if he loses. Which of the choices is kind of like that? Choice **(B)** is.

22. Choice **(A)** is in the passage; see lines 52-55. Look no further.

23. You're asked to look at the structure of the passage. The first half of the passage describes the proposed contingent fee; the second half of the passage raises problems with the proposal. That's best reflected by choice **(E)**.

24. Your common sense isn't going to work—you need to remember or reread what the passage says. You know paragraph 3 is where this problem is discussed. So reread that part. The answer is **(C)** (see lines 35-40).

25. The question is basically, "Why disproportionate? Disproportionate to what?" To answer this question, read the context. The author is concerned with damage awards being eroded. So clearly, the concern is lawyers being paid too much relative to the damage award. That's choice **(B)**.

26. **(D)** is the correct answer: the passage says that the lawyer should use contingent fee arrangements as a last resort. But what's wrong with (C)? It says that the arrangement should be used if the lawyer is "not certain" his client could pay his regular fee. The passage, however, says that the contingency arrangement is only appropriate if the lawyer is certain his client can't pay.

27. The author's criticisms of the proposal are that the investigation of the client's finances and the cost of litigation will be burdensome, and that the contingency arrangement should be available regardless of the client's financial situation. You're looking for something that would undermine one or both of those. How about the fact that lawyers already conduct extensive pre-suit investigations anyway? That would mean that the new rule wouldn't be any more burdensome than what's already in place. So that's choice **(B)**.

# PrepTest 61
## PrepTest 61, Section 1 (RC)

**Passage 1**

Paragraph 1 gives us a history of human rights in the UN. Note the "Although" in line 6, which clearly indicates that while there was human rights language in place, many thought it did not go far enough.

Paragraph 2 goes through the history of the drafting process and the final guarantees agreed to in the document.

Paragraph 3 discusses the UDHR's weakness due to its nonbinding status but indicates the document has been successful in leading to binding human rights conventions.

This is a very basic passage without a lot of nuance. The main idea is that the UDHR was successful in helping human rights despite some flaws and a contentious drafting process.

1. Before you start, think of why the author describes the document as "purely programmatic". S/he is indicating that the document is not legally enforceable. **(D)**

2. The author wants to compare the language of the charter and that of the proposals of opposition groups. **(B)** is correct. (A) might be tempting, but the two documents don't disagree on the definition of rights – only how strongly the documents may be enforced.

3. We know the author is generally positive, though she has some reservations in paragraph 3. **(B)**.

4. **(D)**. The author lays out the practical consequences at the end of paragraph 3, so (D) is in fact false. All of the other statements are explicitly included in the passage.

5. (A) is tempting but wrong; it's not ambiguity that made the initial charter ineffective but its lack of legal consequences. (B) is wrong because the last paragraph suggest the opposite, that the strengths outweigh the weaknesses. (C) is explicitly not true (paragraph 3). (D) is not in the passage. **(E)** is correct –lines 14-22 discuss that the "staunchest proponents" indeed wanted more legal enforceability.

6. We have to review the views of the delegates mentioned. Lines 11-14 mention the proponents of strengthening the charter to require member states to enforce human rights. **(A)** reflects this demand for action on the part of the offending member state.

**Passage 2**

Paragraph 1 makes 2 points: that forgeries are generally considered to be less aesthetically pleasing, and also that forgeries can be confused for originals.

Paragraph 2 asks whether forgery can indeed be art (philosophically).

Paragraph 3 answers the question with the work of Lessing. Lessing argues that art is valuable for it's original vision, not only for its aesthetic qualities.

Paragraph 4 relates Lessing to Vermeer. The forger did not have a unique vision, so it "lacks historical significance."

The author seems to endorse Lessing's writing without reservation, so the main idea is that art should be judged not only by aesthetics but by originality, so forgeries are less artistically valuable.

7. **(C)** relates our prediction. (B) is wrong because it is still talking only about aesthetic value, and Lessing says

we have to move beyond that.

8. **(A)** is correct. The forgery can be aesthetically valuable – Lessing would just argue that the forgery is less artistically valuable overall because of its lack of original vision. (D) is wrong because it is addressing overall artistic success (not just aesthetics); Lessing would say that the forgery is less valuable from this perspective.

9. Make a prediction: the author seems to refer to the critic to show how hard it can be to determine originals from forgeries. **(D)** is correct. While (A) might be true, that's not why the author makes the point.

10. In line 13, critics are embarrassed to learn that the work they praised was in fact done by someone other than the purported author. **(C)** captures this logic. None of the other options discuss this sort of deception.

11. No prediction here so we should move through the choices.
(A) Lessing makes no mention of how many forgeries there are.
**(B)** We know that Lessing doesn't care for forgeries and likes originality. Thus the creation of the work is important in assessing value. Correct.
(C) Lessing doesn't mention influence.
(D) Lesing doesn't discuss different definitions of forgery.
(E) is tempting, but it's too strong. Lessing doesn't say that re-use of techniques "can't be innovative" at all – only that such work should be judged as less successful artistically.

12. **(E)** is correct. The first paragraph is explicit that van Meegeren painted original works under the false signature of Vermeer, but he didn't copy Vermeer works directly.

13. We need to strengthen the contention that aesthetics are separate from artistic value.
(A) This doesn't speak to that distinction.
**(B)** Correct. This is exactly what we're after. Aesthetically pleasing copies are not regarded as high in artistic value.
(C) Again, this only speaks to forgeries and doesn't compare aesthetics to artistic value.
(D) and (E), similarly, are not comparative between aesthetics and artistic value, only discussing one or the other.

**Passage 3, Comparative reading**

Passage A argues that unlike humans, when animals vocalize they don't purposefully do so to alter the behavior of other animals or to provide other animals with information.

Passage B: the first and second paragraphs describe the "common" argument that animals do not communicate with conscious intention. (The discussion of lying is an example in support of this point). The third paragraph begins with the key transition "but." It argues that the previous thinking is circular and that recent research calls previous assumptions made by the "common argument" into question.

How are these two passages related? Well, although they deal with different aspects of intentionality, Passage A and the beginning of Passage B argue that animal communication is qualitatively different from that of humans. But Passage B ends up concluding that recent research shows animal and human communication is more similar than previously thought. So while Passage B doesn't explicitly refute Passage A, the two are in conflict.

14. **(B)** is correct, both passages discuss conscious intention. (A) is only addressed in Passage B. (C) is never discussed. Read (D) carefully as it looks tempting. (D) suggests a comparison between nonhuman primates and all other animals, but both of these passages are about differences between animals and humans. (E) is discussed in Passage B but not Passage A.

15. Read back in the passage to make a prediction here. The author uses Maritain to "exemplify" the common view, which the author goes on to refute in the next paragraph. **(A)** matches this exactly.

## PrepTest 61, Section 1 (RC) Continued...

16. Remember that we already know the author of Passage B is somewhat critical of the thinking in Passage A.
(A) Irrelevant – neither author discusses whether humans act with intentionality all the time, only that they can and often do.
(B) Passage B never calls into question an author's credentials (which would likely be an argument ad hominem!)
(C) While deception is mentioned in Passage B, Passage A doesn't take a stance on it.
(D) Correct. In the last paragraph of Passage B, the author calls into question the assumptions of the argument that animals don't act with intentionality, then points to empirical data to suggest that they might.
(E) Evolutionary benefits are not a central part of either passage.

17. Re-reading those lines, we know we're looking for evidence that animals communicate out of instinct, without doing so intentionally. Sound familiar? (D) is correct; the frog example in Passage A made the very same point.

18. Remember our prediction, that Passage B's author believed that human and animal communication are more similar and that animals act with more intentionality than previously believed. (C) is correct; this is nearly exactly how Passage B's author frames the issue in the final paragraph. For (B), the authors don't really disagree on how important the issue is. (D) is especially tempting here, but read closely. Only Passage A actually discusses attributing mental states to others. Both passages discuss the broad idea of intentionality, but Passage B doesn't discuss the sub-issue of attributing states to other animals at all.

19. As in 18, we should remember that Passage B is generally more critical of the current scientific consensus and presents evidence of alternatives. (B) is correct as Passage B is explicitly critical of other scientists, while Passage A is not. (A) is wrong because neither passage takes up the question of whether science can answer questions. (C) is incorrect; Passage B doesn't accept the validity of conflicting positions, it explicitly says that one of the sides is wrong.

(D) can be deceptive. While we might infer that Passage B supports ongoing research, it never does so explicitly. Furthermore, Passage A doesn't take a stand on whether further research is necessary, so it's impossible to say that the two differ. (E) is wrong because Passage B does not "refuse to commit itself."

**Passage 4**

This passage is particularly important to diagram because it bounces between several different perspectives.

Paragraph 1 introduces the idea that African American histories were transnational "in contrast" to prevailing perspectives.

Paragraph 2 explains why this was – the problem of citizenship. (Curiously and unusually, this example is introduced with "First," but there does not appear to be a second explanation.)

Paragraph 3 returns to the mainstream perspective, finally defining nationalism and explaining why it was prevalent in mainstream historiography. (Note that if you don't know exactly what "historiography" means, you can still intuit what the passage is talking about – a kind of current explanation of historical and current events).

Paragraph 4 changes course – it argues that African American discourse was in fact nationalistic under a certain interpretation. This seems to be the author's final perspective, but it's one that we could not easily have seen coming given the 3 previous paragraphs.

The main idea is that while African American historical perspectives appear to be less nationalistic than mainstream perspectives, they in fact are also nationalistic.

20. If you have already predicted the main idea this shouldn't be too hard:
(A) The paragraph is about historical narrative, not general challenges for African Americans.

## PrepTest 61, Section 1 (RC) Continued...

(B) The motives of African American historians is mentioned but is not the main idea.
(C) This sounds good but is wrong; the last paragraph reveals that African American historians did in fact take a nationalist perspective.
**(D)** Correct. Note how similar this was to our prediction: (D) starts by acknowledging that African American historians seem at first to be transnational, but then concludes that they were in fact more nationalistic than first thought.
(E) This isn't mentioned in the passage.

21. The context of "reconstructing" is creating a glorious African past in order to overcome degrading representations. **(E)** is correct – the authors are shaping a conception. (A) is the closest wrong answer, but note that "reconstructing" involves creating an identity, not simply correcting an old one. The old representations are being "overturned," not simply corrected.

22.
**(A)** is strongly implied in the second paragraph; it was the unresolved citizenship question that led to emigrationist sentiment.
(B) really isn't discussed anywhere in the passage.
(C) has two problems – first, the passage doesn't indicate that nationalist historians were in any way f ictionalizing the glory of their nation, only that they focused on that aspect. Second, (C) ignores the voices of the African American historians.
(D) the passage never addresses foreign policy and nationalism.
(E) While the last paragraph makes the case that African American historians were nationalistic, nowhere do African Americans explicitly endorse nationalism – in fact, just the opposite.

23. Make sure to go back and understand what the transnationalist perspective is. (It's not explicitly defined, so be careful).
(A) Nowhere does transnationalism promote the comparison of 2 different nationalist mythologies.
B) While it is true that transnationalism plays down territorial ambition, there's nothing to say that it involves treatment of minority populations. (While it might make sense that African American transnationlists would be interested in this issue, it's not explicitly a part of transnaitonalism itself).
(C) Simply recounting attempts doesn't have any historical perspective.
(D) is a bit confusing and seems like a possibility. Ultimately we just don't have evidence that transnationalism would be interested specifically in U.S. foreign policy.
**(E)** is correct. Incorporating a variety of cultures without giving credence to national borders seems the most transnational.

24. Make sure to look back at the passage frequently. You can't pick an answer here without specific evidence that the passage supports your answer. **(E)** is correct; Paragraph 2 defines how leaders responded to the citizenship question.

25. This one is tricky and involves more process of elimination than loving the right answer.
(A) False; the author is explicit that African Americans originally came from many different countries.
**(B)** Correct; the final paragraph discussed how African American historians could be seen as creating a nation, even without explicit geographical borders.
(C) Very strong language; we can't say they didn't engage in any myth-making.
(D) We don't know whether the historians mentioned were the most prominent. Again, too extreme.
(E) There isn't any evidence for this.

26. Make sure to have a prediction. We know the second paragraph explains why many African American historians had a trans-national perspective. **(A)** is correct, a very near paraphrase of our prediction. While (D) is technically true, that's not why the paragraph is there.

27. Make sure you know the position of mainstream U.S. historians given in the 3rd paragraph.
 **(B)** Correct. This is very much like a nation's "temperament" leading to its success (lines 32-34).
None of the other options come very close.

# PrepTest 61, Section 2 (LR)

**1. Question Type: Flaw**
Mary concludes that Jamal's argument is absurd because he says she both has a right and doesn't have a right to sell the business. It's clear, however, that there may be a difference between "right" and "legal right," and Jamal distinguishes between them. Mary's mistake is to ignore this distinction, so the answer is (D).
(A) There's no mention of time in the prompt.
(B) This isn't directly related to Mary's argument, which turns on her rights, not the employees'.
(C) Mary's argument isn't that she has a right to sell the business, but that Jamal's claims are contradictory. She doesn't need to provide evidence for these claims in order to show that they contradict each other.
**(D)** Correct.
(E) Mary attacks Jamal's statements by calling them absurd, but says nothing about Jamal's character.

**2. Question Type: Principle**
The principle illustrated is that there's no value in making one part of something work when all the other parts don't work if the whole thing requires all its parts in order to be successful. This same principle is illustrated in (E): Automotive engineers find that there's no value in making a part of a car which will continue working when the car itself is on the junk heap. So (E) is the answer.
(A) The items in a store are sold independently of one another, but the organs in a body work only together, so this is a different situation.
(B) This argument is about the organs working together, so it's not parallel to the prompt, which describes one organ working alone.
(C) The different models sold by a car company don't work together the way the organs in a body do, so this isn't the same principle.
(D) This answer demonstrates the opposite of the principle that the prompt demonstrates: if one organ is overdeveloped, it can actually harm the other organs.
**(E)** Correct.

**3. Question Type: Must be true**
The prompt offers two criteria which, combined, are sufficient for success: protecting individual liberties and helping the economy. Since we know that the present administration protects individual liberties, if it were also successful economically it would be an overall success. Thus (C) must be true.
(A) The prompt doesn't tell us anything about the current administration's economic success.
(B) We know that the current administration doesn't protect the environment, but since the prompt says that such an administration can still be an "overall success," we don't know whether B is true.
**(C)** Correct.
(D) The prompt says nothing about the relationship between economic success and protecting the environment.
(E) The prompt says that one does not need to protect the environment in order to be an overall success.

**4. Question Type: Method of argument**
The prompt argues that the government should enact a ban on fishing. The evidence it cites shows that the fish in Eagle Bay are toxic, and that this presents a risk to public health. So (D) is the answer. Note that the prompt does not provide evidence that the ban would be economically harmful; it merely says that other people ("widespread concern") have said so.
(A) The ban, not the toxin, is described as economically harmful.
(B) The argument seeks to demonstrate that a ban should be enacted, not that a general moral principle is true.
(C) The prompt provides no evidence on what opponents of the ban have or have not thought.
**(D)** Correct.
(E) The prompt shows that fishing in the bay would make expose the public to toxins, not that banning fishing would reduce the level of toxins in the bay.

**5. Question Type: Principle**
Vandenburg says that the art museum is violating the purpose of its founders, since they wanted to pay attention to contemporary art but the collection of contemporary at this museum is smaller than its other collections; Simpson says that it's not violating its purpose, since its purpose is to collect good art and there may be little good contemporary art. Simpson will be correct if the museum would be wrong to collect bad art merely

## PrepTest 61, Section 2 (LR) Continued...

to give equal space to contemporary art. Thus (A) is the answer.
**(A)** Correct.
(B) This would justify Vandenburg, not Simpson.
(C) Simpson's argument is that an art museum should not collect art from periods with no good art, so his argument won't be adequately justified by the claim that it "need not" do so.
(D) The argument is about an art museum, not an ethnographic museum.
(E) Simpson's argument is not that the curators are and should be violating the founders' intentions, but that even if the founders intended to devote equal "attention" to contemporary art this doesn't mean that they have to devote equal space.

### 6. Question Type: Strengthen

This argument is fairly weak as it stands, since it relies merely on correlation (corporations want something and government does that thing) without providing any evidence that the two phenomena are actually linked. It might just be chance that the government cuts funding to projects which corporations object to; perhaps the government has cut funding to all research projects, not just those on alternative energy. We need evidence that the government is cutting funding specifically because corporations object, and (C) provides that evidence: If only projects discouraged by corporations are cut by the government, that makes it likely that corporations influenced the government's decisions.
(A) This provides no evidence for the causal link the prompt is trying to prove.
(B) This weakens the argument, since it suggests that funding may be cut for other reasons besides corporate opposition.
**(C)** Correct.
(D) This weakens the argument, since it suggests that corporations don't have much power over government funding decisions.
(E) This doesn't provide evidence for the causal link the prompt is trying to prove.

### 7. Question Type: Point at issue

Note that Sklar doesn't object to any of Talbert's arguments for teaching chess; he simply provides a completely different reason for thinking it should not be taught. The two speakers don't necessarily disagree on whether chess promotes mental maturity, or whether it diverts attention from social value; they simply disagree on whether, overall, it should be taught. Thus the answer is (D).
(A) Talbert agrees with this, but Sklar doesn't say he disagrees.
(B) Neither speaker expresses an opinion on this.
(C) Sklar agrees with this, but Talbert doesn't say whether he disagrees.
**(D)** Correct.
(E) Neither speaker expresses an opinion on this.

### 8. Question Type: Flaw

Theodora's mistake occurs right in her first sentence: she refutes the idea that vegetarianism cannot lead to nutritional deficiencies, when Marcia merely said vegetarianism doesn't necessarily lead to nutritional deficiencies. So whether or not her argument about poverty is adequate, she's arguing against a straw man, and the answer is (A).
**(A)** Correct.
(B) Theodora makes an argument which is independent of the results cited by Marcia, so she isn't wrong to ignore them.
(C) Theodora doesn't say that industries won't collapse if people don't become vegetarian, only that these industries will if people do become vegetarian.
(D) Marcia and Theodora use "diet" in the same way.
(E) She doesn't say this.

### 9. Question Type: Main point

The musicologist makes a general claim about the classification of instruments in order to prove a specific claim: that pianos are percussion instruments even though they have strings. Thus the answer is (E).
(A) This is a premise of the musicologist's argument but not his main point.
(B) He says nothing about how musicians interact with instruments.

(C) He doesn't mention how pianos sound.
(D) He says the opposite of this.
(E) Correct.

### 10. Question Type: Inference
We can infer that since agricultural runoff adds phosphorus, and phosphorus stimulates the growth of plankton, agricultural runoff stimulates plankton growth. A says this, and none of the other answers follow from the prompt. Thus the answer is (A).
(A) Correct.
(B) We can't infer what the ocean was like before the situation described in the prompt, since the prompt doesn't discuss this.
(C) We can't infer that there would be no bacteria if there were no agricultural runoff, only that there would be less bacteria.
(D) Even if agricultural runoff caused the doubling in phosphorus levels: runoff may have increased only slightly, or quadrupled, for all we know.
(E) We can't infer this general statement from a specific description of a given body of water.

### 11. Question Type: Weaken
This argument clearly isn't rock-solid: there are a number of reasons why it might take one longer to leave a parking space in some situations than others, even if one didn't feel "possessive" of that space. An alternative explanation for the results would severely weaken the argument, and (A) provides such an alternative: drivers leave more slowly not because they feel possessive, but because they feel pressured and drive less well when they're pressured. Thus (A) weakens the argument.
(A) Correct.
(B) The argument is about leaving, not entering.
(C) This answer looks right, since it seems to provide an alternative explanation just like (A). But it's not as good as (A) because it explains only the difference between leaving a space when no one is waiting and leaving when someone is waiting, not the difference between waiting patiently and waiting with honking. Answer (A) explains this difference (there's more pressure if someone's honking), so it's a better answer.
(D) The psychologists don't need parking spaces to be representative of how likely it is that someone is waiting, only of the effect on time when someone is waiting.
(E) This applies only to waiting with honking, not to waiting patiently, so it doesn't weaken the argument.

### 12. Question Type: Paradox
The "paradox" here is that shark teeth are very common, but shark skeletons are very uncommon, in the fossil record. This would be explained if there were a significant difference between shark teeth and shark skeletons. Answer choice A provides such a difference: shark skeletons are made of cartilage, which is less likely to fossilize than teeth. (A) is the answer.
(A) Correct.
(B) This only deepens the paradox.
(C) This is irrelevant.
(D) This implies that there should be more shark teeth than shark skeletons, but doesn't explain why shark skeletons are rarer than other vertebrate skeletons.
(E) This only deepens the paradox, since if the same processes are involved we would expect them to be equally common.

### 13. Question Type: Assumption
In an assumption question, always look for the word or concept that's in the conclusion but not in the premises. Here, that concept is "interpretation of reality"—the premises tell us nothing about this. They merely tell us that photographs "express worldviews." To draw a logical argument we must link these two claims. Only (B) does so: if photographers express a worldview, and expressing a worldview is interpreting reality, then the critic's conclusion follows.
(A) The critic would certainly agree with this, but it's not sufficient for his argument, since it only says that realistic depiction can interpret, whereas he says that photographers always do interpret.
(B) Correct.

## PrepTest 61, Section 2 (LR) Continued...

(C) This doesn't link expression with interpretation, so it's not sufficient.
(D) We're looking for (express a worldview -> interpret reality); this is logically distinct from (interpret reality -> express a worldview), so this can't be the answer.
(E) The critic would agree with this statement, but it doesn't link interpretation and expression.

### 14. Question Type: Weaken

The geologist concludes that, since it's very unlikely that worms made the tracks, they must have been caused by geological processes. He provides no positive evidence for geological processes; he merely excludes an alternative explanation. So if we had reason to believe that geological processes were also a very unlikely cause, that would weaken his argument. Answer choice (D) does just this: if it's impossible that geological processes made the tracks, this certainly works against his conclusion.

(A) We must assume that the geologist's premises are true—that the sandstone really is as old as he says. So even if it's sometimes hard to estimate the age of sandstone, that doesn't matter here.
(B) This strengthens the argument: if a wide variety of marks were made, why not these worm-like ones too?
(C) This is irrelevant, since the life forms would presumably be just as unlikely as worms to be alive half a billion years before the earliest forms of multi-cellular life.
**(D) Correct.**
(E) This raises the possibility that worms may have been around earlier than we suspect, but if the marks are half a billion years earlier than the earliest traces of life it's very unlikely that worms were around then.

### 15. Question Type: Conclusion

The main point of the prompt is clearly that "it should be unsurprising if" unrelated species evolve similar organs. The evidence is that certain organs are the only way to accomplish a given task, so if unrelated species need to accomplish this task they'll need to develop these organs. Thus the answer is (B).

(A) This doesn't mention needs, so it doesn't fit.
**(B) Correct.**
(C) This is too general: the prompt doesn't just say they'll develop organs, but that they'll develop similar organs.
(D) The prompt says that the same needs lead to similar organs, but doesn't say anything about different needs.
(E) Eyes and wings are merely examples, not the main point of the argument.

### 16. Question Type: Assumption

The engineer's argument seems pretty solid: he doesn't claim that his plan is feasible, only that if it could be done the steel plants would reduce their electric bills. However, he makes an important leap: he says not just that they would reduce their electric bills but that they would save money overall. Of course, this is only true if installing the generators saves more money than it costs, so he must assume choice (C).

(A) The engineer doesn't claim that this plan is the best, only that it would save money.
(B) The engineer doesn't say his plan is possible with current technology, only that if it worked it would save money.
**(C) Correct.**
(D) For the engineer's argument to work, it's not necessary that electricity be the primary source of energy, just that it be a source of energy.
(E) The engineer's argument doesn't depend on this being the only way to save money.

### 17. Question Type: Method of argument

The herbalist claims that the bacteria will have an easier time resisting a standard antibiotic than an herbal antibacterial, just as a cook would have an easier time preparing a meal for a single guest than for dozens. So clearly the standard antibiotic corresponds to a single guest.

**(A) Correct.**
(B) This corresponds to the herbal antibacterial.
(C) Irrelevant.
(D) The cook corresponds to the bacteria.
(E) The ingredients aren't part of the analogy.

## PrepTest 61, Section 2 (LR) Continued...

**18. Question Type: Flaw**
The argument turns on showing that owls who have developed an auditory schema based on faulty sight still fail to navigate even when they get their sight back. But this fails to address the question of whether their sight is damaged by the lenses in such a way that it remains faulty even after the lenses are taken off. If this were the case, the owls might be using sight to locate sounds as adults and their errors might result from problems in sight. Thus the answer is (A).
**(A)** Correct.
(B) This is irrelevant.
(C) The argument doesn't imply that the owls reason, merely that they develop an association.
(D) The argument is about owls and doesn't refer to other bird species.
(E) The experimental results discussed are all relevant.

**19. Question Type: Paradox EXCEPT**
We need to explain why journalists still use quotation to report false claims, but no longer challenge those claims. Remember, this is an EXCEPT question, so four of the answer choices will help explain this and one, the correct one, won't. (D) doesn't explain the shift—on the contrary, if debate on controversial issues draws attention, we would expect journalists to do it more, not less. So (D) is the answer.
(A) This would discourage journalists from disagreeing with controversial claims, so it helps explain why journalists don't do so.
(B) If journalists don't know as much about the topics they cover, they may be unqualified to identify false claims and refute them.
(C) If people who make controversial and possibly false claims speak only to journalists who agree with them, other journalists won't get a chance to refute their views.
**(D)** Correct.
(E) If journalists are criticized for refuting false claims, that explains why they do so less often.

**20. Question Type: Weaken**
This argument contains a major flaw which is rather subtle: the computer may be predicting a higher proportion of heart attacks than the human but at the same time generating a lot of false positives. Suppose the computer simply diagnosed every EKG it looked at as a heart attack—then it would correctly diagnose 100% of the things that later turned out to be heart attacks, but clearly it wouldn't be doing a better job than an experienced cardiologist. Answer (C) suggests that something like this is going on: the computer is generating many false positives, so the human may still be better at reading EKGs.
(A) This doesn't weaken the argument, since even if the cardiologist made few mistakes the computer may have made even fewer.
(B) This doesn't affect the fact that in this situation the computer seems to have done better.
**(C)** Correct.
(D) The computer and the human may both have limits, but this doesn't weaken the claim that the computer is better.
(E) The prompt says the cardiologist was better (more experienced and skilled) than most cardiologists, so if even he couldn't beat the computer that only strengthens the claim that the computer is better than humans.

**21. Question Type: Principle**
The prompt provides evidence that taking a given action would reduce the accident rate, then states that this action should be taken. The prompt is assuming, therefore, that if a measure reduces accidents one should adopt it, and the answer is (E).
(A) The prompt says nothing about changing exclusively high-speed roadways, only that at least these should be changed.
(B) This would help to justify the argument in that it would provide support for a uniform national standard, but this isn't sufficient to justify a specific standard speed, so (E) is a better answer.
(C) The prompt doesn't state that all roadways have equal average traffic speeds, so this principle would weakn the argument.
(D) The argument isn't about "good laws," it's about reducing accidents.
**(E)** Correct.

## PrepTest 61, Section 2 (LR) Continued...

**22. Question Type: Strengthen**

Keep in mind that this is an EXCEPT question: all but one of the answer choices will strengthen the psychiatrist's claim, and the one that doesn't is the right answer. (C) clearly doesn't strengthen the argument: it's either irrelevant (since the psychiatrist's argument is about college students) or weakens the argument (since increased spending does help some groups decrease anxiety and depression). So (C) is the answer.

(A) This simply confirms the evidence the psychiatrist cites.
(B) This supports the psychiatrist's view that those with high levels of spending wouldn't be worse off if they decreased spending.
**(C)** Correct.
(D) If the psychiatrist's measurements are argument, his evidence is all the more believable.
(E) Individual cases of very large shifts in spending without shifts in anxiety and depression provide evidence that spending won't increase anxiety and depression.

**23. Question Type: Parallel flaw**

The structure of this argument could be sketched as follows:
BH -> FY
Most FY are TS
Therefore: Most BH are TS

So what's the flaw? Well, even if all the brick houses have front yards, and most houses with front yards have two stories, it could be the case that the brick houses are in the minority of front-yard houses that don't have two stories. Just because most of a class (front yards) has a characteristic (two stories) doesn't mean most of a subset of a class (brick houses) has that characteristic. (Just as it could be true that most days in May this year were sunny but still false that most Wednesdays in May were sunny.) The only answer choice which shares this flaw precisely is D: legislators are parallel to brick houses, public servants are parallel to houses with front yards, and not running for office is parallel to having two stories. So (D) is the answer.

(A) L -> P, Most L are RO, therefore most P are RO. This is almost right, but if you look carefully at the diagram you'll see that it differs from the prompt.
(B) Introduces four groups, legislators, politicians, those who have run for office and public servants, when the prompt contains only three groups.
(C) The conclusion here isn't about "most" of something, so it's ruled out immediately.
**(D)** Correct.
(E) "Most are not" in the conclusion isn't parallel to the prompt.

**24. Question Type: Sufficient assumption**

This question depends on a subtle vocabulary shift: the historian initially talks about "clear and unambiguous moral beliefs" but switches later to "inclination to morally judge human behavior." If these two phrases mean the same thing, the argument is properly drawn—so we need an assumption which says they're equivalent. Only B provides that, so B is the answer.

(A) The argument's conclusion is about what studying history does to a person, not about which events the person focuses on.
**(B)** Correct.
(C) The historian doesn't discuss "understanding human history," only studying it extensively.
(D) The historian says that anyone who views history as a working out of moral themes must have a strong moral belief, but he doesn't imply that the stronger ones moral beliefs the more one sees it that way.
(E) The historian seems to imply that people grow more objective as they learn more, which is the opposite of this.

**25. Question Type: Paradox**

The students express a preference for experience, but among individual candidates they choose one who has no experience. We have to find a piece of information which explains this apparent contradiction between students' expressed preferences. An obvious possibility is that students simply don't know which candidates are experienced; if this is the case, it makes sense that they might choose an inexperienced candidate in ignorance of his inexperience, while still preferring experienced candidates in principle. Thus (D) is the answer.

(A) This still doesn't explain why the one candidate students did choose was inexperienced.
(B) Again, this doesn't explain why students chose a candidate with no experience.

## PrepTest 61, Section 2 (LR) Continued...

(C) This suggests that the students may not have had the option of choosing an experienced candidate, but it doesn't state this explicitly, so (D) is still a better answer.

**(D)** Correct.

(E) This may be true, but the question isn't about who would actually make a good president; it's about the apparent contradiction between who the students think would make a good president. Thus this is irrelevant.

# PrepTest 61, Section 3, Game 1

This is a grouping game with two complications: the issue of the driver, and the fact that we're not sure exactly how many workers go in each car. Note that there are no distinctions in the rules between Car 1 and Car 2, so we'll use 1 and 2 for labels, but we could just as easily switch the occupants between cars without breaking any rules.

F G H J K L = 6

1  d  ___  ___ ..... .....
2  d  ___  ___ ..... .....

## Rules
#1: F or G drives H

#2: F or K drives J

#3: (G L)

Discussion: Make sure to note a position for each driver in each car. (We've put the "d" first in each car, but remember there isn't any relative position between riders in each car; no one is "before or after" anyone else within a car.)

The two rules regarding drivers require consideration. H and J must be driven by a combination of F, G, or K. It's also possible that F drives BOTH H and J. It's work working out the possibilities.

### F and G drive

Fd  J  ___ ..... .....
Gd  L  ___ ..... .....

### F and K drive

Fd  H  ___ ..... .....
Kd  ___  ___ ..... .....

### K and G drive

Kd  J  ___ ..... .....
Gd  L  H  ..... .....

### F drives both H and J

Fd  H  J  ..... .....
___  G  L  ..... .....

If F drives H and J, the block of G and L must go in the other car since there's not room. However, we know nothing about the driver of the second car.

1. List question.
a) **Correct.**
b) Violates Rule 2
c) Violates Rule 3
d) Violates Rule 1
e) Violates Rule 2

2. Look through our options; if F drives we're not sure who the second driver is, but we listed out all of the other options.
  e) **Correct.** K and L can't be drivers.

3. If Lisa drives, looking at our options the only configuration is to have F drive both H and J, giving us:

$$\underline{\text{Fd}} \quad \underline{\text{H}} \quad \underline{\text{J}} \quad \underline{\phantom{X}} \quad \underline{\phantom{X}}$$

$$\underline{\text{Ld}} \quad \underline{\text{G}} \quad \underline{\phantom{X}} \quad \underline{\phantom{X}} \quad \underline{\phantom{X}}$$

  a) **Correct.** K is unrestricted and could go with F, H, and J.

4. If F is not the driver, the only configuration is the one with G and K driving.

$$\underline{\text{Kd}} \quad \underline{\text{J}} \quad \underline{\phantom{X}} \quad \underline{\phantom{X}} \quad \underline{\phantom{X}}$$

$$\underline{\text{Gd}} \quad \underline{\text{L}} \quad \underline{\text{H}} \quad \underline{\phantom{X}} \quad \underline{\phantom{X}}$$

If F travels with 2 other workers, he must go with K and J, as the other car already has 3 workers:

$$\underline{\text{Kd}} \quad \underline{\text{J}} \quad \underline{\text{F}} \quad \underline{\phantom{X}} \quad \underline{\phantom{X}}$$

$$\underline{\text{Gd}} \quad \underline{\text{L}} \quad \underline{\text{H}} \quad \underline{\phantom{X}} \quad \underline{\phantom{X}}$$

  c) **Correct.** F must be driven by K, and the other rider is J.

5. This is trial and error.
  a) Could be true, e.g. GL, FHJK
  b) Could be true, e.g. FH, K G L J
  c) Could be true, e.g. F J, G L K J
  d) **Correct, must be false.** If K doesn't drive, all the configurations with K riding have him with 2+ other workers.
  e) Could be true, see a)

# PrepTest 61, Section 3, Game 2

This is a straightforward linear game with sequencing rules.

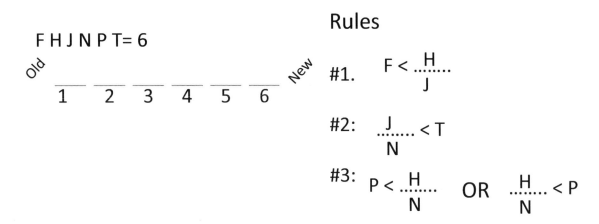

Discussion: Make sure to put in your basic exclusion rules. While variables like J appear multiple times, it's not really possible to combine rules since you won't know all the relationships. You can deduce F < J < T from Rules 1 and 2.

Rule 3 essentially says that P is either before both H and N or after; it just can't be between them.

6. List question.
a) **Correct.**
b) Violates Rule 2
c) Violates Rule 3
d) Violates Rule 1
e) Violates Rule 2

7. Our inferences tell us that none of H, J, and T can go first; the other 3 could.

**c) Correct. Three.**

8. You can do quite a bit of elimination here from other diagrams.
a) **Correct.** With F in 4th we know that J and H must come after it. But J must also go before T, which won't work. (This is also an inference we can add to our main diagram. While it's possible to have found it earlier, it would have been almost by accident and would not have been a good time investment).
b) Could work: P N F H J F
c) Could work: F H N J T P
d) Could work: F J P N T A
e) Could work: F H N P J T

9. If F goes third, we know right away that J and H must go after it. What do we do with Rule 2? Since T must be after J, T must also go after F (in either 5 or 6). We have N and P left for the first 2 spaces. Since P can't go between H and N, N will have to go second with P first.

**c) Correct.** Only the necklace can go third.

10. We are given P is first and need to know what could go second. Right away we can eliminate J and H (which need F before them) and T, which needs N and J. We're left with F and N. They could both work:
    - P F J N H T
    - P N F J H T

**b) Correct.** Only F or N could go second if P is first.

11. In this rule change question, the second rule is eliminated and we need to figure out how to get it back. We know we need to find a way for N and J to both come before T.
a) This gives us the order F < T < H, but that tells us nothing about N and needlessly puts H behind T.
b) F was going to have to go before T anyway, and N<T helps here, but this rule doesn't position J.
c) This rule, written N < T ←→ J < T, doesn't work because it's possible for neither side of the conditional to be triggered. It allows T < N and T < J simultaneously, which breaks our rule twice.
d) **Correct.** This rule tells us that F, J, and N are all older than T. N and J are correctly positioned; F < J was correct in the old setup as well (remember our deduction that F < J < T), so it's just restating something we already knew was true.
e) P < N ←→ P < T. Understanding where P goes doesn't really help us place T.

# PrepTest 61, Section 3, Game 3

This is a hybrid game with linear and grouping components. We must understand which 4 of the 5 runners are in, and also in what order they go.

Q R S T U = 5

```
___  ___  ___  ___
 1    2    3    4
      ~S        ~S
```

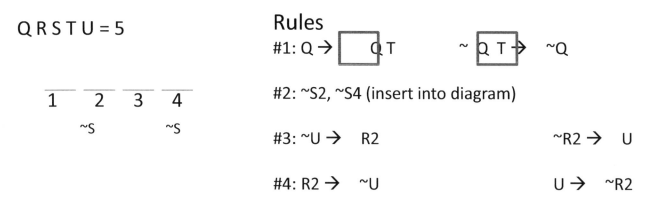

Rules
#1: Q → [Q T]        ~[Q T] → ~Q

#2: ~S2, ~S4 (insert into diagram)

#3: ~U → R2          ~R2 → U

#4: R2 → ~U          U → ~R2

Discussion: Rules 3 and 4 clearly interact. For many students, it's easier to create 2 double-sided arrows to explain the rules:

~U ←→ R2    (Rule 3 and Rule 4)
U ←→ ~R2    (contrapositive of Rule 3 and Rule 4).

What does it all mean? Essentially, we'll have either U or ~R2, but not both.

Since we know that one runner will be out, it might be worth your time to consider all of those options:

~Q
```
     T/U
___  ___  ___  ___
 1    2    3    4
      ~R        ~S
      ~S
```
With Q out, w know U will be in, so ~R2.

~R
```
___  ___  ___  ___
 1    2    3    4
      ~S        ~S
```
No further inferences. With R out, ~R2 is true so we know U, but we know that anyway since each of the other 4 are already in for this option.

~S
```
___  ___  ___  ___
 1    2    3    4
      ~R
```
Since S is out, U will be in, so we know ~R2.

~T

~T doesn't work; if T is out, Q must be in, but if Q is in it must be before T. **This gives us the valuable inference that T must always be in.**

~U
```
 S    R    Q    T
___  ___  ___  ___
 1    2    3    4
```
Since ~U, we know R2. Q and T are both in, so we know they make up a block, and there's only room for that block in 3 and 4. S can only go first.

12. List question.
a) Violates Rule 4
b) Violates Rule 2
c) Violates Rule 1
d) **Correct**
e) Violates Rule 3

13. We learned from our deductions that T must be included. **d) is correct.**

14. Look back at our options; which one was fully determined? The option with ~U. Is that one of the answer choices? Yes! **b) is correct.**

15.
a) **Correct.** If we know that R is directly before S we know that U is in: looking back at the option where ~U, S is before R. So our group is R S U and T. R can't be second because U is in, so the only place the RS block can go is 3 and 4. However, this puts S in 4, which is prohibited by rule.
b) Could be true: S Q T U
c) Could be true: S T U R
d) Could be true: S Q T R
e) Could be true: U T S R

16. If U is first, we know ~R2. So what could go second? S never can, so our only options are Q or T. WE can split them out quickly:

```
 U    Q
___  ___  ___  ___
 1    2    3    4
      ~R        ~S
      ~S
```

```
 U    T
___  ___  ___  ___
 1    2    3    4
      ~R        ~S
      ~S
```

If Q is in, T must be next. Since S can't go 4th, R must go last and S must be out.

```
 U    Q    T    R
___  ___  ___  ___
 1    2    3    4
      ~R        ~S
      ~S
```

If T is second, Q must be out because there's no space for Q to be directly before T. S and R must be in; S can't go 4th by rule, so it must go 3rd, with R in 4th.

```
 U    T    S    R
___  ___  ___  ___
 1    2    3    4
      ~R        ~S
      ~S
```

Either way, R is 4th. **e) Correct.** All of the other choices could be false.

17. S can only go one of two places by rule: first or 4th. Let's see what the options look like:

```
 S   ___  ___  ___
```
If S is first, there are a number of ways to fill in the rest of the diagram.

```
 Q    T    S   ___
```
If S goes third, the block of QT have to go first and second.

**b) Correct.** Only S or Q can go first in this configuration.

PrepTest 61, Section 3, Game 4

This is a linear game.

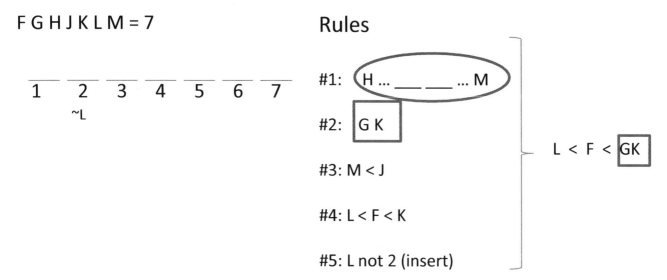

Discussion: Rules 2 and 4 can be combined. There are many simple exclusion inferences to be made. Since 1 and 7 are so heavily restricted, it makes sense to note which variables could go there.

18. List question.
a) Violates Rule 4
b) Violates Rule 5
c) Violates Rule 3
d) **Correct**
e) Violates Rule 1

19. We know J can't go first, but unfortunately that's not an answer choice so we'll need to do more work. Make sure to eliminate from other diagrams.
a) Could work, M J L F G K H
b) Could work, L M J F G K H
c) **Correct,** J can't go 5th.
d) Could work, L M J G K J H
e) Could work, L M J G K H J

20.
a) M going first forces L into second, which violates a rule.
b) K in 5 puts G in 4; we would need L, F, and M to all fit in the first 2 slots.
c) With H in 6, GK must go 4/5. Nothing will be available to go last. (remember only K J H can go last).
d) **Correct.** L M J F G K H
e) F in 2 forces L into 1. There is no way M can fit before J, violating a rule.

21. We are given K<M. We can combine with our other 2 sequencing rules to get:

   L < F < GK < M < J

We just need to place H, taking care to separate it from M.

a) If G is second, L and F must go 1 and 2. H will be too close to M.
b) **Correct.** H can go third: L F H G K M J
c) Juarez must go much later.
d) L can't go third as only H can go before it, leaving an empty spot in 1 or 2.
e) M must have at least 4 variables before it.

22. If G is 5, K will be 6.

b) **Correct.** Only HJK can go last; we know K is 6 here. If we put J into 7, we need to get M H L J into the first 4. Since M and H have to be split, we put M in 1 and H in 4. However, since L must go before F, L would have to go second, which is forbidden by Rule 5. (Students often forget "smaller" rules like this.)

23. We know L has at least 3 variables behind it (F, K, G). Can L go 4? That puts F and the GK block in 5-7. We won't have space in the first 3 spaces to fit in H __ __ M.

# PrepTest 61, Section 4 (LR)

**1. Question Type: Principle**

The situation described is essentially this: Males with large spots are more likely to mate but less likely to survive to adulthood in some environments. Thus the answer is (E).

(A) We don't know whether spots are more dangerous for males than females, so this isn't necessarily true.
(B) This is probably true, but doesn't incorporate the danger of predators, so it doesn't apply that well to the situation.
(C) This is clearly untrue: males with large spots may have more offspring but die young.
(D) We don't know whether females have spots or not, so we can't say whether the spots are helpful are harmful for them.
**(E)** Correct.

**2. Question Type: Requires clarification (this is a relatively unique question stem)**

The Mytheco executive claims that the difference in salary between programmers and technical writers is due to seniority, but she doesn't provide enough information to prove her point: Even if "many of the technical writers" have worked at Mytheco longer than "many of the programmers," that doesn't tell us whether, on average, the technical writers have worked at Mytheco longer and therefore earned their higher pay. We need to know the average difference in the seniority of the two groups to know whether the writers deserve higher pay, so (B) is the answer.

(A) This is irrelevant.
**(B)** Correct.
(C) The question isn't about the relationship between salary and benefits for a given employee but about the difference in those two things combined between two groups of employees.
(D) This wouldn't affect our evaluation of the executive's argument.
(E) The argument is about technical writers vs. programmers, not about executives.

**3. Question Type: Most strongly supported EXCEPT**

Remember, this is an EXCEPT question: four of the statements are supported by the prompt, while one is not.
(A) is unsupported, since we are told only that some cable networks have expanded overseas, not that any broadcast networks have, so (A) is the right answer.
**(A)** Correct.
(B) We are told that cable can offer lower advertising rates than broadcast because it's supported by fees, which implies that broadcast is not supported by fees.
(C) We are told that advertisers are attracted to cable because it offers lower fees, which implies that advertisers care about lower fees.
(D) We are told that cable offers the advantage of a multinational audience to advertisers, which implies that advertisers want such an audience.
(E) We are told that 24-hour news stations are an advantage of cable for advertisers, so they must be something advertisers want.

**4. Question Type: Strengthen**

This argument isn't that strong, because it shows that two things (air pollution and elimination of plant disease) occurred at the same time, then claims that one caused the other. Correlation doesn't imply causation. We're seeking further evidence that these two things were linked and didn't just coincidentally happen at the same time. Answer choice (D) shows that not only did air pollution coincide with the elimination of these diseases, but no air pollution coincided with their reemergence; since two such coincidences are unlikely, (D) supports the idea that air pollution eliminates these diseases.

**(A)** The question isn't about how plants react to air pollution but about how plant diseases react to it.
(B) This is information about the plant diseases, but doesn't provide evidence that they're eliminated by air pollution.
(C) This doesn't strengthen or weaken the argument, it just tells us what we don't know.
(D) Correct.
(E) Since we don't care about plant diseases besides black spot and tar spot, what happened to them is irrelevant.

## PrepTest 61, Section 4 (LR) Continued...

**5. Question Type: Most strongly supported**

We know two things about the abridgement: that it was done from memory (since the person who did it didn't possess a copy of Hamlet), and that whoever did it remembered one character's speeches much better than the other characters' speeches. Who memorizes a whole play, but memorizes one part much better than others? An actor, of course! Thus the answer is (C).

(A) Shakespeare would have possessed a copy of the play, so this isn't supported.
(B) We don't know whether the new version was easier to produce.
**(C)** Correct.
(D) A spectator might conceivably memorize the play, but would have no reason to remember one part better than others, so this is weakly supported.
(E) We can't infer anything about the abridger's motivations.

**6. Question Type: Main point**

The musicologist clearly thinks that people are wrong to criticize repetition in Handel's arias, and he justifies his view by arguing that this repetition serves a role. Only (C) captures this idea, so (C) is the answer.

(A) The musicologist seems to think the proportion of music is justified, not disproportionate, so this isn't his point.
(B) The musicologist doesn't compare Handel's arias to other arias, so we don't know whether he thinks this.
**(C)** Correct.
(D) The musicologist argues that the repetitions serve "a vital function," so they aren't unnecessary.
(E) The critic refutes only one criticism of the arias, so we don't know what he thinks about "most" criticism.

**7. Question Type: Most strongly supported**

The prompt says that Baxe is dominant in the corporate market even though it may not be the best designer. Why? Well, the corporate customers want a company which won't go bankrupt, even if that company isn't necessarily the best. This supports the idea that Baxe may continue to be dominant in the market even if it isn't the best designer, so (E) is the answer.

(A) This is not supported by the prompt, since Baxe has a near monopoly on the market, so it would be hard for other very large firms to exist.
(B) We know Baxe has a monopoly in corporate design, but we don't know anything about other markets.
(C) We know only that some small firms are better than Baxe, not that most are.
(D) The prompt explains that even if corporate customers knew there were better designers in the market, they might still choose Baxe for its size, so we don't know whether the customers are aware of better designers or not.
**(E)** Correct.

**8. Question Type: Weaken**

The prompt tells us that an asteroid strike could not have a worldwide effect, and so could not be responsible for the extinction of all the dinosaurs. But this argument makes sense only if the dinosaurs lived all over the world; if they lived near the impact, the asteroid could well be responsible for their extinction. Thus (E), if true, would weaken the argument.

(A) This would strengthen the argument, since it implies that the asteroid couldn't have been responsible for most dinosaurs' extinctions.
(B) This is irrelevant, since the argument is about dinosaur extinction.
(C) This might seem to weaken the argument, since it implies that the asteroid did kill dinosaurs, but the prompt never claims that no dinosaurs were killed by the asteroid. It merely says that most dinosaurs were killed by something else.
(D) This is irrelevant, since the prompt concerns only the Chicxulub asteroid.
**(E)** Correct.

**9. Question Type: Parallel reasoning**

This argument has a relatively simple structure: it takes two random samples from two groups, finds a difference between the samples, and infers a difference between the groups. Only answer choice (D) has precisely this structure: it takes samples from the Liberals and Conservatives (parallel to lot A and lot B) and then infers something about Liberals and Conservatives as a whole. Thus (D) is the answer.

## PrepTest 61, Section 4 (LR) Continued...

(A) There are no two groups in this argument, so it's not parallel.
(B) This argument isn't about two groups either. It is about plant disease like the prompt, but its reasoning isn't similar.
(C) This argument does involve statistical sampling on a group, but it doesn't compare two groups, so it's not parallel.
**(D) Correct.**
(E) This argument doesn't compare two groups using statistics, so it's not parallel.

### 10. Question Type: Most strongly supported

The economist's argument is a bit complicated: If people had the true belief that job loss was caused by impersonal social forces, they would demand government control of the economy. Government control of the economy, however, would lead to economic disaster. It's not hard to see the conclusion: knowledge of the causes of job loss would lead to an economic disaster. Thus the answer is (A).

**(A) Correct.**
(B) The economist implies that personal abilities are no defense against impersonal social forces, since these forces, and not personal failings, cause job loss.
(C) This is an extreme answer, and you should avoid extreme answers: the economist is against extensive government control, but he doesn't think the government should "never interfere."
(D) The economist doesn't say anything about change over time, so this isn't supported.
(E) The economist does say that people shouldn't feel responsible for job loss, but doesn't discuss responsibility for economic disaster, so this isn't strongly supported.

### 11. Question Type: Find the flaw

On the LSAT, it's extremely important to distinguish between sufficient conditions (if x then y) and necessary conditions (only if x then y). In this prompt we're told that if most residents want the airport, it will be build—them wanting it is a sufficient condition. But the airport may be built even if they don't want it, since them wanting it isn't a necessary condition. The prompt argues that since they don't want it probably won't be built—but this doesn't follow, since it could be built for other reasons. So the flaw is a failure to distinguish between necessary and sufficient conditions, and the answer is (A).

**(A) Correct.**
(B) The prompt takes no stand on whether what "most people believe" (that the airport will cause noise problems) is true or not.
(C) The prompt concludes only that something is unlikely, not that it won't occur.
(D) What people near Dalton think isn't relevant.
(E) This might mean that most people are wrong to hope the airport won't be built, but it doesn't affect whether the airport is likely to be built.

### 12. Question Type: Paradox

It's important, in facing a paradox question, to figure out exactly what the "paradox" is. Why is the result unexpected? We would assume that if the speed limit is lowered, travel time should go up—but instead it went down. What could have happened to decrease travel time? (C) provides an answer to this question: fewer accidents occur with the new speed limit, so fewer delays occur and travel times go down. Thus (C) is the answer.

(A) This would only make the paradox more confusing: if speed is lower during rush hour, how can travel times go down?
(B) This is irrelevant, since the prompt is about rush hour.
**(C) Correct.**
(D) This is irrelevant: if enforcement didn't change, it can't explain change in travel time.
(E) This is irrelevant: if no change occurred in number of cars, this can't explain change in travel time.

### 13. Question Type: Assumption

In an assumption question, always ask: what's in the conclusion that isn't in the premises? In this case, "artistic merit" is in the conclusion, but it's not mentioned in the premises. The premises refer only to enjoyment. So we need an assumption that links enjoyment and merit. Only (A) does so, so (A) is the answer: if critics can affect pleasure, and pleasure determines merit, then critics determine merit.

**(A) Correct.**

## PrepTest 61, Section 4 (LR) Continued...

(B) We need to know something about merit, so the confidence of viewers isn't relevant.
(C) This doesn't support the conclusion, since "understanding what gives an artwork merit" isn't the same as determining the work's merit.
(D) This is irrelevant, since we already know that, one way or another, critical response determines the pleasure people take in a work.
(E) This simply restates more generally a claim which is already made in the prompt: that criticism can affect a viewer's pleasure.

### 14. Question Type: Paradox

We want an answer which explains both of the facts cited in the prompt: thefts declined, and likelihood of conviction went up. Only (A) does both: if there are fewer car thieves, that explains why thefts declined, and if the thieves who are around now stay with the stolen cars, they're more likely to be convicted of having stolen them. Thus (A) is the answer.

**(A)** Correct.
(B) If people ignore the alarms, this shouldn't cause a decrease in car thefts, so this wouldn't explain either of the facts in the prompt.
(C) If more police are chasing burglaries, this would make convictions for car theft go down, not up, so this doesn't explain either fact.
(D) If the market for car parts is more lucrative, we expect theft to go up, not down.
(E) This answer is about sentencing, not conviction rates.

### 15. Question Type: Flaw

The legislator whether his constituents favor "high" taxes, but he didn't define what "high" was. So we don't know what level of taxes his constituents support, and we can't know whether they support a given reduction or increase in taxes. Thus his conclusion that they support the proposed reduction doesn't hold. (B) is the correct answer: the legislator doesn't address what taxes his constituents consider high.

(A) The legislator makes no claim about the country's population as a whole, only about his constituents.
**(B)** Correct.
(C) The legislator does provide evidence that his constituents support the bill; he just misrepresents it.
(D) The claim made in support of the conclusion (that his constituents oppose high taxes) is not the same as the conclusion (that his constituents support tax reduction).
(E) He argues that the public supports his bill, so this doesn't apply.

### 16. Question Type: Main point

The argument provides two pieces of evidence that the ban on pets should be lifted: it provides health benefits and increases quality of life. Thus the main point (the point this evidence supports) is clearly that the ban should be lifted, and the answer is (C).

(A) This is evidence in support of the conclusion, not the conclusion.
(B) This is irrelevant.
**(C)** Correct.
(D) This is evidence in support of the conclusion, not the conclusion.
(E) This is evidence, not the conclusion.

### 17. Question Type: Method of argument

The argument's conclusion is that "water itself is among the biggest water polluters." (You can tell because there's a "thus" before it.) This claim is supported by the point that rainwater runoff pollutes more than industrial discharge. Thus the answer is (D).

(A) The claim that water is a pollutant is the conclusion.
(B) The statement that rainwater is a larger polluter than industrial runoff is a subsidiary conclusion, not the main conclusion.
(C) This isn't a generalization, but a comparison.
**(D)** Correct.
(E) The prompt compares two kinds of pollution; it doesn't give examples of various kinds of pollution.

***PrepTest 61, Section 4 (LR) Continued...***

**18. Question Type: Point at issue**
Wong clearly thinks that democracies are always better, even if autocracies are temporarily necessary; Tate thinks that autocracies are sometimes better. Thus the main thing they disagree on is whether there exist countries which are permanently better of as autocracies, and the answer is (A).
**(A)** Correct.
(B) Neither speaker says that these things are most important.
(C) Both speakers discuss what is better, but neither says any countries can't become democracies.
(D) Both speakers would likely agree with this.
(E) Tate would disagree with this, but Wong expresses no opinion on the subject.

**19. Question Type: Principle**
The principle is that if no fully qualified candidate works for Arvue, the most productive candidate should be hired (regardless of whether he works for Arvue). To know whether the principle is well-applied here, we need to know whether any qualified candidates work for Arvue, and whether Delacruz is the most productive candidate from outside Arvue. So the answer is (E).
(A) We can't know whether Delacruz or Krall will be more productive from this.
(B) This wouldn't justify the application since we don't know whether Krall is fully qualified and works for Arvue. If he is both these things, he should be hired.
(C) This doesn't justify the application since if Krall is "fully qualified," he should be hired.
(D) We don't know whether any of the current candidates who work for Arvue are fully qualified, so we can't say whether one of them should be hired.
**(E)** Correct.

**20. Question Type: Assumption**
Even if the substances which exist in plants not yet studied contain substances of medicinal value, this does not imply that these substances are unknown to medicine: they may be substances which have already been discovered in other plants. The argument assumes that they are new substances; otherwise it would not be the case that medicine could learn from the as yet unstudied plants. Thus the answer is (A).
**(A)** Correct.
(B) This would damage the argument, since it would imply that rain forests do not need to be preserved, so it's certainly not necessary for the argument.
(C) It's not necessary that the majority of plants contain beneficial substances, only that some do.
(D) It's not necessary that all useful substances be discovered, only that some be.
(E) This restates claims already made in the prompt, so it's not an assumption.

**21. Question Type: Weaken**
The argument is relatively weak here: just because porous bones are helpful for divers doesn't mean that every animal with porous bones is a diver (any more than the fact that sharp eyes are useful for looking at computer screens implies that every animal with good eyesight uses computers). If we discovered that porous bones were fairly common, this would work against the idea that all animals who have them are deep divers. (C) provides such information, so (C) weakens the argument.
(A) This suggests that there are other ways for deep divers to surface, but it doesn't imply that porous bones have other uses besides diving.
(B) This strengthens the argument: if porous bones were rare, there's likely a reason that ichthyosaurs have them, and that reason could be diving.
**(C)** Correct.
(E) This merely says that we don't know about ichthyosaurs, so it's not good evidence to either strengthen or weaken the argument.
(E) This slightly weakens the argument, since ichthyosaurs didn't need porous bones to surface, but porous bones may still have been useful, so it doesn't weaken the argument as much as (C) does.

**22. Question Type: Method of argument**
The conclusion of the argument is that the grant money should be spent not on the charter but on other things. The librarian explains that it's more important to restore other documents since the charter is of sentimental but not scholarly interest. Thus the claim that the charter will soon deteriorate beyond repair—evidence that

## PrepTest 61, Section 4 (LR) Continued...

the money should be spent on the charter—is evidence for a conclusion with which the librarian disagrees. The answer is (C).

(A) The librarian doesn't disagree that the charter will soon deteriorate beyond repair; she merely argues that even though this is so, the money should still be spent elsewhere.
(B) The claim that the charter will deteriorate is not a conclusion, but evidence for the conclusion that it should be restored.
**(C)** Correct.
(D) The fact that the charter will deteriorate is evidence against, not for, the librarian's argument.
(E) Even if the claim were false, the librarian's argument would be all the more true: the money should be spent elsewhere, especially if the charter is in no danger.

### 23. Question Type: Principle

The columnist argues that if we care about any species, we should try to preserve all of them, since we don't know whether the species we care about are dependent on other species. In other words, we shouldn't let a change occur (species we don't care about going extinct) unless we know it won't endanger something important to us (the survival of species we care about). The principle which most conforms to this is (D).

(A) The columnist doesn't mention what's in our interest, only what's important to us.
(B) The columnist doesn't argue for not taking action; his argument implies that we should take action to protect all species.
(C) The columnist doesn't mention the flourishing of human populations.
**(D)** Correct.
(E) The columnist implies that we should work for the best long-term consequences, not the best immediate consequences.

### 24. Question Type: Flaw

Answering this question correctly depends on distinguishing between necessary and sufficient conditions. The prompt gives a sufficient condition for feeling comfortable approaching someone (if one is the same age, one feels comfortable), but it clearly assumes that this is also a necessary condition (one will not approach those who are not one's age). This is a mistake: it might be true that one is comfortable approaching strangers who are both one's age and not one's age (in a counterfactual universe, of course). Thus the flaw is that the argument fails to consider that one may be comfortable approaching strangers who are not one's age, and the answer is (E).

(A) The argument gives a condition for comfort, not for discomfort.
(B) The argument makes no claim about a specific situation; it's all about general facts.
(C) The argument states that most friendships begin when someone approaches a stranger, so it doesn't need to deal with the situation in which one approaches a non-stranger.
(D) The argument does not claim that one never approaches strangers unless one is comfortable, only that most friendships begin when someone feels comfortable approaching a stranger.
**(E)** Correct.

### 25. Question Type: Assumption

The argument is structured as follows:
No social integrity -> No individual freedom
No social integrity -> No pursuit of the good life
Therefore: No rule of law -> No individual freedom.
The argument fails to connect rule of law and individual freedom in its premises. The only thing we know about individual freedom from the premises is that it requires social integrity; thus individual freedom must be connected to rule of law through social integrity, and (B) is the answer:
No rule of law -> No social integrity.
(The good life plays no substantial role in this argument.)

(A) This is the opposite of the direction we want.
**(B)** Correct.
(C) The good life isn't relevant since it's not connected to individual freedom by the prompt.
(D) This doesn't help us connect the rule of law to individual freedom.
(E) This merely reverses the conclusion. (No individual freedom -> No rule of law) does not imply that (No

## PrepTest 61, Section 4 (LR) Continued...

rule of law -> No individual freedom), and only the latter is the conclusion we're looking for.

**26. Question Type: Parallel flaw**
The economist's answer could be written as follows:
Uneducated -> Weak E & P
Educated -> Serious commitment
Therefore: Serious commitment -> No weak E & P.
It could be symbolized:
No A-> B
A -> C
Therefore: C -> No B
The argument is fraught with flaws: it improperly reverses conditionals in several ways. The easiest way to solve this problem is simply to try to match its form to that of an answer choice. Only (B) matches:
No empathy -> not good candidate
Empathy -> manipulate
Manipulate -> good candidate.

(A) This involves relative statements (more and less) while the prompt does not, so it's unlikely to be parallel.
**(B)** Correct.
(C) This is a simple incorrect negation of a conditional, which has only two factors (give orders and understand personalities). Since the prompt involves three groups, this can't be parallel.
(D) The structure of this isn't parallel to that of the prompt.
(E) This argument contains no parallel to the split between educated and uneducated people in the prompt; it's all about one group, people who dislike exercise.

We hope you were able to use these explanations to help raise your LSAT score. If you're still struggling or just need help polishing your score for top schools, consider our one-on-one tutoring program.

Next Step Test Preparation is a national leader in providing one-on-one LSAT tutoring. We believe strongly that one-on-one attention is the best way for students to improve their scores. Our students around the country work individually with top-scorers and expert instructors to create customized strategies and study plans. Next Step students improve their scores significantly – even on retakes or after months of self-study.

To learn more, please visit our website http://www.nextsteptestprep.com/ or call us directly at 888-530-NEXT.

## Special Offer

Buyers of our Recent LSATs Explained book receive $100 off our 24-hour tutoring package or $50 off our 16-hour package.

Just mention this discount and be prepared to forward your receipt.

Made in the USA
Lexington, KY
27 September 2017